james halliday

the pocket guide to
wines

of australia

HarperCollins*Publishers*

First published in Great Britain in 2000 by Mitchell Beazley
First published in Australia in 2000
by HarperCollins*Publishers* Pty Ltd
ACN 009 913 517
A member of the HarperCollins*Publishers* (Australia)
Pty Limited Group
25 Ryde Road, Pymble, Sydney NSW 2073, Australia
http://www.harpercollins.com.au

Published in association with Octopus Publishing Group Ltd.,
London, Great Britain

Copyright © Octopus Publishing Group Ltd 2000
Text copyright © James Halliday 2000
Illustrations © Octopus Publishing Group Ltd 2000

This book is copyright.
Apart from any fair dealing for the purposes of private study,
research, criticism or review, as permitted under the Copyright Act,
no part may be reproduced by any process without prior written
permission. Inquiries should be addressed to the publishers.

A CIP record of this book is available from
the National Library of Australia

ISBN 0 7322 6539 8

Commissioning Editor: Rebecca Spry
Managing Editor: Hilary Lumsden
Design: Colin Goody
Cover design: Katie Mitchell
Cover photograph: Kevin Judd
Editor: Jane Hughes
Production: Karen Farquhar
Index: Anne Barrett

Typeset in Veljovic.

Printed and bound in China by Toppan Printing Company

7 6 5 4 3 2 1
03 02 01 00

The author and publishers will be grateful for any information which will assist them in keeping future editions up to date. Although all reasonable care has been taken in the preparation of this book, neither the publishers nor the author can accept any liability for any consequences arising from the use thereof, or the information contained herein.

Contents

Introduction	6
New South Wales	14
Victoria	56
South Australia	110
Western Australia	156
Tasmania	184
Queensland	198
Index	205

Key to Symbols

☆☆☆☆☆	Outstanding winery regularly producing exemplary wines
☆☆☆☆¼	Extremely good; virtually on a par with a five-star winery
☆☆☆☆	Consistently producing high-quality wines
☆☆☆¼	A solid, reliable producer of good wine
☆☆☆	Typically good, but may have a few lesser wines
☆☆¼	Adequate
☆☆	Hard to recommend

- ☎ Telephone number
- Ⓕ Fax number
- est Established in
- ◊ Production (cases)
- ♀ Tastings
- $ Cellar-Door Sales
- ✗ Guided tours
- ¶ Restaurant
- ⇌ Accommodation

Abbreviations

NR	Not Rated; used in a number of situations. Mostly for a new winery which has not released enough wine for a proper judgement to be made. Also for small, perhaps remote, wineries that rely solely on cellar-door trade and are reluctant to submit wines for critical review.
V	Denotes a winery whose wines are particularly well priced in the context of their quality.
NA	Not Available
NFP	Not for Publication
GI	Geographic Indications
NSW	New South Wales
SA	South Australia
WA	Western Australia
EU	European Union

Key to Maps

─ · · ─ · · ─	State border
─ ─ ─ ─	Zone boundary
──────	Official regional boundary
----------	Interim regional boundary
··········	Probable regional boundary

Letters indicate Zones
Numbers indicate Regions (excludes map overleaf)

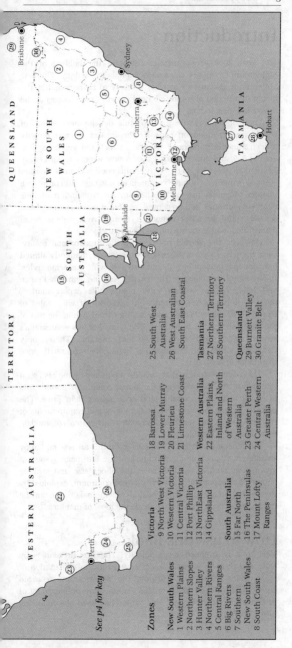

Introduction

The year 2000 sees Australia celebrate the holding of the Millennium Olympic Games in its capital city, Sydney. The new Millennium also arrives at what is likely to be regarded as the height of a period of unprecedented growth (and change) in the Australian wine industry.

There are many measures of this development, some of which are explained on page 7. The impact is most directly reflected in the number of wineries, which ten years ago was around 500, and now exceeds 1,000. A new winery is born every 72 hours in Australia, so by the time this book is printed, another 50 or so wineries will have commenced business. To complicate matters, Australia has no mechanism for registration of new vineyard plantings, and no central register of new wineries. Some sensibly (and proudly) announce their arrival; others seem determined to hide their wine under a bushel.

However, this should not obscure the fundamental reality. Over the past 15 years Australian wine has permanently altered international perceptions of, and tastes in, wine and wine styles. It has dared to challenge the citadels of fine wine in France and Italy. In the world's most competitive export market, the UK, it has now captured over one-third of wine sales of £5 (A$13) or more; France takes another third, while the rest of the world shares the remainder. The United States is Australia's second-largest (and most profitable) market. There, only California wines can command a higher average retail price than those of Australia.

This demonstrates that while Australian wine is seen internationally as offering exceptional value for money, its principal focus is on quality and style rather than price. The industry has deliberately sought the views and requirements of the principal export markets, and endeavoured to accommodate these wherever feasible.

It has been possible for Australia to do this for several happy reasons. Australia is not constrained by the European system of *appellation contrôlée*. And there is the sheer size and striking climatic and topographic diversity of the continent, exploited by the free but tenacious spirit of Australia's winemakers. We may be the lucky country, but we have made the most of that luck.

How to use this Book

This book is arranged geographically. The first division is by State and then by Region. (See page 9-10 for an explanation of these terms.) Once in a Region, the wineries are arranged alphabetically. There is no official classification or hierarchy of producers in Australia, but the author has used the following rating system:

☆☆☆☆☆	Outstanding winery regularly producing exemplary wines
☆☆☆☆✫	Extremely good; virtually on a par with a five-star winery
☆☆☆☆	Consistently producing high-quality wines
☆☆☆✫	A solid, reliable producer of good wine
☆☆☆	Typically good, but may have a few lesser wines
☆☆✫	Adequate
☆☆	Hard to recommend

Then there are the following symbols and abbreviations:

NR Not Rated; this is used in a number of situations. Most frequently it is used for a new winery which has not released enough wine for a proper judgement to be made. Another common usage is for small, perhaps remote, wineries that rely solely on cellar-door trade and are reluctant to submit wines for critical review. (This is examined further on page 55 [NSW rest of state]).

V   Denotes a winery whose wines are particularly well-priced in the context of their quality.

NA Not Available

NFP Not for Publication

History and the Future

A potted history of the Australian wine industry between 1820 and 2000 neatly divides it into four periods. The first period ran from 1820 to 1900, as winemaking spread through New South Wales (NSW), Tasmania, Western Australia (WA), Victoria and South Australia (SA). By 1870 production had risen to 8.7 million litres; 20 years later Victoria alone was producing twice that amount. Both fine table wines and fortified wines were made for domestic and export markets.

Between 1900 and 1955 Australia became an exporter of low-cost sweet 'Sherry' and 'Tawny Port', sourced largely from South Australia's Riverlands and around Griffith on the Murrumbidgee River. The third period, from 1955 to 1985, saw the transition back from fortified wine to table wine. This was also a time of declining exports and of increasing domestic consumption of table wine: per capita it rose from 2 litres per annum in 1960 to 21 litres in 1985. The engine was the development of the bag-in-box, which introduced cheap table wine to all socio-economic sections of the community, combined with a massive shift from red to white wine consumption between 1975 and 1985.

The golden era of wine exports, 1985 to 2000, then follows. This fourth period also marks a fundamental shift in the make-up (and size) of the nation's vineyards. In 1984/'85 Australian exports were 8.7 million litres, worth A$17 million; by late 1999 exports passed 220 million litres of wine, valued in excess of A$1 billion.

Underlying this most recent development were three phases of change in the vineyards. Firstly, the plantings of premium grapes increased from 33.3 per cent to over 80 per cent of the total. The other two phases are interlinked: a complete reversal of the earlier red/white consumption ratio, and a massive explosion in the rate and amount of new vineyard plantings.

Between 1995 and 2000 vineyard plantings increased by 50 per cent from a little over 60,000 hectares to 92,000 hectares, rising to 107,000 hectares by 2002. Official forecasts see exports rising from 220 million litres to 396 million litres by 2002, making Australia the fourth-largest exporter of wine in the world (after France, Italy and Spain). The challenges inherent in this are immense – Australia will have to be lucky, and very clever.

Climate and Soils

Rightly or wrongly, the Australian view is that climate has a far greater influence on wine quality and style than does soil. Linked with that proposition is the belief that it is far easier to modify soil structure and chemical composition than (with one major exception, irrigation) it is to mediate the effect of climate.

Australia has a bewildering number of soil types, many reflecting the extreme age of the continent. Even within a small, 15-hectare vineyard there may be three or four different soil types. Overall, however, these are likely to be the so-called 'duplex soils', marked by a sudden change from sandy or loamy surface soils to a clay subsoil. If there is no hard pan between the soil and clay, and no significant increase in acidity (ie, no drop in pH), these are excellent soils for grape-growing. Australia's most celebrated soil is the *terra rossa* of Coonawarra (also found elsewhere in that corner of South Australia). It is a uniform limestone-derived soil with no major structural change; its red colour comes from oxidised iron traces.

The majority of Australia's wine regions are coastal, and enjoy a Mediterranean climate. Rain falls predominantly in winter and spring, the day-to-night temperature range is not great, and the risk of spring frost is much reduced. But, there is great diversity in the comparative warmth (measured in heat degree days – average daily temperature x number of days in growing season) of these maritime regions. The Swan and Hunter Valleys are hotter than the Midi of France; Margaret River is (deceptively) distinctly warmer than Bordeaux; Langhorne Creek and Coonawarra are on a par with it; the Yarra Valley is cooler than Bordeaux but warmer than Burgundy; and Geelong is cooler than Burgundy.

If you look at the map of Australia on page 4, you will see just how close to the coast most of the continent's wine regions are, and how vast and empty the centre and north are. There are, of course, inland regions, with what are called Continental climates. These are unaffected by the moderating influences of oceans, and have considerable day/night (and seasonal) temperature shifts. The coldest are to be found in the mountain areas of southern NSW, Central and Southern Victoria, and Tasmania.

Grape Varieties

Thanks largely to the extraordinary efforts of James Busby (a Scottish gardener by birth and training) and William MacArthur (best known as the founder of Australia's sheep industry), all the classic grape varieties came to Australia between 1800 and 1850. James Busby's *Journal of a Tour* makes it clear that the varieties came from impeccable vineyards. They were also brought over before *phylloxera* (a virulent vine pest) appeared in Europe.

Nonetheless, by 1955 there were just a handful of premium varieties in significant production. This was due to the total domination of the market by fortified wines, and the shrinking of the viticultural map to irrigated areas and to production centres in the Barossa and Hunter Valleys. Only a few outposts remained.

White wines were restricted to Semillon (spelled here without the è; notably from the Hunter Valley, NSW) and Riesling (the Barossa, Clare and Eden Valleys, SA). There was only one classic red variety, Shiraz, although the winemakers of today would include Grenache and Mourvedre (or Mataro) of which there was plenty used – mind you, in fortified winemaking. The most obvious absentees were Chardonnay (not to mention a raft of other white grapes), Cabernet Sauvignon, Merlot and Pinot Noir. The massive changes that then took place between 1956 and 1999 are best understood from the tables which follow:

White Grape Varieties (tonnes)

	1956	1966	1979	1989	1999
Chardonnay	Nil	Nil	1,471	28,419	235,945
Riesling	2,500	1,958	21,464	41,176	30,875
Semillon	3,000	11,987	28,457	40,232	89,437
Sauvignon Blanc	Nil	Nil	939	7,315	23,327

Red Grape Varieties (tonnes)

	1956	1966	1979	1989	1999
Shiraz	12,410	14,529	62,595	57,823	207,103
Cabernet Sauvignon	500*	621	20,504	31,207	133,383
Pinot Noir	142	150	631	6,007	18,211
Merlot	Nil	Nil	Nil	2334	33,344
Grenache	21,000	32,000	52,000	33,656	24,676
Mourvedre	3,800	4,000	12,500	10,106	9,106

* Estimate

Labels and Laws

Laws of the kind one expects under some form of *appellation contrôlée* system were first introduced by each of the states in 1963. While the regulations were adequate, the states refused to supply the financial and human resources needed to police compliance, and so their impact was minimal.

In 1989 the industry took the matter into its own hands. The regulations were embodied in the federal government's *Food*

Standards Code, and the industry voted for a compulsory levy to provide funds for policing the *Label Integrity Programme*. The core of the legislation covers the control of label claims. If a vintage, single variety and/or single region is claimed on a label, 85 per cent of the wine must be of that stated vintage, variety and region. If more than one region or variety is claimed, they must be named in the order of importance (ie, percentage). There are also lists of permitted additives. Any substance not on the list is banned. Sugar is the most notorious.

In October 1994 the Australian Wine & Brandy Corporation Act was amended to provide for the registration of defined place names. There is now a multi-tiered hierarchy of what are called Geographic Indications (GI). The most general is simply 'Product of Australia'. Next comes 'South East Australia', which takes in all the principal regions of the eastern states (NSW, SA and Victoria). Then come each of the States, a self-explanatory concept. The states are in turn divided into Zones, and next Regions, which is where the fun (or is it tragi-comedy?) starts.

To qualify, a Region must produce at least 500 tonnes of wine grapes a year from at least five individually owned vineyards of at least five hectares each. The Region must also be a single tract of land that is discrete and homogenous in its grape-growing attributes to a degree that is measurable but is less substantial than in a Subregion. A Subregion has similar requirements, except that it must be 'homogenous in its grape-growing attributes to a degree that is substantial'. Sophisticated indeed, and small wonder the registration pace has been painfully slow. It also explains why this book is divided into Regions that are in part legally defined, and in part simply reflect existing practice.

AUSTRALIAN WINES VINTAGE CHART
1 – Worst Vintage 10 – Best Vintage

Vintage	87	88	89	90	91	92	93	94	95	96	97
NEW SOUTH WALES											
Lower Hunter Valley											
red	9	4	5	4	10	4	5	7	5	6	5
white	8	4	5	6	8	8	5	6	7	8	4
Upper Hunter Valley											
red	8	7	8	5	9	5	6	7	8	9	7
white	6	7	7	6	9	6	7	7	8	9	7
Mudgee											
red	5	6	7	8	7	6	5	8	6	8	8
white	7	7	9	8	8	6	7	8	7	8	7
Orange											
red	5	6	5	8	6	8	6	8	7	9	8
white	7	6	5	7	7	9	7	7	8	8	9
Riverina											
red	6	6	5	8	7	9	7	6	8	9	8
white	6	6	5	8	7	8	8	7	8	8	8
Canberra District											
red	6	9	6	8	9	7	8	8	9	8	8
white	7	9	5	8	8	7	7	6	8	8	8
Hastings River											
red	8	8	7	4	7	6	8	6	7	5	5
white	6	6	8	5	6	6	8	7	8	6	8
VICTORIA											
Yarra Valley											
red	7	10	5	8	10	10	7	9	7	8	9
white	6	10	4	8	8	10	8	9	5	7	8
Mornington Peninsula											
red	7	9	6	8	8	7	10	8	7	5	10
white	7	8	6	7	8	7	9	9	8	7	8
Geelong											
red	6	8	6	9	7	8	6	8	9	8	8
white	8	8	7	7	8	8	8	9	9	8	8
Macedon											
red	6	8	6	9	9	7	8	8	8	7	8
white	7	8	5	9	9	7	8	8	8	6	7
Grampians											
red	5	8	7	7	9	8	9	9	10	9	10
white	7	7	6	8	7	8	7	7	9	7	9
Pyrenees											
red	7	10	6	10	10	8	8	8	8	10	7
white	7	9	6	7	9	8	8	7	8	10	7
Far South West Victoria											
red	6	8	7	8	8	8	9	8	7	8	8
white	8	9	9	8	8	9	7	9	8	9	8

Vintage	87	88	89	90	91	92	93	94	95	96	97
VICTORIA *continued*											
Bendigo											
red	7	9	6	10	8	8	6	8	7	9	10
white	7	8	7	9	6	8	5	7	6	8	9
Goulburn Valley											
red	8	7	5	8	9	8	6	7	8	7	9
white	7	8	6	7	6	9	6	8	7	8	6
Glenrowan and Rutherglen											
red	6	8	4	7	7	8	5	7	5	8	5
white	6	8	6	7	7	8	6	7	6	5	5
King Valley											
red	6	8	4	7	7	8	5	7	5	6	5
white	6	8	6	7	7	8	6	7	6	5	5
Gippsland											
red	7	9	6	8	9	8	6	9	8	7	9
white	8	9	6	6	9	8	7	8	8	6	8
SOUTH AUSTRALIA											
Barossa Valley											
red	6	7	7	9	8	7	8	8	7	9	8
white	7	8	7	9	8	7	7	8	8	9	7
Eden Valley											
red	6	7	7	10	8	8	8	9	7	9	7
white	9	6	6	9	6	7	7	7	8	8	9
Clare Valley											
red	8	8	6	10	8	8	7	8	7	7	8
white	9	7	5	10	7	7	8	9	8	7	10
Adelaide Hills											
red	5	9	4	9	9	7	6	8	8	9	7
white	6	7	4	7	6	9	6	7	8	9	7
Adelaide											
red	7	8	5	8	10	9	7	8	9	8	9
white	8	8	6	9	9	8	8	8	8	9	9
Coonawarra											
red	6	7	6	10	9	6	8	9	6	9	7
white	6	8	6	7	7	6	8	9	7	9	6
Padthaway											
red	5	8	5	7	7	5	6	9	6	8	6
white	7	5	7	8	9	7	8	10	8	9	8
McLaren Vale											
red	7	8	7	10	9	9	8	9	8	9	7
white	8	8	6	10	9	9	8	9	8	9	7
WESTERN AUSTRALIA											
Margaret River											
red	8	8	6	7	10	8	7	9	9	8	8
white	8	7	6	8	8	8	9	8	9	8	6
Great Southern											
red	6	8	8	10	9	8	7	10	9	8	7
white	7	8	7	9	7	8	7	9	8	8	9

Vintage	87	88	89	90	91	92	93	94	95	96	97
WESTERN AUSTRALIA *continued*											
Swan District											
red	5	5	6	6	8	6	7	6	6	6	7
white	9	6	7	7	10	6	10	7	7	6	5
TASMANIA											
Northern Tasmania											
red	5	7	6	7	8	8	5	8	9	7	8
white	7	7	8	8	9	9	8	9	9	7	9
Southern Tasmania											
red	6	8	6	9	7	8	9	9	8	5	8
white	6	8	7	8	7	8	9	8	9	6	8
QUEENSLAND											
red	8	8	10	9	9	8	10	10	9	9	7
white	8	7	9	8	8	8	9	9	9	10	6

New South Wales

1994 14,332 hectares 21.37 per cent of total plantings
1998 21,887 hectares 22.23 per cent of total plantings
NSW has slightly exceeded the national growth rate in plantings; a significant contributor has been the increase in the number and size of the vineyards on the western side of the Great Dividing Range.

Lower Hunter Valley

The chief reason for the birth in 1825 and consequent survival of the Hunter Valley is its proximity to Sydney. In best parochial fashion, the city has come to regard the region as its own. Theoretically, however, the Hunter is by no means a natural winemaking area. The Lower Hunter surely has to be one of the most capricious and vexatious wine regions in the world. It produces one of Australia's greatest – and unique – wines: the long-lived Semillon, and some very fine Shiraz. It can even be cajoled into making excellent Chardonnay (Tyrrell's, Lake's Folly) and Cabernet Sauvignon (Lake's Folly). It can do all this in spite of the fact that it is (or ought to be) far too warm for fine

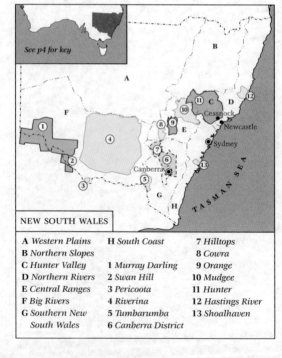

NEW SOUTH WALES

A *Western Plains*	**H** *South Coast*	**7** *Hilltops*
B *Northern Slopes*		**8** *Cowra*
C *Hunter Valley*	**1** *Murray Darling*	**9** *Orange*
D *Northern Rivers*	**2** *Swan Hill*	**10** *Mudgee*
E *Central Ranges*	**3** *Pericoota*	**11** *Hunter*
F *Big Rivers*	**4** *Riverina*	**12** *Hastings River*
G *Southern New South Wales*	**5** *Tumbarumba*	**13** *Shoalhaven*
	6 *Canberra District*	

table wine; only small patches of its soils are truly suitable for grape-growing, and – most of all – rainfall tends to be concentrated during vintage time when the tail-ends of summer monsoons sweep down the coast from Queensland. Yet none of this deters the winemakers – or wine-lovers, for the Lower Hunter is, of course, a Mecca for wine tourists.

Tourism began in a tentative way in the early 1970s, grew strongly in the '80s, and became a gale in the '90s. There are now luxury hotels, vineyard cottages, restaurants of every variety. Visitors are also drawn by the peculiarly Australian beauty of the gently undulating valley. The smoky blue of the Brokenback Range is a significant part of the landscape, wherever in the valley you are. Its stark outline rises threateningly above the nearest vineyards along the Broke Road, and is distantly though clearly etched as you look back from Allandale and Wilderness Roads. All this, and only one-and-a-half hours' drive north of Sydney.

Allandale ☆☆☆☆ V
Lovedale Road, Lovedale, NSW 2320, ☎ (02) 4990 4526, ℻ (02) 4990 1714; est 1978; ♦ 15,000 cases; ♀; A$; Mon-Sat 9-5, Sun 10-5

Winemaker Bill Sneddon presides over an unpretentious and very reliable, good-quality winery using both Hunter Valley and Central Ranges (Mudgee, Hilltops) grapes. Riesling, Semillon and Chardonnay are all good.

Allanmere NR
Allandale Road, Allandale via Pokolbin, NSW 2321, ☎ (02) 4930 7387, ℻ (02) 4930 7900; est 1984; ♦ 7,000 cases; ♀; A$; 7 days 9.30-5

Now owned by Monarch Winemaking Services. While relatively low profile in conventional retail markets, cellar-door sales are flourishing in response to the ever-increasing tourist traffic in the Hunter Valley.

Bacchus Estate NR
381 Milbrodale Road, Broke, NSW 2330, ☎ (02) 6579 1069, ℻ (02) 6579 1069; est 1993; ♦ 1,000 cases; ♀; A$; by appt

This is another of the wineries that are springing up like mushrooms after spring rain. Ten hectares of vineyard have been established, with a further 12 underway, focussing on Chardonnay and Shiraz.

Belbourie ☆☆☆ ♦
Branxton Road, Rothbury, NSW 2330, ☎ (02) 4938 1556; est 1963; ♦ 2,000 cases; ♀; A$; wkds & hols 10am to sunset

The late Jim Roberts' wildly alternative winemaking is now more conventional under the direction of son John. Cellar-door and mailing-list club sales only.

Beyond Broke Vineyard NR
Cobcroft Road, Broke, NSW 2330, ☎ (02) 6026 2043, ℻ (02) 6026 2043; est 1996; ♦ 4,000 cases; ♀; A$; at Broke Village Store 10-4

This is the reincarnation of a former Lindemans vineyard

purchased by Bob and Terry Kennedy in 1996. In a somewhat ironic twist, the 1997 Beyond Broke Semillon won two trophies at the Hunter Valley Wine Show that year.

Bimbadgen Estate NR
Lot 21 McDonalds Road, Pokolbin, NSW 2321, ☏ (02) 4998 7585, Ⓕ (02) 4998 7732; est 1968; ♦ 50,000 cases; ☆; A$; wkds & hols 10-5; ⑩; ⌂

Five owners (and name changes) since 1968 say much. The 45 hectares of estate vineyards and arrival of Kees Van De Scheur, a veteran Hunter winemaker, should eventually give this estate a firm footing.

Blaxlands Wines NR
Broke Road, Pokolbin, NSW 2320, ☏ (02) 4998 7550, Ⓕ (02) 4998 7802; est 1976; ♦ 400 cases; ☆; A$; 7 days 10.30-4.30; ⑩; ⌂

Fair-haired and highly articulate, Chris Barnes, has long been an avid promoter of the Hunter. Blaxlands Restaurant and Wine Centre is his principal business – where he sells many Hunter wines in addition to his own.

Bluebush Estate NR
Wilderness Road, Cessnock, NSW 2325, ☏ (02 4930 7177, Ⓕ (02) 4930 7666; est 1991; ♦ NA; No visitors

Two hectares of vineyards have been established by David McGain. The two wines (Chardonnay and Shiraz) are contract-made and sold by mail order.

Briar Ridge ☆☆☆☆
Mount View Road, Mount View, NSW 2325, ☏ (02) 4990 3670, Ⓕ (02) 4990 7802; est 1972; ♦ 16,000 cases; ☆; A$; Mon-Fri 9-5, wkds 9.30-4.30; ⌂

An unlikely winemaking duo, Neil McGuigan (ex McGuigan Bros) and Karl Stockhausen (ex Lindemans), operate here. Crisp, minerally, lemony Semillon, generous but not flabby Chardonnay and bright, earthy/cherry Shiraz are all very good.

Broke Estate ☆☆☆½
Wollombi Road, Broke, NSW 2330, ☏ (02) 6579 1065, Ⓕ (02) 6579 1065; est 1989; ♦ 5,000 cases; ☆; A$; by appt

The region, not the bank balance, provides the name. Consultant viticulturist Richard Smart and contract winemaker Simon Gilbert initially produced startling Chardonnay and Cabernet, but recent displays have been less convincing.

Brokenwood ☆☆☆☆☆
McDonalds Road, Pokolbin, NSW 2321, ☏ (02) 4998 7559, Ⓕ (02) 4998 7893; est 1970; ♦ 70,000 cases; ☆; A$; 7 days 10-5

A deservedly fashionable winery producing consistently excellent wines, partly from estate-grown grapes (notably Graveyard Shiraz, in the top Australian league), as well as from fruit purchased in the Hunter (Semillon) and across South

East Australia (Cricket Pitch). For the record, I was one of the founders, but cut my ties in 1983.

Brushbox Vineyard NR
Lot 3 Rodd Street, Broke, NSW 2101, ☎ (02) 9913 1419,
Ⓕ (02) 9913 1419; est 1991; ❦ NA; No visitors
Paul and Suzanne Mackay have established their 6.5-hectare Brushbox Vineyard at Broke. It is planted with Chardonnay, Verdelho, Cabernet Sauvignon and Merlot, and so far sold by mail order only.

Calais Estates ☆☆☆
Palmers Lane, Pokolbin, NSW 2321, ☎ (02) 4998 7654, Ⓕ (02) 4998 7813; est 1987; ❦ 11,000 cases; ☙; A$; Mon-Fri 9-5, wkds 10-5
Somewhat off the beaten track in its location and in the varying style and quality of its wines.

Capercaillie ☆☆☆
London Road, Lovedale, NSW 2325, ☎ (02) 4990 2904,
Ⓕ (02) 4991 1886; est 1995; ❦ 5,000 cases; ☙; A$; Mon-Sat 9-5,
Sun 10-5; art gallery
Formerly Dawson Estate, now run by veteran Alasdair Sutherland. Draws on a fruit salad of estate-grown Chardonnay (rich, peachy), Hastings Valley Chambourcin, Orange Merlot and Coonawarra Cabernet Sauvignon.

Carindale Wines NR
Palmers Lane, Pokolbin, NSW 2321, ☎ (02) 4998 7665,
Ⓕ (02) 4998 7665; est 1996; ❦ 1,000 cases; ☙; A$; Fri-Tues 10-4.30
Still in its infancy, producing small quantities of Chardonnay, Cabernet Franc and Merlot from 3.6 hectares of estate vineyards.

Catherine Vale Vineyard ☆☆☆½
Milbrodale Road, Bulga, NSW 2330, ☎ (02) 6579 1334,
Ⓕ (02) 6579 1334; est 1994; ❦ 725 cases; ☙; A$; 7 days 10-5
Former schoolteachers Bill and Wendy Lawson run the 3.5-hectare vineyard, selling grapes to contract winemaker John Hordern and taking back wine in part payment.

Chateau Francois ☆☆☆ V
Broke Road, Pokolbin, NSW 2321, ☎ (02) 4998 7548, Ⓕ (02) 4998 7805; est 1969; ❦ 700 cases; ☙; A$; wkds 9-5 or by appt
Former fisheries director-turned-winemaker Don Francois is an old friend who sells his strongly regional and absurdly cheap wines from his lovely hillside house-cum-winery.

Chateau Pato ☆☆☆☆
Thompson's Road, Pokolbin, NSW 2321, ☎ (02) 4998 7634;
est 1978; ❦ 400 cases; ☙; A$; by appt
Nicholas and Roger Paterson are in charge of this tiny estate operation, producing rich, velvety Shiraz. Several vintages usually on offer.

Cockfighter's Ghost Vineyard ☆☆☆
Lot 251 Milbrodale Road, Broke, NSW 2330, ☏ (02) 9667 1622,
⊚ (02) 9667 1442; est 1994; ❦ 12,000 cases; No visitors
The story of the name is too long to tell... part of the mini wine empire of prominent Sydney merchant banker and man-about-town David Clarke. Effectively a second label to Poole's Rock, with the wines contract-made at various wineries.

Constable & Hershon NR
1 Gillards Road, Pokolbin, NSW 2320, ☏ (02) 4998 7887,
⊚ (02) 4998 7887; est 1981; ❦ 3,000 cases; ⚑; A$; 7 days 10-5; gardens
Features four spectacular formal gardens: the Rose, Knot and Herb, Secret and Sculpture. Typically offers a range of several vintages of Chardonnay and Cabernet/Merlot.

Crisford Winery NR
556 Hermitage Road, Pokolbin, NSW 2022, ☏ (02) 9387 1100,
⊚ (02) 9387 6688; est 1990; ❦ NA; No visitors
Carol and Neal Crisford's 2.6 hectares of Merlot and Cabernet Franc vines yield a single wine marketed under the Crisford Synergy label.

De Iuliis NR
Lot 1 Lovedale Road, Keinbah, NSW 2321, ☏ (02) 4930 7403,
⊚ (02) 4968 8192; est 1990; ❦ 6,500 cases; ⚑; A$; by appt
Three generations of the De Iuliis family have been involved in the establishment of this 40-hectare vineyard at Keinbah. Under current generation Michael de Iuliis they have moved from contract grape-growing into winemaking.

Drayton's Family Wines ☆☆☆✦ V
Oakey Creek Road, Cessnock, NSW 2321, ☏ (02) 4998 7513,
⊚ (02) 4998 7743; est 1853; ❦ 100,000 cases; ⚑; A$; Mon-Fri 8-5,
wkds & public hols 10-5
Approaching its 150th birthday in direct family ownership. The flinty Semillon and Bin 5555 Hermitage are both good mid-range wines; William Shiraz and Joseph Shiraz, from very old vines, are stylish, gently oaked flagships.

Drews Creek Wines NR
558 Wollombi Road, Broke, NSW 2330, ☏ (02) 6579 1062,
⊚ (02) 6579 1062; est 1993; ❦ 300 cases; ⚑; A$; by appt
Two wines are contract-made for owner Graeme Gibbson from estate-grown Chardonnay and Merlot.

Elyssium Vineyard NR
393 Milbrodale Road, Broke, NSW 2330, ☏ (02) 9664 2368,
⊚ (02) 9664 2368; est 1990; ❦ 500 cases; ⚑; A$; by appt; ⛌;
wine education wkds
Victoria Foster has one hectare of Verdelho and runs weekend wine and food courses at her award-winning (tourism) cottage that sleeps six.

Evans Family ☆☆☆☆⁂
Palmers Lane, Pokolbin, NSW 2321, ☏ (02) 4998 7333,
℻ (02) 4998 7798; est 1979; ❦ 3,000 cases; ♀; A$; by appt
Centred on the plantings of Gamay (which is rare in Australia) and Chardonnay grown around the ancestral mansion of Leonard Paul Evans OBE, OA. The Chardonnay is voluptuous, the Gamay flirtatious.

Farrell's Limestone Creek ☆☆☆⁂
Mount View Road, Mount View, NSW 2325, ☏ (02) 4991 2808,
℻ (02) 4991 3414; est 1982; ❦1,000 cases; ♀; A$; wkds & public hols 10-5
A substantial grape grower in the beautiful Mount View area. Most fruit is sold to McWilliam's, with small amounts of Semillon, Chardonnay, Late Harvest Verdelho, Shiraz, Merlot and Cabernet/Merlot competently contract-made.

Fordwich Estate NR
390 Milbrodale Road, Fordwich, NSW 2330, ☏ (02) 9968 1764,
℻ (02) 9960 3454; est 1998; ❦ 2,500 cases; No visitors
The Bainton family, headed by eminent Sydney QC Russell Bainton, has 48 hectares of vineyard. They currently sell most of the grapes, yet intend to steadily increase production in-house.

Gartlemann Hunter Estate NR
Lovedale Road, Lovedale, NSW 2321, ☏ (02) 4930 7113,
℻ (02) 4930 7114; est 1996; ❦ NA; ♀; A$; by appt
In 1996 Jan and Jorg Gartlemann purchased what was previously the 16-hectare George Hunter Estate, established by Sydney restaurateur Oliver Shaul in 1970. Chardonnay, Semillon and Shiraz are contract-made.

Glenguin NR
River Oaks Vineyard, Lot 8 Milbrodale Road, Broke, NSW 2330,
☏ (02) 6579 1009, ℻ (02) 6579 1009; est 1993; ❦ 6,000 cases; ♀;
A$; at Boutique Wine Centre, Broke Road, Pokolbin
Named for the Scottish distillery and Barony of WWII Air Chief Marshall Sir Arthur Tedder, grandfather of current owner Lord Robin Tedder. Robin also happens to be a Master of Wine, and oversees the making of this estate's pleasant, if unspectacular, white wines.

Golden Grape Estate NR
Oakey Creek Road, Pokolbin, NSW 2321, ☏ (02) 4998 7588,
℻ (02) 4998 7730; est 1985; ❦ NFP; ♀; A$; 7 days 10-5; ⑂; museum
This estate is a thoroughly curious part of the German Pieroth business. General tourists are its prey and, judging by the number of cars and coaches always parked outside, it's definitely feasting well.

Hill of Hope NR
Cobcroft Road, Broke, NSW 2330, ☏ (02) 6579 1161, ℻ (02) 6579 1373; est 1996; ❦ 30,000 cases; ♀; A$; 7 days 10-5

The (perhaps temporarily) re-named Saxonvale Winery is now principally a crush facility for other wineries. The challenge to the name has come from Henschke, seeking to protect its Hill of Grace label.

Hollyclare NR
Lot 6 Milbrodale Road, Broke, NSW 2330, ☎ (02) 6579 1193, ℱ (02) 6579 1269; est 1987; ❦ 1,500 cases; ⚏; A$; wkds 10-5

A 3-hectare vineyard planted in 1987 is the weekend refuge for John Holdsworth, whose wine is contract-made at Tamburlaine using Holdsworths' tanks and barrels.

Honeytree Estate NR
16 Gillards Road, Pokolbin, NSW 2321, ☎ (02) 4998 7693, ℱ (02) 4998 7693; est 1970; ❦ 3,600 cases; ⚏; A$; Fri-Mon 10-5; ⌂

Honeytree was set up in 1970, then lapsed into obscurity before a change of ownership and revitalisation by Henk and Robyn Strengers. Produces a trophy-winning Semillon via competent contract winemaking.

Howards Way Vineyard NR
Cobcroft Road, Broke, NSW 2330, ☎ (02) 4998 1336, ℱ (02) 4938 3775; est NA; ❦ 3,500 cases; No visitors

Another brand-new venture with 13 hectares of Shiraz, Pinot Noir and Semillon. Their first wine is to be released in late 1999.

Hungerford Hill NR
McDonalds Road, Pokolbin, NSW 2321, ☎ (02) 4998 7666, ℱ (02) 4998 7682; est 1967; ❦ 18,000 cases; ⚏; A$; Mon-Fri 9-4.30, wkds 10-4.30

A much-transformed brand of the giant Southcorp, with *avant-garde* labels. The wines are made at Tulloch winery using high-quality grapes from the Central Ranges and Southern NSW Zones of NSW. The author has titular responsibility for the wines, hence no rating.

Hunter Ridge NR
Hermitage Road, Pokolbin, NSW 2320, ☎ (02) 4998 7500, ℱ (02) 4998 7211; est 1996; ❦ NFP; ⚏; A$; 7 days 10-5

The winery is that of McGuigan Bros, but the Hunter Ridge brand-name and wines are BRL Hardy's, providing it with a Hunter flag of convenience. A somewhat curious arrangement but presumably financially rewarding.

Ivanhoe Wines NR
Cnr Oakey Creek and Marrowbone Roads, Pokolbin, NSW 2320, ☎ (02) 4998 7325, ℱ (02) 4998 7848; est 1995; ❦ NA; ⚏; A$; 7 days 10-5

Stephen Drayton is the third branch of the family to be actively involved in this winery, with 25 hectares of 30-year-old vines providing a first-class base. The Ivanhoe property has been so-called since 1840.

Jackson's Hill ☆☆☆
Mount View Road, Mount View, NSW 2321, ☏ (02) 4990 1273, Ⓕ (02) 4991 3233; est 1984; ❦ 1,000 cases; ▼; A$; Thurs-Mon & public hols 10-5

A resident of the spectacularly scenic Mount View Road quixotically specialising in Cabernet Franc (and Semillon in various guises). The quality of the homemade chocolates is another reason to visit the cellar door.

Kevin Sobels Wines NR
Cnr Broke and Halls Roads, Pokolbin, NSW 2321, ☏ (02) 4998 7766, Ⓕ (02) 4998 7475; est 1992; ❦ 5,000 cases; ▼; A$; 7 days 10-5; pottery, crafts

Kevin Sobels has had a peripatetic career in the Hunter spanning 30 years. He now has eight hectares of estate plantings and specialises in his cellar-door/mail-order sales, offering arts and crafts as well as wine.

Kulkunbulla ☆☆☆☆
Brokenback Estate, Cnr Broke and Hermitage Roads, Pokolbin, NSW 2320, ☏ (02) 9954 1873, Ⓕ (02) 9954 1930; est 1996; ❦ 2,400 cases; No visitors

A reincarnation of part of the former Rothbury Brokenback Estate. This smoothly-run owner-syndicate has produced cleverly packaged Semillon and Chardonnay with excellent flavour, concentration and style.

Lake's Folly ☆☆☆☆☆
Broke Road, Pokolbin, NSW 2321, ☏ (02) 4998 7507, Ⓕ (02) 4998 7322; est 1963; ❦ 4000 cases; ▼; A$; Sat 10-4 when wine is available

Dr Max Lake pioneered the concept of 'weekend winemaking' by untrained winemakers in Australia (hence the name). His son Stephen is now in sole control, making superb, complex stone-fruit/tangy Chardonnay and finely structured Cabernets. If you can find it, enjoy!

Latara NR
Cnr McDonalds and Deaseys Roads, Pokolbin, NSW 2320, ☏ (02) 4998 7320; est 1979; ❦ 250 cases; ▼; A$; Sat 9-5, Sun 9-4

Most of the grapes from the 5-hectare, 20-year-old vineyard are sold to the Brokenwood winery, which in turn makes a tiny amount of Semillon, Cabernet Sauvignon and Shiraz for the Latara label.

Lindemans (Hunter Valley) NR
McDonalds Road, Pokolbin, NSW 2320, ☏ (02) 4998 7684, Ⓕ (02) 4998 7682; est 1843; ❦ 12,000 cases; ▼; A$; Mon-Fri 9-4.30, wkds & public hols 10-4.30; museum

The historic Ben Ean winery was completely restored in 1999 as an Olympic showplace, while a major upgrade was given to the winemaking base across the road at Tulloch (both owned by

Southcorp). The multi-million dollar expenditure will surely result in a continuing renaissance in the quality of the long-lived Semillon and Shiraz in particular. (The author is *inter alia* group winemaker for Lindeman, Tulloch and Hungerford Hill.)

Little's Winery ☆☆✔
Lot 3 Palmers Lane, Pokolbin, NSW 2321, ☏ (02) 4998 7626,
℻ (02) 4998 7867; est 1984; ❖ 6,000 cases; ♀; A$; 7 days 10-4.30
A bright and friendly family enterprise run by Ian Little. Off the beaten track, but has the habit of bobbing up with excellent wines that, individually, would receive a higher rating.

Louis-Laval Wines NR
160 Cobcroft Road, Broke, NSW 2330, ☏ (02) 6579 1105,
℻ (02) 6579 1105; est 1987; ❖ 600 cases; ♀; A$; by appt
Roy Meyer runs a 2.5-hectare organic vineyard and is proud of the fact that the winery has no refrigeration and no stainless steel. Both the Cabernet Sauvignon and Shiraz have had successes at wine shows.

Macquariedale Estate NR
40 Rusty Lane, Branxton, NSW 2335, ☏ (02) 4938 1408,
℻ (02) 4938 1408; est 1993; ❖ 2,000 cases; No visitors
In 1993 Ross McDonald began planting a small vineyard at Branxton. One thing led to another, he and his family moved from Sydney to the Hunter Valley, and purchased a 25-year-old vineyard to supplement production. The wines are contract-made, and sold through the Boutique Wine Centre in Broke Road, Pokolbin.

Margan Family Winegrowers ☆☆☆☆
1238 Milbrodale Road, Broke, NSW 2330, ☏ (02) 6579 1317,
℻ (02) 6579 1317; est 1989; ❖ 15,000 cases; ♀; A$; Mon-Fri 9-5
Flying winemaker Andrew Margan has returned to the roost with hospitality and marketing wife Lisa. A brand-new 700-tonne winery is producing excellent wine from ten hectares of estate vineyards and 13 under lease. The Chardonnay and Shiraz in particular stand out.

Marsh Estate ☆☆☆ V
Deasey Road, Pokolbin, NSW 2321, ☏ (02) 4998 7587,
℻ (02) 4998 7884; est 1971; ❖ 4,000 cases; ♀; A$; Mon-Fri 10-4.30, wkds 10-5
Peter Marsh, a former pharmacist, is one of the elder statesmen of the Hunter renaissance, quietly and competently making and selling all his wines via cellar door and mail order. His style of wines is always direct, with oak playing a minimal role, and cellaring paying dividends.

McGuigan ☆☆☆
PO Box 31, Cessnock, NSW 2335, ☏ (02) 4998 7400, ℻ (02) 4998 7401; est 1992; ❖ 400,000 cases; ♀; A$; 7 days 10-5; ⇌, ⦿

A highly successful Stock Exchange-listed public company, relentlessly driven by the awesome energy and peerless marketing skills of Brian McGuigan. Its grape sources are, to put it mildly, diverse, and its labels quite garish.

McWilliam's Mount Pleasant ☆☆☆☆☆ V
Marrowbone Road, Pokolbin, NSW 2320, ☏ *(02) 4998 7505,*
℻ *(02) 4998 7761; est 1880;* ❀ *NFP* ⚑*; A$; 7 days 10-4.30;* ✗*;* ⑩*; gift shop*

One of the Hunter Valley's treasures. The Elizabeth Semillon, released for a song when five years old, is the best-value white in Australia. Rose Hill and O'Shea Shiraz are silky classics, too.

Milbrovale NR
520 Milbrovale Road, Broke, NSW 2330, ☏ *(02) 9362 4915,*
℻ *(02) 9363 5716; est 1995;* ❀ *11,500 cases; No visitors*

Former chemists and chain-store owners Richard Owens and wife Mary are investing A$5 million in two substantial vineyards and a 500-tonne, 30,000-case winery. Watch this space.

Mistletoe Wines NR
Lot 1 Hermitage Road, Pokolbin, NSW 2335, ☏ *(02) 4998 7770,*
℻ *(02) 4998 7792; est 1967;* ❀ *2,000 cases;* ⚑*; A$; Mon-Fri 10-6 or by appt*

A name that has come and gone at various times since 1909 has been revived by the Sloan family. The pleasant wines are made by contract winemaker Jon Reynolds and sold exclusively through cellar door and mail order.

Molly Morgan Vineyard ☆☆☆½
Talga Road, Lovedale, NSW 2321, ☏ *(02) 4930 7695,* ℻ *(02) 9235 1876; est 1968;* ❀ *1,400 cases;* ⚑*; A$; wkds & public hols 10-5*

New ownership by powerful former wine retailers, 30-year-old vines, skilled winemaking, and the raunchy history of convict Molly Morgan has revitalised interest in this picturesque vineyard. Powerful, lemony Semillon is setting the pace.

Montagne View Estate NR
555 Hermitage Road, Pokolbin, NSW 2335, ☏ *(02) 4998 7822,*
℻ *(02) 6574 7276; est 1993;* ❀ *500 cases;* ⚑*; A$; 7 days 10-5;* ⑩*;* 🛏

Luxury is the operative word at this eight-suite guest-house and restaurant; set among five hectares of Chardonnay and Merlot. The wines are contract-made.

Moorebank Vineyard NR
Palmers Lane, Pokolbin, NSW 2320, ☏ *(02) 4998 7610,*
℻ *(02) 4998 7367; est 1977;* ❀ *1,750 cases;* ⚑*; A$; Fri-Mon 10-5 or by appt; museum*

Most of the grapes from the mature 5.5-hectare vineyard owned by Ian Burgess and Debra Moore are sold to Brokenwood, which contract-makes part for Moorebank. The packaging is immaculate in an *avant-garde* style; peachy Chardonnay is best.

Mount Eyre Vineyard NR
Wollombi Road, Broke, NSW 2330, ☏ (02) 6579 1087, ℻ (02) 6579 1087; est 1996; ❖ NA; ♀; A$; at Broke Store

The 20-hectare estate is planted with Semillon, Chardonnay, Shiraz, Cabernet Franc and Cabernet Sauvignon. The wines, made by Simon Gilbert at Muswellbrook, are available for tasting (and purchase) at the Broke Store.

Mount View Estate ☆☆☆☆
Mount View Road, Mount View, NSW 2325, ☏ (02) 4990 3307, ℻ (02) 4991 1289; est 1971; ❖ 3,000 cases; ♀; A$; Mon-Fri 10-4, wkds & hols 10-5

With the return of the prodigal winemaker-son Keith Tulloch (trained by Len Evans at Rothbury), wine quality here has soared across the board. Look for its unusual Verdelho fortified wines.

Murray Robson Wines NR
'Bellona', Old North Road, Rothbury, NSW 2335, ☏ (02) 4938 3577, ℻ (02) 4938 3577; est 1993; ❖ 4,000 cases; ♀; A$; 7 days 9-5

Third time lucky, perhaps. In his third incarnation, regional veteran Murray Robson still signs every label by hand. The wines come from four hectares of estate plantings supplemented by grapes purchased from elsewhere in the Hunter Valley.

Oakvale ☆☆☆
Broke Road, Pokolbin, NSW 2321, ☏ (02) 4998 7520, ℻ (02) 4998 7747; est 1893; ❖ 5,000 cases; ♀; A$; 7 days 10-5

Former Sydney solicitor Barrie Shields makes big, golden-hued, buttery/toasty Semillon and Chardonnay and almost delicate reds at this historic winery once owned by the late Doug Elliott.

Peacock Hill Vineyard NR
Cnr Branxton Road and Palmers Lane, Pokolbin, NSW 2320, ☏ (02) 4998 7661, ℻ (02) 4998 7661; est 1969; ❖ 2,000 cases; ♀; A$; Fri-Mon, public & school hols 10-5; ⊭

The Peacock Hill Vineyard was first planted in 1969 as part of the Rothbury Estate; after several further changes of ownership it was acquired by George Tsiros and Silvi Laumets in October 1995. They have rejuvenated the vineyard and established a small lodge; the wines are contract-made.

Pendarves Estate ☆☆☆✓
110 Old North Road, Belford, NSW 2335, ☏ (02) 6574 7222, ℻ (02) 9970 6152; est 1986; ❖ 9,000 cases; ♀; A$; wkds 11-5, Mon-Fri by appt; ⊭

Wine and health activist, wine historian and general practitioner Dr Philip Norrie also finds time to grow grapes and (via contract) make worthwhile wines of assorted variety and hue.

Pepper Tree ☆☆☆☆
Halls Road, Pokolbin, NSW 2321, ☏ (02) 4998 7539, ℻ (02) 4998 7746; est 1993; ❖ 40,000 cases; ♀; A$; 7 days 9-5; ⊧⊧; ⊭

With vineyards in both the Hunter Valley and Coonawarra, Pepper Tree winemaker Chris Cameron has made a determined and quite successful effort to establish Pepper Tree as one of Australia's leading producers of Merlot. Chardonnay and Shiraz are also good.

Peppers Creek NR
Broke Road, Pokolbin, NSW 2321, ☏ (02) 4998 7532, Ⓕ (02) 4998 7531; est 1987; ❖ 700 cases; ♀; A$; Wed-Sun 10-5; cafe, ⌂; antiques
A combined café, antique shop and winery, selling all its eclectic range of wine through the cellar door.

Peterson Champagne House NR
Cnr Broke and Branxton Roads, Pokolbin, NSW 2320, ☏ (02) 4998 7881, Ⓕ (02) 4998 7882; est 1994; ❖ 7,000 cases; ♀; A$; 7 days 9-5; ¶
This house specialises in sparkling wine (which is fine), which it obstinately calls Champagne (which it is not).

Petersons ☆☆☆✓
Mount View Road, Mount View, NSW 2325, ☏ (02) 4990 1704, Ⓕ (02) 4991 1344; est 1971; ❖ 15,000 cases; ♀; A$; Mon-Sat 9-5, Sun 10-5
One of the older wineries of this region, established by Newcastle pharmacist Colin Peterson, with 20 hectares of beautifully located vineyards. It has had various moments of glory along the way, with rich Semillon, Chardonnay and powerful, earthy/cherryish Back Block Shiraz.

Piggs Peake NR
697 Hermitage Road, Pokolbin, NSW 2335D, ☏ (02) 6574 7000, Ⓕ (02) 6574 7070; est 1998; ❖ 8,000 cases; ♀; A$; 7 days 10-5; gallery
The derivation of the name remains a mystery to me. It is one of the newest wineries to be constructed in the Hunter Valley, sourcing most of its grapes from other growers to complement the one hectare of estate plantings.

Pokolbin Estate ☆☆✓
McDonalds Road, Pokolbin, NSW 2321, ☏ (02) 4998 7524, Ⓕ (02) 4998 7765; est 1980; ❖ 3,500 cases; ♀; A$; 7 days 10-6; ¶
This is more a regional wine shop than a winery, offering a wide range of wines (eg Lake's Folly, Pothana) in addition to its own contract-made wines, which come from 12 hectares of estate plantings.

Poole's Rock ☆☆☆✓
Lot 41 Wollombi Road, Broke, NSW 2330, ☏ (02) 9667 1622, Ⓕ (02) 9667 1442; est 1988; ❖ 4,000 cases; No visitors
There are five hectares of estate-grown Chardonnay, providing the single peachy/creamy wine for Sydney banker David Clarke (*see* Cockfighter's Ghost), made for him at McWilliam's by Phil Ryan.

Pothana NR
Carramar, Belford, NSW 2335, ☎ (02) 6574 7164, Ⓕ (02) 6574 7209; est 1984; ❖ 2,000 cases; ⚑; A$; by appt

The Chardonnay is made as a soft, buttery/toasty wine in the mainstream Hunter Valley style. It is principally sold through Pokolbin Estate and by mailing list.

Reg Drayton Wines ☆☆☆☆ V
Cnr Pokolbin Mountain and McDonalds Roads, Pokolbin, NSW 2321, ☎ (02) 4998 7523, Ⓕ (02) 4998 7523; est 1989; ❖ 3,000 cases; ⚑; A$; 7 days 10-5; museum

Fifth-generation Robyn Drayton (billed as the Hunter's first female *vigneron*) and husband Craig inherited the business after her parents were killed in an air crash. Very good vineyards and skilled contract winemaking by Tyrrell's helps produce good Chardonnay, Shiraz, and solidly built Semillon.

Rothbury Estate ☆☆☆☆ V
Broke Road, Pokolbin, NSW 2321, ☎ (02) 4998 7555, Ⓕ (02) 4998 7553; est 1968; ❖ 30,000 cases; ⚑; A$; 7 days 9.30-4.30; ⦿

Rothbury was wrestled from the hands of Len Evans by Fosters/Mildara-Blass in a bitterly contested takeover battle in 1998, but it is still a Hunter landmark. Its slimmed-down portfolio of wines in three ranges are well-made and well-priced. Chardonnay and Shiraz are best.

Rothbury Ridge NR
Wilderness and Talga Roads, Rothbury, NSW 2320, ☎ (02) 4930 7206, Ⓕ (02) 4930 7944; est 1988; ❖ NA; ⚑; A$; by appt

The 17-hectare Rothbury Ridge vineyard has nothing to do with Rothbury Estate – Rothbury is a place-name, and hence cannot be protected as a trade name or trademark. Its wines are contract-made at Wandin Valley Estate – which, I suspect, purchases a significant proportion of the production.

Saddlers Creek ☆☆☆☆
Marrowbone Road, Pokolbin, NSW 2321, ☎ (02) 4991 1770, Ⓕ (02) 4991 1778; est 1989; ❖ 10,000 cases; ⚑; A$; 7 days 9-5

This house made an impressive start with consistently full-flavoured, rich wines. Marrowbone Chardonnay and Equus Hunter Shiraz are its best wines in a kaleidoscopic array of labels and sub-brands.

Sandalyn Wilderness Estate NR
Wilderness Road, Rothbury, NSW 2321, ☎ (02) 4930 7611, Ⓕ (02) 4930 7611; est 1988; ❖ 3,500 cases; ⚑; A$; 7 days 10-5; musical events

Sandra and Lindsay Whaling preside over the picturesque cellar-door building at Sandalyn, on the evocatively named Wilderness Road. You will also find a one-hole golf range and views to the Wattagan, Brokenback and Molly Morgan ranges. The estate has 8.85 hectares of vineyards.

Scarborough ☆☆☆☆
Gillards Road, Pokolbin, NSW 2321, ☏ (02) 4998 7563,
⒡ (02) 4998 7786; est 1985; ❧ 10,000 cases; ⚐; A$; 7 days 9-5
The vastly experienced Ian Scarborough crafts two styles of Chardonnay: richer (for the local market) and finer (for export). Both are sold with several years' bottle age.

Sutherland ☆☆☆⟡
Deasey's Road, Pokolbin, NSW 2321, ☏ (02) 4998 7650,
⒡ (02) 4998 7603; est 1979; ❧ 7,000 cases; ⚐; A$; 10-4.30; ⌂
With substantial and now fully mature vineyards to draw upon, Sutherland is a more or less consistent producer of generous, mainstream Hunter whites and reds, albeit with a high level of phenolic extraction. Chenin Blanc Crémant harks back to the Loire Valley.

Tamburlaine ☆☆☆☆⟡
McDonalds Road, Pokolbin, NSW 2321, ☏ (02) 4998 7570,
⒡ (02) 4998 7763; est 1966; ❧ 40,000 cases; ⚐; A$; 7 days 9.30-5
A thriving business, which, notwithstanding the fact that it has doubled its already substantial production in recent years, sells over 90 per cent of its wines through cellar door and by mailing list (with an active tasting-club members' cellar programme offering wines held and matured at Tamburlaine). Unashamedly and deliberately focused on the tourist trade (and of course, its club members).

Tempus Two Wines ☆☆☆☆⟡ V
Hermitage Road, Pokolbin, NSW 2321, ☏ (02) 9818 7222,
⒡ (02) 9818 7333; est 1997; ❧ 20,000 cases; ⚐; A$; 7 days 10-5
Formerly Hermitage Road Wines, this is now a brand loosely based at the McGuigan Bros Hunter Ridge Winery. It draws on grapes from all over South East Australia to produce some surprisingly good, cleverly polished wines. Very good lemon, mineral, and herb-flavoured Riesling, and Semillon.

Terrace Vale ☆☆☆
Deasey's Lane, Pokolbin, NSW 2321, ☏ (02) 4998 7517,
⒡ (02) 4998 7814; est 1971; ❧ 8,000 cases; ⚐; A$; 7 days 9-5
Long-established but relatively low-profile winery heavily dependent on its local trade. Smart new packaging has lifted the presentation, and there are one or two very good wines.

Thalgara Estate ☆☆☆☆
De Beyers Road, Pokolbin, NSW 2321, ☏ (02) 4998 7717,
⒡ (02) 4998 7774; est 1985; ❧ 3,000 cases; ⚐; A$; 7 days 10-5; ⌂
Steve Lamb runs this relatively small and low-profile 6-hectare estate, producing an outstanding Show Reserve Shiraz.

The Belgenny Vineyard NR
92 DeBeyers Road, Pokolbin, NSW 2320, ☏ (02) 9247 5300,
⒡ (02) 9247 7273; est 1992; ❧ 5,000 cases; No visitors

Established by Norman Seckold with the planting of 5.8 hectares of Chardonnay, 1.2 of Semillon, 4.5 of Shiraz and 2.1 of Merlot. The wines are contract-made, with a cellar door and function rooms planned to open in January 2000.

Tinklers Vineyard NR
Pokolbin Mountains Road, Pokolbin, NSW 2330, ☎ *(02) 4998 7435,* ⓕ *(02) 4998 7529; est 1997;* ❖ *NA;* ⚑; *A$; by appt*
Ian and Usher Tinkler own a large vineyard (32 hectares) on the slopes of the Pokolbin Mountain Road. Most of the production is sold, with a small amount contract-made for cellar-door sales.

Tinonee Vineyard NR
Milbrodale Road, Broke, NSW 2330, ☎ *(02) 6579 1308,* ⓕ *(02) 6579 1146; est 1997;* ❖ *3,000 cases;* ⚑; *A$; wkds & public hols 10-5; gallery*
Ian Craig has established 14 hectares of vineyards on a mix of red volcanic and river flat soils at Broke. Once all the vines come into bearing (by 2000-01), annual production will reach 5,000 cases.

Tintilla Wines NR
725 Hermitage Road, Pokolbin, NSW 2335, ☎ *0411 214 478,* ⓕ *(02) 9767 6894; est 1993;* ❖ *1,000 cases;* ⚑; *A$; by appt*
The Lusby family has established 7.5 hectares of Semillon, Sangiovese, Shiraz and Merlot, making a promising start with a cherry-and-chocolate 1998 Shiraz. Estate-grown olives and olive oil add interest.

Tulloch NR
'Glen Elgin', De Beyers Road, Pokolbin, NSW 2321, ☎ *(02) 4998 7580,* ⓕ *(02) 4998 7682; est 1895;* ❖ *26,000 cases;* ⚑; *A$; Mon-Fri 9-4.30, wkds 10-4.30*
A once-famous family-owned company that passed through several hands before becoming part of Southcorp. Inoffensive, unoaked Verdelho is its *forté*. Not rated because the author has titular responsibility for the brand.

Tyrrell's ☆☆☆☆☆ V
Broke Road, Pokolbin, NSW 2321, ☎ *(02) 4993 7000,* ⓕ *(02) 4998 7723; est 1858;* ❖ *620,000 cases;* ⚑; *A$; Mon-Sat 8-5*
1971 Vat 47 Chardonnay launched a thousand ships. This craftily crafted wine is still one of the flagbearers. Vat 1 Semillon, released when five years old, is a superb mix of lemon, honey and toast; the elegant Vat 9 Shiraz is also very good. These icons head a cascade of wines down all price points to Long Flat White and Long Flat Red.

Undercliff NR
Yango Creek Road, Wollombi, NSW 2325, ☎ *(02) 4998 3322,* ⓕ *(02) 4998 3322; est 1990;* ❖ *1,000 cases;* ⚑; *A$; wkds 10-4 or by appt; etching gallery*
James and Janet Luxton run a winery-cum-art studio at

Wollombi on the very edge of the Hunter Valley, producing etchings and prints as well as nice wines which have had success in local wine shows over recent years.

Van de Scheur NR

O'Connors Lane, Pokolbin, NSW 2321, ☎ (02) 4998 7789, ⓕ (02) 4998 7789; est 1995; ❖ 1,500 cases; ♀; A$; wkds 10-5

After 25 years making wine, Kees Van de Scheur has finally moved to establish his own winery and vineyard on part of the Ingleside Vineyard, which was planted in 1872 but went out of production in the 1930s. While the estate vineyards come into bearing, Van de Scheur is making Semillon, Chardonnay and Shiraz from purchased grapes. Worth watching.

Verona Vineyard NR

Small Winemakers Centre, McDonalds Road, Pokolbin, NSW 2321, ☎ (02) 4998 7668, ⓕ (02) 4998 7430; est 1972; ❖ NA; ♀; A$; 7 days 10-5

Verona has had a chequered history, yet remains a significant business acting as a sales centre for a number of other Hunter Valley winemakers from its premises directly opposite Brokenwood. Fruit for the Verona wines comes from 22 hectares at Muswellbrook, and five hectares surrounding the winery.

Vinden Estate NR

Lot 17 Gillards Road, Pokolbin, NSW 2320, ☎ (02) 4998 7410, ⓕ (02) 4998 7421; est 1998; ❖ 950 cases; ♀; A$; wkds & public hols 10-5

Sandra and Guy Vinden have bought their dream home with landscaped gardens and 2.5 hectares of vineyard in the foreground, and the Brokenback mountain range in the distance. The inaugural 1998 Semillon and 1998 Chardonnay were both competently made and will improve with time in bottle.

Wandin Valley Estate ☆☆☆☆

Wilderness Road, Rothbury, NSW 2321, ☎ (02) 4930 7313, ⓕ (02) 4930 7317; est 1973; ❖ 10,000 cases; ♀; A$; 7 days 10-5; ⌘; café, cricket ground

Australian television producer James Davern and family run a quality winery, village green cricket oval and extensive cottage accomodation. Reserve Chardonnay (toasty, spicy) and Reserve Cabernet Sauvignon (lush, cassis, blackcurrant) lead the way.

Warraroong Estate NR

Wilderness Road, Lovedale, NSW 2321, ☎ (02) 4930 7594, ⓕ (02) 4930 7199; est 1988; ❖ NA; ♀; A$; 7 days 10-5

Warraroong Estate was formerly Fraser Vineyard, and adopted its new name after it changed hands in 1997. The name 'Warraroong' is an Aboriginal word for hillside, reflecting the southwesterly aspect of the property that looks back towards the Brokenback Range and Watagan Mountains. The label design is from a painting by local Aboriginal artist Kia Kiro.

Wines of Australia

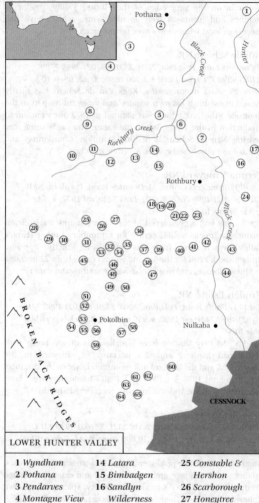

LOWER HUNTER VALLEY

1 *Wyndham*	14 *Latara*	25 *Constable &*
2 *Pothana*	15 *Bimbadgen*	*Hershon*
3 *Pendarves*	16 *Sandlyn*	26 *Scarborough*
4 *Montagne View*	*Wilderness*	27 *Honeytree*
5 *Murray Robson*	17 *Wandin*	28 *Oakvale*
6 *Belbourie*	*Valley*	29 *Chateau*
7 *Molly Morgan*	18 *Little's*	*Francois*
8 *Tintilla*	19 *Carindale*	30 *Tyrell's*
9 *Mistletoe*	20 *Moorebank*	31 *Peppers Creek*
10 *Hunter Ridge*	21 *Calais*	32 *McGuigan*
11 *Marsh*	22 *Evans Family*	33 *Brokenwood*
12 *Terrace Vale*	23 *Peacock Hill*	34 *Verona*
13 *Sutherland*	24 *Allanmere*	35 *Glenguin*

New South Wales 31

36 *Rothbury*	**47** *Windarra*	**58** *Van de Scheur*
37 *Blaxlands*	**48** *Pokolbin*	**59** *McWilliam's*
38 *Pepper Tree*	**49** *Tulloch*	*Mount Pleasant*
39 *Kevin Sobels*	**50** *Thalgara*	**60** *Saddlers Creek*
40 *Lake's Folly*	**51** *Lindemans*	**61** *Jackson's Hill*
41 *Peterson*	**52** *Hungerford Hill*	**62** *Mount View*
Champagne	**53** *Reg Drayton*	**63** *Petersons*
42 *Wilderness*	**54** *Tinklers*	**64** *Farrell's*
43 *Allandale*	**55** *Ivanhoe*	*Limestone Creek*
44 *Capercaillie*	**56** *Drayton's*	**65** *Briar Ridge*
45 *Chateau Pato*	*Family*	
46 *Tamburlaine*	**57** *Golden Grape*	

Wilderness Estate NR

Branxton Road, Pokolbin, NSW 2321, ☎ (02) 4998 7755, ℻ (02) 4998 7750; est 1986; ❖ 25,000 cases; ⚲; A$; 7 days 9-5
Long-term Wyndham winemaker John Baruzzi and grape-grower/winemaker Joe Lesnik have 37 hectares of mature vineyards.

Windarra NR

DeBeyers Road, Pokolbin, NSW 2321, ☎ (02) 4998 7648, ℻ (02) 4998 7648; est NA; ❖ NA; ⚲; A$; Tues-Sun 10-5
The Andresen family has six hectares of Semillon, Chardonnay and Shiraz, producing contract-made wines.

Wyndham Estate ☆☆☆

Dalwood Road, Dalwood, NSW 2335, ☎ (02) 4938 3444, ℻ (02) 4938 3422; est 1828; ❖ NFP; ⚲; A$; Mon-Fri 9.30-5, wkds 10-4; ᛃ

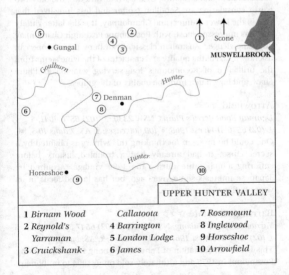

UPPER HUNTER VALLEY

1 *Birnam Wood*	*Callatoota*	**7** *Rosemount*
2 *Reynold's*	**4** *Barrington*	**8** *Inglewood*
Yarraman	**5** *London Lodge*	**9** *Horseshoe*
3 *Cruickshank-*	**6** *James*	**10** *Arrowfield*

The Hunter Valley fiefdom of the vast Orlando-Wyndham octopus, producing wines of utterly consistent quality and style that will never frighten the fish.

Upper Hunter Valley

Perversely, the distinction between the Lower and Upper Hunter is not one made under the GI framework. Technically they are one region, which fragments into small areas such as Pokolbin, Rothbury and Broke Fordwich. It is an idiosyncratic approach that undoubtedly pleases the *vignerons* of the Upper Hunter, for which you might as well read Rosemount, the utterly dominant force in the region.

Rosemount has come to this position by a slightly unusual path. Viticulture had come and gone between 1870 and 1910. Fifty years later, in 1960, Penfolds made the brave – though not necessarily correct – decision to uproot itself from the Lower Hunter Valley and move lock, stock and barrel to the Upper Hunter Valley. In 1969 Rosemount Estate arrived and opened its doors for business. By 1978 Penfolds decided it had made a major mistake and sold its winery to Rosemount, an act that marked its exit from NSW.

While Rosemount now dominates the Upper Hunter Valley scene, its viticultural and winemaking empire extends to Mudgee and Orange (NSW); McLaren Vale, Coonawarra and Adelaide Hills (SA); and the Yarra Valley (Victoria). The reasons for this spread – and Rosemount is not the only winery to draw on fruit from outside the region – are the inherent limitations on viticulture in the Upper Hunter Valley.

It is simply not suited to red wine production. The wines lack concentration and structure. Of the white varieties, the only two worth considering are Semillon (softer and less long-lived that that of the Lower Hunter) and Chardonnay. It is the latter variety that has impressed most, with Rosemount Roxburgh Chardonnay an acknowledged Australian classic. Even here, though, one can ask how much of the quality and character of the wine stems from the brilliance of Rosemount's long-serving winemaker Philip Shaw, and how much from the quality of the grapes.

Arrowfield ☆☆☆
Denman Road, Jerry's Plains, NSW 2330, ☎ *(02) 6576 4041,*
℻ *(02) 6576 4144; est 1968;* ❖ *100,000 cases;* ⚱; *A$; 7 days 10-5;* ⎸⚬⎹
One could be forgiven for thinking this winery is blighted by a secret curse; it had already had a troubled history before suffering a major fire during the 1999 vintage. Acquired by Japanese interests some years ago, but has lacked focus in its wines both before and since.

Barrington Estate ☆☆☆✓
Yarraman Road, Wybong, NSW 2333, ☎ *(02) 6547 8118,*
℻ *(02) 6547 8039; est 1967;* ❖ *20,000 cases;* ⚱; *A$; by appt;* ⇌
This is the reincarnation of Penfolds' Wybong Estate, bought by Rosemount in 1978 and ultimately sold on in 1994 to millionaire

entrepreneur Gary Blom. Blom has big plans for the estate. Yarraman Road is the top label; Barrington Estate the second.

Birnam Wood Wines NR
Turanville Road, Scone, NSW 2337, ☏ (02) 6545 3286, ℻ (02) 6545 3431; est 1994; ❖ 4,000 cases; ⚑; A$; 7 days 10-4
Former Sydney car dealer Mike Eagan and wife Min originally moved to Scone to establish a horse stud farm. The vineyard came later but is now a major part of the business, with over 30 hectares of vines. The majority of the production is sold, with a small part vinified for Birnam Wood.

Cruickshank-Callatoota Estate ☆☆☆
2656 Wybong Road, Wybong, NSW 2333, ☏ (02) 6547 8149, ℻ (02) 6547 8144; est 1973; ❖ 7,000 cases; ⚑; A$; 7 days 9-5; ✗
Owned by Sydney management consultant John Cruickshank and family. Wine quality has definitely improved in the 1990s, although the wines still show strong regional, rather earthy, characteristics; and the label itself likewise doggedly remains old-fashioned.

Horseshoe Vineyard NR
Horseshoe Road, Horseshoe Valley via Denman, NSW 2328, ☏ (02) 6547 3528; est 1986; ❖ NFP; ⚑; A$; wkds 9-5
Seems to have fallen by the wayside after its wonderful start in 1986, making rich, full-flavoured, barrel-fermented Semillons and Chardonnays that were still drinking well ten years later. Younger vintages do not have the same magic.

Inglewood Vineyards ☆☆☆
Yarrawa Road, Denman, NSW 2328, ☏ (02) 6547 2556, ℻ (02) 6547 2546; est 1988; ❖ 18,000 cases; No visitors
A very significant addition to the viticultural scene, with almost 170 hectares of established vineyards, involving an investment of around A$7 million. Much of the fruit is sold to Southcorp but some is vinified under contract for Inglewood's expanding winemaking and marketing operations.

James Estate NR
Mudgee Road, Baerami via Denman, NSW 2333, ☏ (02) 6547 5168, ℻ (02) 6547 5164; est 1971; ❖ 20,000 cases; ⚑; A$; 7 days 10-4.30
The former Serenella Estate, sold in 1997 to David James, and still undergoing a period of transition. There are 60 hectares of estate vineyards and a substantial winery which yield the James Estate, Serenella, Southern Cross and Terra Australis brands.

London Lodge Estate NR
Muswellbrook Road, Gungal, NSW 2333, ☏ (02) 6547 6122, ℻ (02) 6547 6122; est 1988; ❖ NA; ⚑; A$; 7 days 10-9; ⑩; arts and crafts
This is a 16-hectare vineyard belonging Stephen and Joanne

Horner. It is planted with Chardonnay, Pinot Noir, Shiraz and Cabernet Sauvignon, and sold through a cellar door that also offers a full array of tourist attractions.

Meerea Park ☆☆☆✓
2 Denton Close, Windella via Maitland, NSW 2321, ☎ 0417 693 310, ⓕ (02) 4930 7100; est 1991; ❖ 15,000 cases; ⚲; A$; at The Boutique Wine Centre, Broke Road, Pokolbin

This is a particularly interesting venture and the brainchild of Rhys Eather, great-grandson of Alexander Munro, a famous local *vigneron*. Eather buys grapes from here, there and everywhere, and makes the wine at Simon Gilbert's contract winery at Muswellbrook.

Minimbah NR
Minimbah House, Whittingham, NSW 2330, ☎ (02) 6572 4028, ⓕ (02) 6572 1513; est 1996; ❖ NA; No visitors

This is a venture in its infancy. There are four hectares of Chardonnay and one of Shiraz which were planted in 1996. The first releases are due in 2000, and will be made under contract by Simon Gilbert.

Reynolds Yarraman ☆☆☆☆ V
Yarraman Road, Wybong, NSW 2333, ☎ (02) 6547 8127, ⓕ (02) 6547 8013; est 1967; ❖ 15,000 cases; ⚲; A$; Mon-Sat 10-4, Sun & public hols 11-4; ⦿

Jon Reynolds surprised many industry observers when he quit his high-profile job as chief winemaker at Houghton in the Swan Valley in 1984, ultimately buying this stone winery and vineyard in the Upper Hunter Valley. Following an initial struggle, the flair and polish has returned with a portfolio that focuses on Hunter Semillon and Chardonnay, and Cabernet Sauvignon from Orange.

Rosemount Estate (Hunter Valley) ☆☆☆☆☆ V
Rosemount Road, Denman, NSW 2328, ☎ (02) 6549 6400, ⓕ (02) 6549 6499; est 1969; ❖ 700,000 cases; ⚲; A$; Mon-Sat 10-4; Sun summer 10-4, winter 12-4; ⦿

Rosemount Estate has achieved a miraculous balancing act over the past years, maintaining – indeed increasing – wine quality while presiding over an ever-expanding empire and ever-increasing production. The wines are consistently of excellent value. All have real character and individuality; not a few are startlingly good.

Southern Grand Estate NR
c/o 111 Goulburn Street, Sydney, NSW 2333, ☎ (02) 9282 0987, ⓕ (02) 9211 8130; est 1997; ❖ 1,600 cases; No visitors

Based on the long-lost Hollydene Estate, the label of which (though not the vineyards) disappeared over 20 years ago. A holiday and convention resort is planned by new owners, the Kho family.

Mudgee

It is not hard to see why the aborigines bestowed the name *Mudgee*, meaning 'nest in the hills', on this region. The hills in question are a gentler part of the Great Dividing Range. It is easy to see why the three German families – Roth, Kurtz and Bucholz – were drawn to this area, establishing vineyards in 1858, and why the Roth and Kurtz families were still actively involved in grape-growing and winemaking 100 years later.

The other key figure in the early days was the remarkable Italian, Dr Thomas Fiaschi, who first arrived in far north Queensland in 1874. In '79 he established a 20-hectare vineyard on the banks of the Hawkesbury River and went on to combine an extraordinary army career with his winemaking interests, founding the Tizzana (on the Hawkesbury) and establishing the Augustine Vineyards and Winery in Mudgee. From this point on the 55 vineyards that existed in Mudgee in 1893 slowly dwindled away until by 1963 only the Roth family's Craigmoor Vineyard was in production. The following year Alf Kurtz established Mudgee Wines, and the recovery of Mudgee was underway. By 1993 there were once again 55 growers in the district, tending 430 hectares; by 1999 the area under vine exceeded 1,200 hectares and is still rapidly growing.

Mudgee has the distinction of providing a virus-free, pre-*phylloxera* clone of Chardonnay identified by the famous French ampelographer Professor Paul Truel. But it is as a red wine region that Mudgee has made its mark, primarily with deeply coloured Shiraz and Cabernet Sauvignon. The berry-and-chocolate Shiraz develops earthy overtones with ten years' bottle age, while the Cabernet offers lush fruit laced through with balanced tannins.

Abercorn ☆☆☆
Cassilis Road, Mudgee, NSW 2850, ☎ (02) 6373 3106, ⓕ (02) 6373 3108; est 1996; ❦ NA; ⛿; A$; by appt

Former journalist Tim Stevens and wife Connie acquired the run-down Abercorn vineyard in 1996. Chardonnay and Cabernet Sauvignon are currently contract-made, but the Stevens plan to build a winery and do it themselves within the next three years.

Andrew Harris Vineyards ☆☆☆☆⌁
Sydney Road, Mudgee, NSW 2850, ☎ (02) 6373 1213, ⓕ (02) 6373 1296; est 1991; ❦ 12,000 cases; No visitors

Andrew and Debbie Harris lost no time and spared no expense in establishing 90 hectares of vineyards. Careful fruit selection and skilled contract winemaking has resulted in high-quality wines in three ranges: Premium, Reserve and The Vision (a super-premium Cabernet/Shiraz). All have abundant fruit and polished oak.

Botobolar ☆☆☆⌁ V
89 Botobolar Road, Mudgee, NSW 2850, ☎ (02) 6373 3840, ⓕ (02) 6373 3789; est 1971; ❦ 5,000 cases; ⛿; A$; Mon-Sat 10-5, Sun 10-3

Kevin Karstrom has taken over the mantle of Gil Wahlquist in running this pioneering organic vineyard. His portfolio includes a preservative-free dry red and dry white; but the conventional Shiraz and Cabernet Sauvignon are the best of the bunch.

Brittens Wines NR
Lot 8, Stoney Creek Road, Cooyal via Mudgee, NSW 2850,
☎ *(02) 6373 5320, est 1993;* ❖ *NA;* ♀; *A$; Sat 9-4, Sun & public hols 9-3*

A relatively new producer in Mudgee, with eight hectares of Semillon, Chardonnay, Merlot and Cabernet Sauvignon, much of it still coming into production. The contract-made wines are all sold through cellar door and mail order.

Burnbrae NR
Hill End Road, Erudgere via Mudgee, NSW 2850, ☎ *(02) 6373 3504,* Ⓕ *(02) 6373 3601; est 1976;* ❖ *NFP;* ♀; *A$; Wed-Mon 9-5*

The Mace family, who were the founders of Burnbrae, sold to Alan Cox in 1996. It continues as an estate-based operation with 23 hectares of vineyards. The winemaking techniques and equipment are traditional.

Burrundulla NR
Sydney Road, Mudgee, NSW 2850, ☎ *(02) 6372 1620,*
Ⓕ *(02) 6372 4058; est 1996;* ❖ *NA; No visitors*

A very substantial venture but still in its infancy. The Cox family (Chris, Michael and Ted) is busy establishing 54 hectares of vineyards, with Chardonnay, Shiraz and Cabernet vines.

Craigmoor ☆☆☆
Craigmoor Road, Mudgee, NSW 2850, ☎ *(02) 6372 2208,*
Ⓕ *(02) 6372 4464; est 1858;* ❖ *NFP;* ♀; *A$; Mon-Fri 9-4, wkds 10-4;* ⦿; *museum*

One of the oldest wineries in Australia to remain in continuous production. It is now the chief public face of Orlando-Wyndham's substantial winemaking operations in Mudgee (*qv* Montrose), with an atmospheric cellar door.

Eurunderee Flats Winery NR
Henry Lawson Drive, Mudgee, NSW 2850, ☎ *(02) 6373 3954,*
Ⓕ *(02) 6373 3750; est 1985;* ❖ *1,500 cases;* ♀; *A$; Sun-Fri 10-4, Sat 9-5*

Sometimes called Knights Vines, although the wines are marketed under the Eurunderee Flats label. There are five hectares of vineyards that yield white wines of variable quality, and rather better dry red table wines.

Half Mile Creek ☆☆☆
George Campbell Drive, Mudgee, NSW 2850, ☎ *(02) 6372 3880,*
Ⓕ *(02) 6372 2977; est 1981;* ❖ *10,000 cases;* ♀; *A$; 7 days 10-4*

Now part of the Mildara-Blass empire, Half Mile Creek has a great history. It was once the Augustine Vineyard, established by the Roth family in the 19th century, and purchased by

Dr Thomas Fiaschi (one of the great unsung heroes of the Australian wine industry) in 1917. A chequered career followed but it remains a substantial producer.

Huntington Estate ☆☆☆☆☆ V
Cassilis Road, Mudgee, NSW 2850, ☏ (02) 6373 3825, ℉ (02) 6373 3730; est 1969; ☙ 25,000 cases; Mon-Fri 9-5, wkds 10-4

The remarkable Roberts family members have a passion for wine that is equalled only by their passion for music. The Huntington Music Festival is a major annual event. The velvety red wines are outstanding, and sell for absurdly low prices.

Knowland Estate NR
Mount Vincent Road, Running Stream, NSW 2850, ☏ (02) 6358 8420, ℉ (02) 6358 8423; est 1990; ☙ 250 cases; ☥; A$; by appt

The former Mount Vincent Winery sells much of its grape production from the 3.5 hectares of vineyards to other makers, but proposes to increase production under its own label.

Lawson's Hill ☆☆☆
Henry Lawson Drive, Eurunderee, Mudgee, NSW 2850, ☏ (02) 6373 3953, ℉ (02) 6373 3948; est 1985; ☙ 3,300 cases; ☥; A$; Mon, Thurs, Fri, Sat 10-4.30, Sun 10-4; ⊨

Former music director and arranger (for musical acts in Sydney clubs) José Grace and wife June run a strongly tourist-oriented operation offering an array of wines, contract-made from their eight hectares of vineyard. The reds are richly representative of the deeply coloured, flavoursome Mudgee style.

Lowe Family Wines ☆☆☆
9 Paterson Road, Bolwarra, NSW 2320, ☏ (02) 4930 0233, ℉ (02) 4930 0233; est 1987; ☙ 6,000 cases; No visitors

Former Rothbury winemaker David Lowe and Jane Wilson make the Lowe Family Wines at the Oakvale Winery, sourced from 15 hectares of family-owned vineyards in Mudgee supplemented by purchases from Orange and the Hunter Valley.

Mansfield Wines NR
204 Eurunderee Road, Mudgee, NSW 2856, ☏ (02) 6373 3871, ℉ (02) 6373 3708; est 1975; ☙ 3,680 cases; ☥; A$; Mon-Sat 9-5, Sun 10-5

Mansfield Wines is one of the old-style wineries, offering a mix of varietal and generic table wines at low prices, and an even larger range of miscellaneous fortified wines, not all of which are locally produced.

Martins Hill Wines NR
Sydney Road, Mudgee, NSW 2850, ☏ (02) 6373 1248, ℉ (02) 6373 1248; est 1985; ☙ 800 cases; ✗; No visitors

Janette Kenworthy and Michael Sweeny are committed organic grape growers and members of the Organic Vignerons Association. While there is no cellar door (only a mailing list), vineyard tours and talks can be arranged by appointment.

Miramar ☆☆☆☆ V
Henry Lawson Drive, Mudgee, NSW 2850, ☏ *(02) 6373 3874,*
℻ *(02) 6373 3854; est 1977;* ❖ *8,000 cases;* ⚑; *A$; 7 days 9-5*

The silver-bearded, elfin-eyed Ian MacRae runs 38 hectares of vineyard, selling part of the crop to others, and vinifying the remainder. Early benchmark success with Rosé and Chardonnay has since been supplemented, indeed supplanted, by dense, long-lived Shiraz and Cabernet Sauvignon.

Montrose ☆☆☆↓ V
Henry Lawson Drive, Mudgee, NSW 2850, ☏ *(02) 6373 3853,*
℻ *(02) 6373 3795; est 1974;* ❖ *50,000 cases;* ⚑; *A$; Mon-Fri 9-4, wkds 10-4*

Now the major production facility for Orlando-Wyndham in New South Wales. The Montrose label is deliberately downplayed in favour of the three Poet's Corner wines: two white and one red. However, Montrose Sangiovese and Barbera from 25-year-old vines are worth the hunt.

Mount Vincent Mead NR
Common Road, Mudgee, NSW 2850, ☏ *(02) 6372 3184,*
℻ *(02) 6372 3184; est 1972;* ❖ *2,000 cases;* ⚑; *A$; Mon-Sat 10-5, Sun 10-4*

Does make a Shiraz and a Liqueur Muscat, but not in the class of the meads... these can be absolutely outstanding, dramatically reflecting the impact of the different plants from which the honey-bees collect pollen.

Mountilford NR
Mount Vincent Road, Ilford, NSW 2850, ☏ *(02) 6358 8544,*
℻ *(02) 6358 8544; est 1985;* ❖ *NFP;* ⚑; *A$; 7 days 10-4;* ⌂

Offers a decidedly eclectic range of sometimes oddly named wines, which owner/winemaker Don Cumming sells almost entirely through cellar door and by mail order.

Mudgee Wines NR
Henry Lawson Drive, Mudgee, NSW 2850, ☏ *(02) 6372 2258;*
est 1963; ❖ *1,000 cases;* ⚑; *A$; Thur-Mon 10-5, hols 7 days*

All the wines are naturally fermented here with wild yeasts, and made without the addition of any chemicals or substances, including SO_2. A very demanding route, particularly with white wines, but any shortcomings in quality will be quite acceptable to some.

Pieter van Gent ☆☆☆
Black Springs Road, Mudgee, NSW 2850, ☏ *(02) 6373 3807,*
℻ *(02) 6373 3910; est 1978;* ❖ *10,000 cases;* ⚑; *A$; Mon-Sat 9-5, Sun 11-4;* ⌂

Many years ago, Pieter van Gent worked for Lindemans before joining Craigmoor and then moving to his own winery in 1979. Here, he and his family have forged a strong following, notably for his fortified wines.

Platt's NR
Mudgee Road, Gulgong, NSW 2852, ☎ (02) 6374 1700,
ℱ (02) 6372 1055; est 1983; ❖ 4,000 cases; ⚑; A$; 7 days 9-5
Barry Platt is a local veteran and very experienced winemaker. Sadly for some, the wines have limited distribution outside their cellar-door location.

Red Clay Estate NR
269 Henry Lawson Drive, Mudgee, NSW 2850, ☎ (02) 6372 4569,
ℱ (02) 6372 4596; est 1997; ❖ NA; ⚑; A$; Jan-Sept 7 days 10-5,
Oct-Dec: Mon-Fri 10-5 or by appt
Ken Heslop and Annette Bailey are among the most recent arrivals in Mudgee, with a 2.5-hectare vineyard planted with a diverse range of varieties. The wines are sold exclusively through cellar door and by mail order.

Seldom Seen Vineyard NR
Craigmoor Road, Mudgee, NSW 2850, ☎ (02) 6372 4482,
ℱ (02) 6372 1055; est 1987; ❖ 4,500 cases; ⚑; A$; 7 days 9.30-5
This estate is a substantial grape-grower (with 18 hectares of vineyards), which reserves a portion of its crop for making and releasing under its own label. There seems to be an unconscious irony in the name, as with Platt's – but I have not tasted the wines for some years.

Stein's ☆☆☆
Pipeclay Lane, Mudgee, NSW 2850, ☎ (02) 6373 3991,
ℱ (02) 6373 3709; est 1976; ❖ 5,000 cases; ⚑; A$; 7 days 10-4;
motorbike museum
The sweeping panorama from the winery is its own reward for cellar-door visitors to Robert Stein's set-up. Quality jumps around somewhat, but truly excellent Chardonnay and Shiraz have been made from time to time.

Tallara NR
Cassilis Road, Mudgee, NSW 2850, ☎ (02) 6372 2408,
ℱ (02) 6372 6924; est 1973; ❖ 1,800 cases; No visitors
Tallara's large, 54-hectare vineyard was established in 1973 by KPMG partner Rick Turner. Only a fraction of the production has ever been retained for the Tallara label (currently made by Simon Gilbert). It is principally sold via a mailing list, with a little local distribution.

Thistle Hill ☆☆☆☆ V
McDonalds Road, Mudgee, NSW 2850, ☎ (02) 6373 3546,
ℱ (02) 6373 3540; est 1976; ❖ 4,000 cases; ⚑; A$;
Thurs-Mon 10-4; ⛺
David and Leslie Robertson produce supremely honest wines, always full of flavour and appropriately reflecting the climate and *terroir*. Some may be a little short on finesse, but never on character. Chardonnay and Cabernet Sauvignon lead the way, and age well.

Cowra

Until 1973, when the first vines were planted, Cowra's chief claim to fame (apart from grazing) was as the site of Australia's prisoner-of-war camp for captured Japanese soldiers and airmen. The war memorial is well worth a visit. The vineyards are situated on gentle slopes within a broad valley in the western side of the Great Dividing Range. They are planted at a lower altitude than Orange, Mudgee or Hilltops (around 300 metres) and, although further south, have a significantly warmer climate.

Cowra now faces a challenge. It was established on the crest of the white wine boom, and was an early and highly successful entrant in the Chardonnay game. Now Australia is part of a worldwide red wine boom, and the supply of Chardonnay is in excess of demand. Cowra's principal grape has lost the lustre it once had, and its red wines are by and large mediocre, lacking concentration and flavour. A second problem has been the lack of real identity. Until very recently, no wine was made in Cowra; all the grapes were trucked to far-away destinations. Cowra's *vignerons* are certainly working hard to create a regional image and identity, and the first few wineries have appeared. Yet, it is unlikely that Cowra will break out of the 'fighting varietal' sector.

Cowra Estate ☆☆☆ V
Boorowa Road, Cowra, NSW 2794, ☏ (02) 6342 1136, ℻ (02) 6342 4286; est 1973; ❖ 20,000 cases; ♀; A$; 7 days 9-6; ¶; ⌫

A large vineyard acquired by South African businessman and cricket-lover John Geber in 1995. The ever-energetic Geber has worked ceaselessly to lift the brand, introducing the Classic Bat series of Chardonnay, Pinot Noir and Cabernet/Merlot at the top of the range. Whether Victor Trumper (featured on the label) would be pleased, I do not know.

Danbury Estate NR
*Canowindra, NSW 2794 (PO Box 605, Cowra, NSW 2794),
☏ (02) 6341 2204, ℻ (02) 6341 4690; est 1996; ❖ NA; ♀; A$; by appt*

This estate specialises in Chardonnay and was established by Jonathan Middleton, with a little over eight hectares of vines. The wines are contract-made.

Hamiltons Bluff NR
*Ryegates Lane, Canowindra, NSW 2804, ☏ (02) 6344 2079,
℻ (02) 6344 2165; est 1995; ❖ 2,000 cases; ♀; A$; wkds & hols 10-4, Mon-Fri by appt*

Owned by the Andrews family, who planted 45 hectares of vines in 1995. The first releases came with the 1998 vintage; three different Chardonnays were contract-made by Andrew Margan and two won medals at the 1998 Cowra Wine Show.

Hermes Morrison Wines NR
*253 Swan Ponds Road, Woodstock, NSW 2793, ☏ (02) 6345 0153,
℻ (02) 6345 0153; est 1990; ❖ 750 cases; ♀; A$; 7 days summer, wkds & public hols 10-5, winter by appt; ✗*

The Morrison family established the Hermes Pol Dorset Stud in 1972, later adding Hermes Morrison wines. Only a 10-minute walk from the cellar door takes you to the summit of Mount Palatine, with spectacular views of the Canobolas Mountains sitting 80 km away.

Kalari Vineyards NR
120 Carro Park Road, Cowra, NSW 2794, ☏ (02) 6342 1465, ℻ (02) 6342 1465; est 1995; ❖ NA; ⚲; A$; 7 days 10-4
Kalari Vineyards, with 14.5 hectares of esablished vines, is yet another of the new brands to appear in the Cowra region. The initial release included a Verdelho, Chardonnay and Shiraz.

Wallington Wines NR
Nyrang Creek Vineyard, Canowindra, NSW 2904, ☏ (02) 6344 7153, ℻ (02) 6344 7153; est 1992; ❖ 800 cases; ⚲; A$; by appt
Anthony and Margaret Wallington have progressively planted 14 hectares to the classic varieties. Most of the grapes are sold; some Chardonnay, Shiraz and Cabernet are contract-made.

Windowrie Estate NR
Windowrie, Canowindra, NSW 2804, ☏ (02) 6344 3234, ℻ (02) 6344 3227; est 1988; ❖ 42,000 cases; ⚲; A$; 7 days 10-6
Windowrie Estate was established in 1988 on a substantial grazing property at Canowindra, 30 km north of Cowra. While much of the fruit from the 240-hectare vineyard is sold to other makers, rapidly increasing quantities are made for the Windowrie Estate and The Mill labels. The Chardonnays enjoy show success.

Orange

Centred on the undulating slopes of Mount Canobolas (an extinct volcano and part of the Great Dividing Range), at 600–900 metres above sea-level, Orange has long been an important orchard area. An experimental vineyard was planted at Molong in the 1940s, but was soon forgotten. It was not until 1980 that the first commercial vineyards were planted (at Bloodwood Estate). Vineyard plantings increased slowly in the 1980s, but – as in so much of Australia – have expanded with almost frightening rapidity in the second half of the 1990s.

Orange's major development has been the establishment of a 490-hectare vineyard to the northeast of Molong. Little Boomey, as it is called, will produce over 6,800 tonnes of grapes (the equivalent of 470,000 cases of wine) a year. While most is contracted to be sold to Southcorp, in 1999 Little Boomey announced plans to build a substantial grape-processing plant and winery on its vineyard site.

In late 1997 the Orange Agricultural College Campus of Sydney University entered into an agreement with a private wine company to build a 1,000-tonne winery (rising to 3,000 tonnes) on university property. Yet to be built, the intention is for the winery to provide winemaking services for Orange growers. This should hopefully lead to more Orange-based brands, as much of the production is still sold to producers outside the region. In the last decade Orange has become an exciting vineyard area. It has shown the ability to produce first-class Chardonnay, Semillon, Shiraz and Cabernet Sauvignon, all reflecting the temperate, continental climate of this pretty corner of NSW.

Belubula Valley Vineyards NR
Golden Gully, Mandurama, NSW 2798, ☎ (02) 6367 5236, ℻ (02) 9362 4726; est 1986; ❧ 1,000 cases; No visitors
Belubula is a Cabernet Sauvignon specialist, and was founded by David Somervaille, a leading Sydney lawyer. Most of the production from the 1-hectare vineyard (primarily planted with Cabernet Sauvignon, but also a little Semillon, Chardonnay and Pinot Noir) is sold by word of mouth.

Bloodwood Estate ☆☆☆☆ V
4 Griffin Road, Orange, NSW 2800, ☎ (02) 6362 5631, ℻ (02) 6361 1173; est 1983; ❧ 3,500 cases; ♀; A$; by appt
Rhonda and Stephen Doyle were the principal pioneers of this region. Their wines gain both consistency and quality year on year. The cherry-flavoured, crisp Rosé of Malbec is always good, a new Merlot Noir (a 100 per cent Merlot) is worthwhile and the Cabernet, with some leaf and mint characters, also appeals.

Brangayne of Orange ☆☆☆☆½ V
49 Pinnacle Road, Orange, NSW 2880, ☎ (02) 6365 3229, ℻ (02) 6365 3170; est 1994; ❧ 5,000 cases; ♀; A$; by appt
Orchardists Don and Pemela Hoskins are exciting newcomers who diversified into viticulture in 1994 and now have 25 hectares of high quality vineyards. Skilled contract winemaking has produced supremely elegant and complex Chardonnay and a spectacular first release of The Tristan, a Cabernet/Shiraz/Merlot blend bursting with ripe fruit.

Canobolas-Smith ☆☆☆½
Boree Lane, Off Cargo Road, Lidster via Orange, NSW 2800, ☎ (02) 6365 6113, ℻ (02) 6365 6113; est 1986; ❧ 1,800 cases; ♀; A$; wkds & public hols 11-5; ⊫
Murray Smith has six hectares of Chardonnay, Pinot Noir, Cabernet Sauvignon, Merlot, Shiraz and Cabernet Franc. Don't be fooled by the psychedelic blue wrap-around label design: a quite delicious and serious Chardonnay leads the range.

Cargo Road Wines NR
Cargo Road, Orange, NSW 2800, ☎ (02) 6365 6100, ℻ (02) 6365 6001; est 1983; ❧ 650 cases; ♀; A$; wkds 11-5
Originally called The Midas Tree, the vineyard was planted in 1984 by Roseworthy graduate John Swanson. He established a 2.5-hectare vineyard that included Zinfandel 15 years ahead of his time. The property was acquired in 1997 by a syndicate, which is expanding the vineyard, particularly Zinfandel.

Faisan Estate ☆☆⌒
Amaroo Road, Borenore, NSW 2800, ☎ (02) 6365 2380; est 1992;
❖ 500 cases; No visitors

The quickly developing vineyard of Colin and Trish Walker, currently with ten hectares coming into bearing. Some of the early releases were rustic, but the barrel-fermented 1998 Chardonnay, with its crème-brûlée character, represents great value at A$12.

Golden Gully Wines NR
5900 Midwestern Highway, Mandurama, NSW 2792,
☎ (02) 6367 5148; est 1994; ❖ 60 cases; No visitors

Kevin and Julie Bate have progressively established five hectares of vineyard on the banks of the Belubula River. Planted mainly with Cabernet Sauvignon and Shiraz, the vines are still coming into production.

Habitat NR
Old Canobolas Road, Nashdale, NSW 2800, ☎ (02) 6365 3294,
🄵 (02) 6362 3257; est 1989; ❖ 120 cases; ♀; A$ at Ibis Wines

The 2.5-hectare vineyard is sited on deep-red basalt soil on the northern slope of Mount Canobolas. At an altitude of 1,100 metres, it is one of the highest – if not the highest – vineyards in Australia. Previously, grapes were sold to Charles Sturt University for sparkling (and table) wines; the wines are now made at Ibis.

Highland Heritage Estate ☆☆☆⌒
Mitchell Highway, Orange, NSW 2800, ☎ (02) 6361 3612,
🄵 (02) 6361 3613; est 1984; ❖ 3,500 cases; ♀; A$; Mon-Fri 9-3, wkds 9-5; ❣

Vineyard plantings have progressively grown from 4 to 20 hectares, with full production by 2001. At present, much of the wine is sold through a converted railway carriage overlooking the vineyard and a 300-seat convention and function centre.

Ibis Wines ☆☆⌒
237 Kearneys Drive, Orange, NSW 2800, ☎ (02) 6362 3257,
🄵 (02) 6362 5779; est 1988; ❖ 700 cases; ♀; A$; wkds & public hols 11-5 or by appt

Phil Stevenson makes his Ibis wines from a 1-hectare vineyard, half planted with Cabernet Sauvignon, the rest a scattering of seven other classic varieties. He sells six wines, all necessarily in micro-quantities except the Cabernet, which is powerful when young, becoming Italianate when mature.

Indigo Ridge NR
Icely Road, Orange, NSW 2800, ☎ (02) 6362 1851, 🄵 (02) 6362 1851; est 1995; ❖ NA ♀; A$; by appt

The newly established Indigo Ridge has two hectares each of Sauvignon Blanc and Cabernet Sauvignon, and sells the small wine production by cellar door and mail order.

Nashdale Wines NR
*Borenore Lane, Nashdale, NSW 2800, ☎ (02) 6365 2463,
⊕ (02) 6361 4495; est 1990; ❖ 1,000 cases; ⚑; A$; wkds 2-6;
|●|; swimming pool*

At an altitude of 1,000 metres, Orange solicitor Edward Fardell's 10-hectare Nashdale Vineyard offers panoramic views of Mount Canobolas and the Lidster Valley. Restaurant is open at weekends.

Templer's Mill ☆☆☆❖
*Orange Agricultural College, Leeds Parade, Orange, NSW 2800,
☎ (02) 6360 5509, ⊕ (02) 6360 5698; est 1997; ❖ 4,000 cases; ⚑;
A$; Fri 2-5 or by appt; |●|*

The Orange Agricultural Campus of Sydney University has established 20 hectares of vineyards in anticipation of a substantial joint-venture winery to be built on the campus grounds. Meanwhile Jon Reynolds (*qv* Reynolds Yarraman), one of the partners in the project, is making the wine.

Riverina

This extensive, unprepossessingly flat vineyard area to the southeast of the state stands as a lasting testament to the skills and vision of a group of dedicated Australians. Riverina is hot and dry: the introduction of irrigation by these pioneers was the key to its creation as 'The Murrumbidgee Irrigation Scheme Area' between 1906 and 1912. Its subsequent development owes a debt to successive generations of the remarkable McWilliam family, not to mention the influence (both pre-and post-WWII) of Italian immigrants. Until the late 1950s, the Riverina produced only cheap fortified wines. It prospered in so doing until changes in the pattern of wine consumption forced the region to rethink its whole approach to grape-growing and winemaking.

It was Glen McWilliam who then showed the same vision (and skill) as the region's founders. He proved that Riesling, Semillon and Cabernet Sauvignon could be successfully grown and made into table wines, which, by the standards of the day, were very good. The 1963 Cabernet Sauvignon was a freakish landmark, still vibrant almost 20 years after it was made.

In the following years the focus was relentlessly placed on holding down the cost of production, and selling wines on price and price alone. It was left to De Bortoli, with its superb botrytised Noble One Semillon, and to wineries such as Riverina Wines, to show just how far viticultural quality can be pushed, principally by limiting yields. Time alone will reveal the extent of the next generation's changes and their performance.

Baratto's NR
Farm 678, Hanwood, NSW 2680, ☎ (02) 6963 0171, ⊕ (02) 6963 0171; est 1975; ❖ NA; ⚑; A$; 7 days 10-5

The 15-hectare Baratto's is in many ways a throwback to the old days. Peter Baratto sells his wine in bulk or in 10- and 20-litre casks from the cellar door at old-time prices, from as little as A$3 per litre.

Casella ☆☆☆
Wakley Road, Yenda, NSW 2681, ☏ (02) 6968 1346, ⓕ (02) 6968 1196; est 1969; ❦ 650,000 cases; No visitors

Casella is typical of the new wave sweeping through the Riverina. The Botrytis Semillon is the outstanding release.

Cranswick Estate ☆☆☆ V
Walla Avenue, Griffith, NSW 2680, ☏ (02) 6962 4133, ⓕ (02) 6962 2888; est 1976; ❦ 750,000 cases; ♟; A$; Mon-Fri 10-4.30, wkds 10-4

Cranswick Estate made a highly successful entry to the Australian Associated Stock Exchange in 1997. The substantial capital raised will see the further expansion of an already thriving business, firmly aimed at the export market in the UK and Europe, US, Japan and South East Asia.

De Bortoli ☆☆☆☆ V
De Bortoli Road, Bilbul, NSW 2680, ☏ (02) 6964 9444, ⓕ (02) 6964 9400; est 1928; ❦ 3,000,000 cases; ♟; A$; Mon-Sat 9-5.30, Sun 9-4; ✗

Famous among the cognoscenti for its superb Botrytis Semillon, which in fact accounts for only a minute part of its total production. This winery releases low-priced varietal and generic wines that are invariably competently made, and equally invariably excellent value for money.

Lillypilly Estate ☆☆☆☆ V
Lillypilly Road, Leeton, NSW 2705, ☏ (02) 6953 4069, ⓕ (02) 6953 4980; est 1982; ❦ 10,000 cases; ♟; A$; Mon-Sat 10-5.30, Sun by appt

Robert Fiumara was the first winemaker to set up a modern, boutique winery in Griffith. He helped bring a sense of identity and character to the Riverina, notably with his Traminer Semillon blend, Tramillon™, and with his unique botrytised Noble Muscat of Alexandria.

McManus NR V
Rogers Road, Yenda, NSW 2681, ☏ (02) 6968 1064; est 1972; ❦ 500 cases; ♟; A$; 7 days 9-5

An extremely idiosyncratic winery run by Griffith GP Dr David McManus, his sister and other family members. Natural winemaking methods lead to considerable variation in quality, but the prices are from another era; some of the vintages on offer likewise.

McWilliam's ☆☆☆☆ V
Winery Road, Hanwood, NSW 2680, ☏ (02) 6963 0001, ⓕ (02) 6963 0002; est 1877; ❦ NFP; ♟; A$; Mon-Sat 9-5

The most important winery in the region, although with the exception of its Liqueur Muscat, the best wines are limited-release wines sourced from other (premium) regions. Those made from Riverina grapes are carefully crafted, well-balanced and keenly priced, but are not heart-stopping.

Miranda ☆☆☆⅓ V

*57 Jondaryan Avenue, Griffith, NSW 2680, ☎ (02) 6962 4033,
℻ (02) 6962 6944; est 1939; ❖ 1.5 million cases; ♀; A$; 7 days 9-5*

The home base for Miranda, which also has separate wineries (and label identities) in the King and Barossa Valleys. The plethora of Riverina brands includes Mirrool Creek, Somerton and Christy's Land. Mirrool Creek Chardonnay often rises above its station, but needs to be drunk while young.

Riverina Wines ☆☆☆☆⅓ V

*700 Lidman Way, Griffith, NSW 2680, ☎ (02) 6962 4122,
℻ (02) 6962 4628; est 1969; ❖ 220,000 cases; ♀; A$; 7 days 9-5.30*

Having scaled vinous mountains over the previous few years, Riverina Wines unexpectedly hit insurmountable financial rocks in 1999. Hopefully, the viticultural and winemaking skills that brought a cascade of richly deserved gold medals in major wine shows for both white and red wines will not disappear. Watch for Warburn Estate and Ballingal Estate labels.

Rossetto ☆☆⅓

*Farm 576 Rossetto Road, Beelbangera, NSW 2686, ☎ (02) 6963 5214, ℻ (02) 6963 5542; est 1930; ❖ 500,000 cases; ♀; A$;
Mon-Sat 8.30-5.30*

Another family-owned and -run winery endeavouring to lift the profile of its wines, but not with the same spectacular success as Riverina Wines. Much of the production is sold to other makers.

St Peter's Edenhope Winery NR

*Whitton Stock Route, Yenda, NSW 2681, ☎ (018) 421 000,
℻ (02) 4285 3180; est 1978; ❖ 250 tonnes; No visitors*

Managing director Stephen Chatterton is a fanatical fly-fisher and tier, which means he is made of the right stuff. The wines are made by St Peter's tenant, Wilton Estate, and sold at low prices under the Edenhope, St Peter's and Sydey labels.

Toorak Estate NR

Toorak Road, Leeton, NSW 2705, ☎ (02) 6953 2333, ℻ (02) 6953 4454; est 1965; ❖ 10,000 cases; ♀; A$; Mon-Sat 9-5

A traditional, long-established Riverina producer with a strong Italian-based clientele across Australia. Production has been increasing, drawing on 65 hectares and purchased grapes.

Vico NR

Farm 1687 Beelbangera Road, Griffith, NSW 2680, ☎ (02) 6962 2849; est 1973; ❖ 1,200 cases; ♀; A$; Mon-Fri 9-5

Ray Vico has been growing grapes on his 9-hectare estate for many years. More recently he decided to bottle and sell part of the production under the Vico label, with some show success.

Westend ☆☆☆⅓ V

*1283 Brayne Road, Griffith, NSW 2680, ☎ (02) 6964 1506,
℻ (02) 6962 1673; est 1945; ❖ 25,000 cases; ♀; A$; Mon-Fri 9-4.30*

Another winery sharply lifting both its quality and its packaging, run by Bill Calabria. Particularly successful 3 Bridges Cabernet Sauvignon and Golden Mist Botrytis Semillon, exuding kumquat and mandarin flavours off-set by precisely balanced acidity.

Wilton Estate ☆☆☆
Whitton Stock Route, Yenda, NSW 2681, ☏ (02) 6968 1303, Ⓕ (02) 6968 1328; est 1977; ❖ 250,000 cases; ♟; A$; Mon-Fri 9-5
Wilton Estate sources grapes and wine from various parts of South East Australia for its dry table wines, while enjoying outstanding success with its Botrytis Semillon from locally grown fruit. It shares the winemaking facilities at St Peter's.

Zappacosta Estate NR
Farm 161 Hanwood Road, Hanwood, NSW 2680, ☏ (02) 6963 0278, Ⓕ (02) 6963 0278; est 1996; ❖ 22,000 cases; ♟; A$; by appt
The most recent arrival in the region is owned and run by Judy and Dino Zappacosta; the winery was briefly known as Hanwood Village Wines.

Canberra District

It has always struck me as a wry commentary on the unreality of the political hothouse that is Canberra that none of the Canberra District *vignerons* actually owns a vineyard in Canberra. It is even more appropriate that none of them is a politician. Freehold does not exist within the Australian Capital Territory. Land used for anything other than housing, commerce or industry is liable to be requisitioned (and the lease terminated) at short notice.

It took the clout of Australia's second-largest wine company to overcome this problem, with an enterprise to dwarf all others. In 1997 BRL Hardy entered into an agreement with the territory government for the erection of a 2,000-tonne winery and the establishment of a 250-hectare vineyard within the Canberra Territory. The region's other, much smaller, *vignerons*, remain clustered in two areas just outside the territory's borders: in the Yass Valley around Murrumbateman, and along the shores of Lake George. Spring frosts are the main threat here – they struck with vicious results in 1998 – and so very careful site selection is a must. That selection in turn can throw up surprises: Riesling, Chardonnay, Shiraz and Cabernet Sauvignon have traditionally been the most successful varieties, but out of the blue (as it were) some impressive Pinot Noirs have emerged. All in all, a once somnolent, introspective region is now taking on a new life.

Affleck NR
154 Millynn Road off Gundaroo Road, Bungendore, NSW 2621, ☏ (02) 6236 9276, Ⓕ (02) 6236 9090; est 1976; ❖ 200 cases; ♟; A$; wkds & public hols, or by appt
The cellar-door and mail-order price-list says that the wines are 'grown, produced and bottled on the estate by Ian and Susie Hendry, with much dedicated help from family and friends'. The original 2.5-hectare vineyard was virtually doubled by the

planting of another two hectares of Merlot in 1998. A new tasting room (offering light lunches) was planned for the end of 1999.

Brindabella Hills ☆☆☆☆½
Woodgrove Close, via Hall, ACT 2618, ☏ (02) 6230 2583, Ⓕ (02) 6230 2023; est 1989; ❦ 1,500 cases; ♀; A$; wkds & public hols 10-5
Distinguished research scientist Dr Roger Harris developed the method for measuring (in unbelievably tiny amounts) the biochemical flavour agent in Cabernet Sauvignon. He also makes elegant and distinctive hand-crafted Sauvignon Blanc-Semillon, Chardonnay, Shiraz and Cabernet Sauvignon from his estate vineyards.

Clonakilla ☆☆☆☆
Crisps Lane, Off Gundaroo Road, Murrumbateman, NSW 2582, ☏ (02) 6227 5877, Ⓕ (02) 6227 5871; est 1971; ❦ 1,500 cases; ♀; A$; 7 days 11-5
Noted scientist Dr John Kirk and energetic schoolteacher son Tim, who has a passion for wine, make an impressive team. The Shiraz (with a percentage of Viognier) can scale the heights, echoing the single-vineyard wines of Guigal in the Rhône Valley. Riesling and Semillon/Sauvignon Blanc can also be impressive.

Doonkuna Estate ☆☆☆☆½
Barton Highway, Murrumbateman, NSW 2582, ☏ (02) 6227 5811, Ⓕ (02) 6227 5085; est 1973; ❦ 2,000 cases; ♀; A$; Sun-Fri 12-4
Founded by the late Sir Brian Murray, a former governor general of Victoria. Purchased by Barry and Maureen Moran in late 1996, who have extended both the vineyard and winery.

Gidgee Estate Wines NR
441 Weeroona Drive, Wamboin, NSW 2621, ☏ (02) 6236 9506, Ⓕ (02) 6236 9070; est 1996; ❦ 300 cases; ♀; A$; first wkd of each month or by appt
Brett and Cheryl Lane purchased a run-down 1-hectare vineyard in 1996 and are now nursing it back to life and doubling its size. Peachy Chardonnay is best.

Helm's ☆☆☆☆½
Butt's Road, Murrumbateman, NSW 2582, ☏ (02) 6227 5536, Ⓕ (02) 6227 5953; est 1973; ❦ 2,500 cases; ♀; A$; Thur-Mon 10-5
Ken Helm is yet another viticultural scientists based in Canberra, and one of the wine industry's more stormy petrels. He is an indefatigable promoter of his wines, and frequently has cause to issue press releases recording the show successes of his tightly structured Rieslings and blackberry and cassis Cabernet/Merlots.

Jeir Creek ☆☆☆
Gooda Creek Road, Murrumbateman, NSW 2582, ☏ (02) 6227 5999, Ⓕ (02) 6227 5900; est 1984; ❦ 3500 cases; ♀; A$; Fri-Sun & hols 10-5

Rob Howell came to part-time winemaking through a love of drinking fine wine. Jeir Creek is now a substantial (and still growing) business, the vineyard plantings increased to 11 hectares by the establishment of more Cabernet Sauvignon, Shiraz and Merlot. Rob is intent on improving both the quality and consistency of his wines.

Kyeema Estate ☆☆☆☆

PO Box 282, Belconnen, ACT 2616, ☎ (02) 6254 7536,
Ⓕ (02) 6254 7536; est 1986; ❖ 700 cases; No visitors

The Canberra *vignerons* tend to be a prickly lot and Kyeema's winemaker/owner Andrew McEwin is no exception. But, take note that every wine ever released under this label has won a show award of some distinction!

Lake George Winery ☆☆☆

Federal Highway, Collector, NSW 2581, ☎ (02) 4848 0039,
Ⓕ (02) 4848 0039; est 1971; ❖ 500 cases; No visitors

Dr Edgar Riek (yes, yet another research scientist) is not so much prickly as impishly, wilfully idiosyncratic. One of the pioneers of the region, and founder of the National Wine Show in Canberra, he will continue to experiment to the end. He is seeking someone to take over his small vineyard and even smaller winery.

Lark Hill ☆☆☆☆☆

RMB 281 Gundaroo Road, Bungendore, NSW 2621, ☎ (02) 6238 1393, Ⓕ (02) 6238 1393; est 1978; ❖ 6,000 cases; ⚐; A$; 7 days 10-5

Dr David (yes, yet another) and Sue Carpenter can – and do – lay claim to being the region's foremost winemakers. They make elegant but complex Chardonnay, utterly disconcertingly powerful Pinot Noir that shows more varietal character than it ought, and polished, flavourful Cabernet-Merlot.

Madew Wines NR

Westering, Federal Highway, Lake George, NSW 2581,
☎ (02) 4848 0026; est 1984; ❖ 2,500 cases; ⚐; A$; wkds & public hols 11-5; ⦿; cricket pitch and pavilion

Originally established within the city limits of Queanbeyan but forced out by urban pressure. The owners then acquired the Westering Vineyard, established by Captain GP Hood. It now boasts scenic views of Lake George, a cricket pitch and a warning sign reading 'Look out for the Great Dane'.

Milimani Estate NR

92 The Forest Road, Bungendore, NSW 2621, ☎ (02) 6238 1421,
Ⓕ (02) 6238 1424; est 1989; ❖ NA; ⚐; A$; first wkd of each month: Sat 2-4, Sun 10-4

The Preston family (Mary, David and Rosemary) has established a 4-hectare vineyard at Bungendore planted to Sauvignon Blanc, Chardonnay, Pinot Noir, Merlot and Cabernet Franc. Contract winemaking at Lark Hill should guarantee quality.

Mount Majura Wines ☆☆☆☆
RMB 311 Majura Road, Majura, ACT, 2609, ☎ (02) 9222 3100, ⓕ (02) 9222 3124; est 1988; ❦ 500 cases; No visitors

A change of ownership in 1999 means a change of contract winemaker from Lark Hill to Brindabella and the expansion of the vineyard from 1 to 5 hectares. Good Pinot Noir should continue through this change.

Murrumbateman Winery NR
Barton Highway, Murrumbateman, NSW 2582, ☎ (02) 6227 5584; est 1972; ❦ 1,000 cases; ♀; A$; Thur-Mon 10-5; ¶

Revived after a change of ownership, the Murrumbateman Winery draws upon 4.5 hectares of vineyard. It also offers an *à la carte* restaurant, function room, picnic and barbecue areas.

Pankhurst NR
Old Woodgrove, Woodgrove Road, Hall, NSW 2618, ☎ (02) 6230 2592, ⓕ (02) 6230 2592; est 1986; ❦ 4,000 cases; ♀; A$; Sun & public hols, or by appt

Agricultural scientist Allan Pankhurst and wife Christine established a 3-hectare split-canopy vineyard and turned to Sue Carpenter as contract winemaker. Results are convincing, particularly the stylish Pinot Noir.

Ruker Wines NR
Barton Highway, Dickson, ACT 2602, ☎ (02) 6230 2310, ⓕ (02) 6230 2818; est 1991; ❦ 500 cases; ♀; A$; wkds & public hols 10-5; ¶

The cellar-door-cum-winery-cum-restaurant began life as a farmshed. It is now finished with heavy wooden railway-bridge beams and clad with the remains of an old slab hut.

Surveyor's Hill Winery NR
215 Brooklands Road, Wallaroo, NSW 2618, ☎ (02) 6230 2046, ⓕ (02) 6230 2048; est 1986; ❦ 1,000 cases; ♀; A$; wkds & public hols or by appt

Most of the grapes from the 7.5-hectare vineyard are sold to Hardy's, which also vinifies the remainder for Surveyor's Hill. This should guarantee the quality of the wines.

Wimbaliri Wines NR
Barton Highway, Murrumbateman, NSW 2582, ☎ (02) 6227 5921; est 1988; ❦ 600 cases; ♀; A$; by appt and at Doonkuna

John and Margaret Andersen chose a smart location to plant a mix of Bordeaux blends, Chardonnay and Shiraz, using sophisticated trellising. The quality of the Cabernet/Merlots made in 1995 and '97 has been very good.

Yass Valley Wines NR
9 Crisps Lane, Murrumbateman, NSW 2582, ☎ (02) 6227 5592, ⓕ (02) 6227 5592; est 1979; ❦ 800 cases; ♀; A$; wkds & public hols 11-5 or by appt

Michael Withers and Anne Hillier, sharing scicentific and viticultural qualifications, purchased Yass Valley in 1991. They have revived and extended the existing run-down vineyards.

Hilltops

A brief flirtation with winemaking occurred here at the end of the 19th century, but it was not until the 1970s that the modern romance began. It was left to a local, the late Peter Robertson, to re-introduce vines in 1975. When McWilliam's purchased his 400-hectare Barwang property in 1989, there were still only 13 hectares under vine. There are now in excess of 100 hectares.

Briefly known as Young, confusingly also the name of the major town around which the region centres, the Hilltops region runs south and east of Young and is defined by the 450-metre contour line as its low point. The climate is cool, with snow in winter, followed by spring frosts that mean careful site selection is needed. Cabernet Sauvignon, Semillon, Chardonnay and Shiraz are the four most widely planted varieties, and are likely to remain so. There are only two small local wineries. Most of the fruit is sold, or, in the case of Barwang, taken to McWilliam's Hanwood winery at Griffith. Both Hungerford Hill and Allandale (in the Hunter Valley) release wines made from Hilltops grapes.

Barwang Vineyard ☆☆☆☆ V

Postal c/o McWilliam's Wines, Doug McWilliam Road, Yenda, NSW 2681, ☎ (02) 9722 1200, Ⓕ (02) 9707 4408; est 1975; ❖ NA; No visitors

These wines (made at McWilliam's) have been of consistent style and quality right from the outset. The range now extends to Chardonnay, Semillon, Shiraz and Cabernet Sauvignon. In each case, oak influence is deliberately downplayed, the powerful fruit character providing ample structure and flavour.

Demondrille Vineyards NR

RMB 97 Prunevale Road, Kingsvale, NSW 2587, ☎ (02) 6384 4272, Ⓕ (02) 6384 4292; est 1979; ❖ NA; ♟; A$; Fri-Mon 10-5 or by appt

Pamela Gillespie and Robert Provan purchased the former Hercynia Vineyard and winery in 1995. The names given to the wines, including The Dove (a Semillon/Sauvignon Blanc), Purgatory, The Raven and Black Rose, suggest this winery marches to the tune of its own drum. The second-label range sold through the cellar door is entitled The Tin Shed.

Grove Estate NR

Boorowa Road, Young, NSW 2594, ☎ (02) 6382 4527, Ⓕ (02) 6382 4527; est 1989; ❖ NA; No visitors

Brian Mullany has established a 30-hectare vineyard planted to Semillon, Chardonnay, Merlot, Shiraz, Cabernet Sauvignon and Zinfandel. Most of the grapes are sold (principally to Southcorp), but a limited amount of wine is contract-made at Charles Sturt University for the Grove Estate label.

Hansen Hilltops NR
Barwang Ridge, 1 Barwang Road, Young, NSW 2594, ☎ (02) 6382 6363, ⓕ (02) 6382 6363; est 1979; ❖ NA; ❣; A$

Peter Hansen acquired the former Nioka Ridge vineyard, the second oldest in the region. Wines made under his Hansen Hilltops label draw upon five hectares of mature vineyards planted to eight classic varieties.

Woodonga Hill NR
Cowra Road, Young, NSW 2594, ☎ (02) 6382 2972, ⓕ (02) 6382 2972; est 1986; ❖ 4,000 cases; ❣; A$; 7 days 9-5

Jill Lindsay, winemaker/proprietor, found the going difficult in the early years, notwithstanding her degree in wine science from Charles Sturt University. Recent years have seen the quality of the wines become more consistent, and Jill has taken on contract-winemaker work for others.

Tumbarumba

This is one of the newest wine regions. It also marks the southernmost extension of the state's wine regions, a line that begins just below the Queensland border and runs along the western side of the Great Dividing Range. This is true Alpine country, frequented by skiers in winter and by bushwalkers and trout fishermen in summer.

The vineyards lie between 300-800 metres, with snow-clad peaks towering above. Spring frosts are a major threat, demanding ultra-careful site selection and (wherever possible) frost protection. The inversion of night-time temperatures – cold air falling, warmer rising – can play tricks, but elevation remains the key factor in the choice of varietal. Chardonnay and Pinot Noir dominate the plantings. In many years, the grapes are destined for sparkling wine, but high-quality table wine can be made in the best warmer vintages. Southcorp is the largest player, both as vineyard owner and grape purchaser, but since 1997 BRL Hardy has also become active.

Excelsior Peak NR
22 Wrights Road, Drummoyne, NSW 2047 (postal address), ☎ (02) 9719 1916, ⓕ (02) 9719 2752; est 1980; ❖ 1,150 cases; No visitors

Proprietor Juliet Cullen established the first vineyard in Tumbarumba in 1980. That vineyard was sold to Southcorp, and Juliet established another vineyard. Plantings total nine hectares, with 6.5 hectares in production, and the wines are released under the Excelsior Peak label.

Tumbarumba Wine Cellars NR
Sunnyside, Albury Close, Tumbarumba, NSW 2653, ☎ (02) 6948 3055, ⓕ (02) 6948 3055; est 1990; ❖ 600 cases; ❣; A$; wkds & public hols, or by appt

Tumbarumba Cellars has taken over the former George Martin's Winery (itself established in 1990) to provide an outlet for

Tumbarumba wines. It is a cooperative venture, involving local growers and businessmen, with modest aspirations to growth.

Tumbarumba Wine Estates NR
Maragle Valley via Tumbarumba, NSW 2653, ☎ (02) 6948 4457, ℻ (02) 6948 4457; est 1995; ❦ NA; No visitors

Having progressively established his vineyards since 1982, Frank Minutello decided to seek to add value (and interest) to the enterprise by vinifying part of his production at Charles Sturt University, commencing with the 1995 vintage.

Hastings River

Viticulture and winemaking in the Hastings River region date back to 1837, when the first vineyard was planted by Henry Fancourt White, a colonial surveyor. By the 1860s there were 33 vineyards in the area. Following Federation and the shift to fortified wines, production inevitably declined. It ceased in the Hastings region during the early years of this century.

Sixty years later, in 1980, the French-descended Cassegrain family decided to expand into real estate and associated viticultural and winemaking interests in the region. As a result they significantly – if improbably – expanded the modern viticultural map of Australia. In the course of meeting the unique climatic challenges of the region, they also pioneered new varieties and new ways of managing vineyards. And they have indirectly encouraged the development of other vineyards and wineries along the northern coast of NSW.

Bago Vineyards NR
Milligans Road, off Bago Road, Wauchope, NSW 2446,
☎ (02) 6585 7099, ℻ (02) 6585 7099; est 1985; ❦ 1,000 cases;
⚲; A$; 7 days 11-5

Jim and Kay Mobs began planting the Broken Bago Vineyards in 1985 with one hectare of Chardonnay. There are now 12 hectares of vines, and contract winemaking has moved to the Hill of Hope winery in the Hunter Valley.

Cassegrain ☆☆☆½
Hastings River Winery, Fernbank Creek Road, Port Macquarie, NSW 2444, ☎ (02) 6583 7777, ℻ (02) 6584 0354; est 1980;
❦ 55,000 cases; ⚲; A$; 7 days 9-5; ⚑

This is a substantial operation. In earlier years, fruit was drawn from many parts of Australia, but the estate now has a 162-hectare vineyard planted with 14 varieties, including the rare Chambourcin, a French-bred cross.

Charley Brothers ☆☆½
The Ruins Way, Inneslake, Port Macquarie, NSW 2444,
☎ (02) 6581 1332, ℻ (02) 6581 0391; est 1988; ❦ 1,500 cases;
⚲; A$; Mon-Fri 1-5, wkds 10-5

The property on which the vineyards sit has been in the family's ownership since the turn of the century. Since 1988, 10.5

hectares of vines have been established. Cassegrain purchases most of the grapes, vinifying part for the Charley Brothers label.

Great Lakes Wines NR
Herivals Road, Wootton, NSW 2423, ☎ (02) 4997 7255, ℻ (02) 4997 7255; est 1990; ♦ 1200 cases; ♀; A$; 7 days 8.30-6
John Webber and family began planting their vineyard in 1990. They are proud that (in their words) 'we are a fair-dinkum winery where we grow the grapes and we make the wine'. The Chambourcin is best, and has won several show awards.

Shoalhaven

All the wineries hugging the NSW coast from north to south are heavily reliant on general (rather than wine) tourism. They also share humid and often wet summer and autumn seasons, which create difficult viticultural challenges. One solution has been the propagation of Chambourcin, a French-bred hybrid, which is strongly resistant to mildew and has extraordinarily good colour. The other solution, adopted by the two best producers in the Shoalhaven area, has been to have their wines contract-made in the Hunter Valley. It has paid big dividends for both. Their wines are immeasurably better than most of the other small wineries dotted along the coast of NSW.

Cambewarra Estate ☆☆☆✓
520 Illaroo Road, Cambewarra NSW 2540, ☎ (02) 4446 0170, ℻ (02) 4446 0170; est 1991; ♦ 3,500 cases; ♀; A$; Mon-Fri by appt, wkds & public hols Wed-Sun 10-5
Founded by Geoffrey and Louise Cole in 1991, Cambewarra became a pace-setter virutally overnight. It reached a pinnacle of success at the 1998 Royal Sydney Wine Show, where its entries topped two small producer classes. Juicy blackberryish Chambourcin is always good, as is a minty, cassis Cabernet.

Coolangatta Estate ☆☆☆✓
1335 Bolong Road, Shoalhaven Heads, NSW 2535, ☎ (02) 4448 7131, ℻ (02) 4448 7997; est 1988; ♦ 5,000 cases; ♀; A$; 7 days 10-5; ⑩; ⇌; museum, golf course
Coolangatta Estate is part of a 150-hectare resort. Some of its oldest buildings were constructed by convicts in 1822. One might expect that the wines are tailored purely for the tourist market, but in fact the standard of viticulture is exceptionally high (immaculate Scott-Henry trellising) and the winemaking is wholly professional (contract-made by Tyrrell's).

Jasper Valley NR
RMB 880 Croziers Road, Berry, NSW 2535, ☎ (02) 4464 1596, ℻ (02) 4464 1596; est 1976; ♦ 1,100 cases; ♀; A$; 7 days 9.30-5.30
A strongly tourist-oriented winery that purchases most of its wine as 'cleanskins' (bottled but unlabelled, sometimes without a capsule) from other makers. The site includes about one hectare of lawns, barbecue facilities, and sweeping views.

The Silos Estate NR
Princes Highway, Jaspers Brush, NSW 2535, ☏ *(02) 4448 6082,*
⨍ *(02) 4448 6246; est 1985;* ❖ *1,000 cases;* ⚲; *A$; Wed-Sun 10-5;*
⦿; ⛃; *bookshop*

Since 1995, Gaynor Sims and Kate Khoury, together with viticulturist Jovica Zecevic, have worked hard to improve quality at this estate, both in the 5-hectare estate vineyard and in the winery. For the moment, the winery continues to rely on the tourist trade for sales.

NSW: Rest of State

The process of formally mapping Australia's wine regions under the GI framework grinds slowly on, with no time limit to focus the minds of those involved. As with the other states, NSW has been divided into Zones, but there is a long way to go with delineating Regions. Yet even when all the nascent Regions of NSW have been formally defined and declared, there will remain a large scattering of wineries across the state that won't fall into any one of those regions. By their very nature, these far-flung wineries live a shadowy and isolated existence. Their wines are sold through cellar-door operations to tourists and to local residents (and occasionally to local restaurants and shops). Seldom do the wines find their way on to the wider marketplace. There is a little-discussed phenomenon that I call the 'isolation factor'. It affects grape growing, winemaking and wine-marketing in more or less equal parts. In its most extreme form it engenders a kind of autism: the *vigneron* has no one with whom to discuss whether his vines are growing well or badly; no one to help solve problems in the vineyard or winery; and no means of finding points of comparison to even identify the existence of those problems.

And to be perfectly honest, it is difficult to find out how well (or not) the wineries are coping with these difficulties. It can likewise be difficult to discern whether they are winemakers at all, or whether they are 'tourist shopfronts' buying bulk or cleanskin wine from a winery 1,000 km away and simply putting a label on it. Most of these wineries are heavily dependent on the tourist trade, although a handful in Sydney's western suburbs also have an ethnic (primarily Italian) client base. Some are the by-product of history (notably those adjacent to Sydney), and others are the result of quixotic lifestyle decisions.

Victoria

1994 21,047 hectares 31.39 per cent of total plantings
1998 26,072 hectares 25.48 per cent of total plantings

The only state not to keep up with the pace; on the other hand, there has been growth in the plantings in the premium areas in the centre and south.

Yarra Valley

When the Swiss settlers came to the Valley in the 1850s, they proved to be highly skilled grape-growers and winemakers. By the late 1880s the Yarra was one of the most important producers of high-quality wines in Australia. Its demise over the next 20 years was even more rapid than its growth. This was due to a combination of the abolition of state tariffs in 1901, declining soil fertility and, most importantly, the Australia-wide move from fine table wines to cheap fortified wines – a style of wine impossible for the Yarra to achieve. The rebirth came in the late 1960s, with slow, steady growth in the 1980s, and frenetic pace in the 1990s.

With a climate cooler than Bordeaux and slightly warmer than Burgundy, the Yarra Valley succeeds best with Chardonnay and Pinot Noir, and sparkling wine made from those varieties. Sauvignon Blanc is easy, Riesling curiously reticent, Marsanne and Roussanne excellent. With appropriate site selection and disciplined canopy and yield management, great results can be achieved with Shiraz, Merlot and Cabernet Sauvignon, especially in the warmer, drier vintages.

Allinda NR
119 Lorimers Lane, Dixons Creek, Vic 3775, ☏ (03) 5965 2450, ℻ (03) 5965 2467; est 1991; ❖ 2,000 cases; ⚑; A$; wkds & public hols 10-6; gourmet picnic baskets

One of the local low-profile Yarra Valley wineries. All the wines are produced on-site by owner/winemaker Al Fencaros from the three hectares of vineyards.

Arthur's Creek Estate ☆☆☆☆☆
Strathewen Road, Arthur's Creek, Vic 3099, ☏ (03) 9827 6629, ℻ (03) 9824 0252; est 1976; ❖ 1,500 cases; No visitors

SEK Hulme planted 1.5 hectares each of Semillon, Chardonnay, and Cabernet in the mid-1970s, with the wines contract-made by various people. It was 15 years before he took the decision to sell any of it. The deep, ripe but classic Cabernet Sauvignon is outstanding, the elegant Chardonnay an eyelash behind.

Badger's Brook NR
874 Maroondah Highway, Coldstream, Vic 3770, ☏ (03) 5962 4130, ℻ (03) 5962 4238; est 1993; ❖ NA; ⚑; A$

Situated prominently on the Maroondah Highway, next door to the well-known Eyton-on-Yarra. Location is all, though not for the wines, which come from various sources.

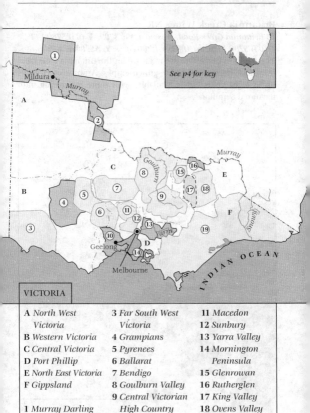

VICTORIA

A *North West Victoria*	**3** *Far South West Victoria*	**11** *Macedon*
B *Western Victoria*	**4** *Grampians*	**12** *Sunbury*
C *Central Victoria*	**5** *Pyrenees*	**13** *Yarra Valley*
D *Port Phillip*	**6** *Ballarat*	**14** *Mornington Peninsula*
E *North East Victoria*	**7** *Bendigo*	**15** *Glenrowan*
F *Gippsland*	**8** *Goulburn Valley*	**16** *Rutherglen*
	9 *Central Victorian High Country*	**17** *King Valley*
1 *Murray Darling*		**18** *Ovens Valley*
2 *Swan Hill*	**10** *Geelong*	**19** *Gippsland*

Bianchet ☆☆☆☆ V

*Lot 3 Victoria Road, Lilydale, Vic 3140, ☎ (03) 9739 1779,
℻ (03) 9739 1277; est 1976; ❦ 2,000 cases; ♀; A$; 7 days 10-6; café*

Recently acquired from the founding family by a small Melbourne-based syndicate. Most of the wines are sold through cellar door. One of the more unusual offerings is Verduzzo Gold, a late-harvest, sweet white wine made from the Italian grape variety. Chardonnay can also be good.

Brahams Creek NR

*Woods Point Road, East Warburton, Vic 3799, ☎ (03) 9560 0016,
℻ (03) 9560 0016; est 1985; ❦ 1,000 cases; ♀; A$; wkds & public hols 10-5*

Owner Geoffrey Richardson did not start marketing his wines until 1994, and a string of older vintages are available for sale at the cellar door.

Britannia Creek Wines NR

75 Britannia Creek Road, Wesburn, Vic 3799, ☎ (03) 5780 1426, ℻ (03) 5780 1426; est 1982; ❦ 1,200 cases; ⚲; A$; wkds 10-6

The wines of this estate are made under the Britannia Falls label from four hectares of estate-grown grapes. A range of vintages up to eight years old is available, with some interesting, full-flavoured Semillon.

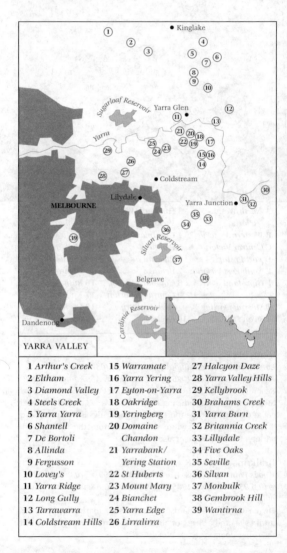

YARRA VALLEY

1 *Arthur's Creek*
2 *Eltham*
3 *Diamond Valley*
4 *Steels Creek*
5 *Yarra Yarra*
6 *Shantell*
7 *De Bortoli*
8 *Allinda*
9 *Fergusson*
10 *Lovey's*
11 *Yarra Ridge*
12 *Long Gully*
13 *Tarrawarra*
14 *Coldstream Hills*
15 *Warramate*
16 *Yarra Yering*
17 *Eyton-on-Yarra*
18 *Oakridge*
19 *Yeringberg*
20 *Domaine Chandon*
21 *Yarrabank/ Yering Station*
22 *St Huberts*
23 *Mount Mary*
24 *Bianchet*
25 *Yarra Edge*
26 *Lirralirra*
27 *Halcyon Daze*
28 *Yarra Valley Hills*
29 *Kellybrook*
30 *Brahams Creek*
31 *Yarra Burn*
32 *Britannia Creek*
33 *Lillydale*
34 *Five Oaks*
35 *Seville*
36 *Silvan*
37 *Monbulk*
38 *Gembrook Hill*
39 *Wantirna*

Coldstream Hills NR
31 Maddens Lane, Coldstream, Vic 3770, ☏ (03) 5964 9410,
℻ (03) 5964 9389; est 1985; ❖ 50,000 cases; ⚑; A$; 7 days 10-5
Founded by the author, who continues in charge of winemaking following the acquisition of Coldstream by Southcorp in mid-1996. Expansion plans already underway have been accelerated, with well in excess of 100 hectares of owned or managed estate vineyards as the base. Chardonnay and Pinot Noir are the focus; Merlot came on-stream from the 1997 vintage.

De Bortoli (Victoria) ☆☆☆☆☆ V
Pinnacle Lane, Dixons Creek, Vic 3775, ☏ (03) 5965 2271,
℻ (03) 5965 2442; est 1987; ❖ 150,000 cases; ⚑; A$; 7 days 10-5; ✗;
¶; gardens
The quality arm of the bustling De Bortoli group, run by Leanne De Bortoli and husband Stephen Webber, an ex-Lindemans winemaker. The top label (De Bortoli), the second (Gulf Station) and the third label (Windy Peak) offer wines of consistently good quality and excellent value. Chardonnay is outstanding.

Diamond Valley Vineyards ☆☆☆☆☆
2130 Kinglake Road, St Andrews, Vic 3761, ☏ (03) 9710 1484,
℻ (03) 9710 1369; est 1976; ❖ 6,000 cases; No visitors
Run by the tightly-knit Lance family, one of the Yarra Valley's finest producers of Pinot Noir and an early pace-setter for the variety. They make true Pinot Noirs, fragrant and intense wines of tremendous style and crystal-clear varietal character.

Domaine Chandon ☆☆☆☆☆
Maroondah Highway, Coldstream, Vic 3770, ☏ (03) 9739 1110, ℻
(03) 9739 1095; est 1986; ❖ 90,000 cases; ⚑; A$; 7 days 10.30-4.30; ¶
Wholly owned by Champagne Moët & Chandon, in a superb location with luxurious tasting facilities. A complex blend of French and Australian style, thought by many to be the best Moët produces overseas. Exported under the Green Point label.

Eltham Vineyards ☆☆☆
225 Shaws Road, Arthurs Creek, Vic 3099, ☏ (03) 9439 4688,
℻ (03) 9439 5121; est 1990; ❖ 850 cases; ⚑; A$; by appt
Drawing on vineyards at Arthurs Creek and Eltham, John Graves (brother of David Graves of the illustrious Californian Pinot producer Saintsbury) produces tiny quantities of quite stylish Chardonnay and Pinot Noir, the former showing nice barrel-fermented characters.

Evelyn County Estate NR
35 New Road, Kangaroo Ground, Vic 3097, ☏ (03) 9437 1668,
℻ (03) 9437 1232; est 1994; ❖ NA; ⚑; A$; by appt
The 7-hectare estate is that of former Coopers & Lybrand managing partner Roger Male and his wife Robyn. Features an architect-designed cellar-door sales, and a gallery that will open in 2000. Wines are good, contract-made by Diamond Valley.

Eyton-on-Yarra ☆☆☆✩ V
Cnr Maroondah Highway and Hill Road, Coldstream, Vic 3370, ☏ *(03) 5962 2119,* ⓕ *(03) 5962 5319; est 1991;* ❖ *15,000 cases;* ⚑*; A$; 7 days 10-5;* ✗*;* 🍴*; concerts*

Owned and run by the energetic and innovative Deidre Cowan, who oversees a capacious restaurant, a sound shell for concerts of every shape and hue and, of course, the winemaking side of a substantial business that has 40 hectares of estate vineyards.

Fergusson ☆☆☆☆
Wills Road, Yarra Glen, Vic 3775, ☏ *(03) 5965 2237,* ⓕ *(03) 5965 2405; est 1968;* ❖ *10,000 cases;* ⚑*; A$; 7 days 11-5;* 🍴*; hot air balloon flights;* ⛳

Best known as a popular tourist destination, particularly for coach parties. Offers hearty fare in comfortable surroundings, accompanied by estate-grown wines (more expensive), or the Tartan range from other regions (less expensive). The Yarra wines are consistently full-flavoured.

Five Oaks Vineyard NR
Aitken Road, Seville, Vic 3139, ☏ *(03) 5964 3704,* ⓕ *(03) 5964 3064; est 1997;* ❖ *1,500 cases;* ⚑*; A$; wkds & public hols 10-5*

Formerly Oakridge Estate (now relocated elsewhere in the Valley), and acquired by Wally and Judy Zuk. Wally, with a background in physics, spends part of his time working in Sydney and Canberra as a physicist and the rest as winemaker (with help from Michael Zitzlaff of Oakridge) at Five Oaks.

Gembrook Hill ☆☆☆☆
Launching Place Road, Gembrook, Vic 3783, ☏ *(03) 5968 1622,* ⓕ *(03) 5968 1699; est 1983;* ❖ *2,000 cases;* ⚑*; A$; by appt*

Ian Marks, Melbourne dentist by day and fastidious viticulturist otherwise, tends the 6-hectare vineyard planted on red volcanic soil. He is now committing the ultimate folly: building an on-site winery for the 2000 vintage. All the wines are delicate, the best a fragrant gooseberry-and-herb Sauvignon Blanc.

Halcyon Daze ☆☆☆
19 Uplands Road, Lilydale, Vic 3140, ☏ *(03) 9726 7111,* ⓕ *(03) 9726 7111; est 1982;* ❖ *500 cases;* ⚑*; A$; by appt*

Richard Rackley runs one of the lower-profile wineries with a small, estate-grown production. Most of the grapes from its 6.5 hectare of vines are sold. Immaculate viticulture ensures that the grapes have a strong market.

Hanson ☆☆☆
340 Old Healesville Road, Yarra Glen, Vic 3775, ☏ *(03) 9439 7425,* ⓕ *(03) 9435 9183; est 1983;* ❖ *800 cases; No visitors*

Dental surgeon Ian Hanson is a red-wine specialist, producing Pinot Noir and various Cabernet-based wines from two vineyard resources, the oldest dating back to the late 1960s. What the wines lack in finesse, they make up for in flavour.

Henkell Wines NR
PO Box 2160, Fitzroy, Vic 3065, ☎ (03) 9417 4144, ℻ (03) 419 8873; est 1989; ❖ NA; No visitors

Hans Henkell started with a Heinz 57-mix of varieties in the vineyard, but has now rationalised it to a total of 18 hectares of Sauvignon Blanc, Chardonnay, Pinot Noir and Cabernet. Most of the grapes are sold, a small amount are contract-made.

Kellybrook ☆☆☆☆
Fulford Road, Wonga Park, Vic 3115, ☎ (03) 9722 1304, ℻ (03) 9722 2092; est 1960; ❖ 3,000 cases; ♀; A$; Mon-Sat 9-6, Sun 11-6; ⦿; petanque

The 8-hectare vineyard at Wonga Park lies at the entrance to the principal wine-growing areas of the Yarra Valley, replete with picnic area and a full-scale restaurant. Also a very competent producer of both cider and apple brandy (in Calvados style).

Lillydale Vineyards ☆☆☆☆ V
Lot 10, Davross Court, Seville, Vic 3139, ☎ (03) 5964 2016, ℻ (03) 5964 3009; est 1976; ❖ NFP; ♀; A$; 7 days 11-5; ⦿

Acquired by McWilliam's Wines in 1994 from founders Alex and Judy White. The elegant wines are now made at McWilliam's in the Riverina. Good Sauvignon Blanc, Chardonnay and Pinot Noir.

Lirralirra Estate ☆☆☆
Paynes Road, Lilydale, Vic 3140, ☎ (03) 9735 0224, ℻ (03) 9735 0224; est 1981; ❖ 400 cases; ♀; A$; wkds & hols 10-6, Jan 7 days

Off the beaten track. Owner Alan Smith originally intended to make a Sauternes-style wine from Semillon, Sauvignon Blanc and Muscadelle, but found the conditions unfavourable for the development of botrytis. He now makes dry red and white wines.

Long Gully Estate ☆☆☆
Long Gully Road, Healesville, Vic 3777, ☎ (03) 9807 4246, ℻ (03) 9807 2213; est 1982; ❖ 30,000 cases; ♀; A$; wkds & hols 11-5

One of Yarra's larger producers to have successfully established a number of export markets. Offers a range of wines; quality is consistent rather than exhilarating. Recent vineyard extensions underline its commercial success.

Lovey's Estate NR
1548 Melba Highway, Yarra Glen, Vic 3775, ☎ (03) 9965 2444, ℻ (03) 5965 2460; est 1989; ❖ 1,000 cases; ♀; A$; Wed-Sun 12-5; ⦿, ⛌, gardens (including a maze), brewery

Owned by Brian Love, the majority of the fruit from the 11-hectare vineyard is sold. Some is made under contract at Tarrawarra, and sold through the cellar door and the restaurant.

Monbulk Winery ☆☆☆
Macclesfield Road, Monbulk, Vic 3793, ☎ (03) 9756 6965, ℻ (03) 9756 6965; est 1984; ❖ 800 cases; ♀; A$; wkds & public hols 12-5, or by appt

Originally made kiwi fruit wines, but has now extended to table wines. While the very cool Monbulk subregion should be capable of producing grapes of distinctive style, these are, unfortunately, not as appealing as the delicious kiwi fruit wines.

Mount Mary ☆☆☆☆☆
Coldstream West Road, Lilydale, Vic 3140, ☎ (03) 9739 1761, ℻ (03) 9739 0137; est 1971; ❖ 3,000 cases; No visitors
The grand old lady of the Yarra Valley, producing superbly refined, elegant and intense Cabernets, and usually outstanding, long-lived Pinot Noirs that justify its exalted reputation. Owner and founding winemaker Dr John Middleton does not suffer fools (for which read wine writers) gladly.

Oakridge Estate ☆☆☆☆
864 Maroondah Highway, Coldstream, Vic 3770, ☎ (03) 9739 1920, ℻ (03) 9739 1923; est 1982; ❖ 15,000 cases; ⚑; A$; 7 days 10-5; ⦿
Moved to its new location and purpose-built winery on the back of capital raised from listing on the Stock Exchange in 1997, and has ambitious plans for expansion. The standard-bearer is a very stylish berry-and-mint Reserve Merlot.

Seville Estate ☆☆☆☆☆ ⌇
Linwood Road, Seville, Vic 3139, ☎ (03) 5964 2622, ℻ (03) 5964 2633; est 1970; ❖ 7,000 cases; No visitors
In early 1997 the controlling interest in Seville Estate was acquired by Brokenwood from founder Dr Peter McMahon. Produces Chardonnay and Pinot Noir in the usual precise Yarra Valley style; the spicey, peppery and cherryish Shiraz, always good, will drive the planned expansion.

Shantell ☆☆☆☆ V
1974 Melba Highway, Dixons Creek, Vic 3775, ☎ (03) 5965 2264, ℻ (03) 5965 2331; est 1980; ❖ 1,500 cases; ⚑; A$; Thurs-Mon 10.30-5
Dr Shan Shanmugam and biochemist Turid have slowly but surely developed Shantell. They still sell some of the grapes from the 10-hectare estate, but also make some marvellous wines that at times reach multiple-trophy standard. One such is the extraordinarily intense and richly tangy 1997 Chardonnay.

Silvan Winery NR
Lilydale-Silvan Road, Silvan, Vic 3795, ☎ (03) 9737 9392; est 1993; ❖ 500 cases; ⚑; A$; wkds & public hols 11-6
John Vigliaroni runs one of the newest Yarra Valley wineries, with six hectares of vineyards coming into bearing. Tastings are held in his Italianate villa set in beautiful grounds and gardens.

St Huberts ☆☆☆☆
Maroondah Highway, Coldstream, Vic 3770, ☎ (03) 9739 1118, ℻ (03) 9739 1096; est 1966; ❖ 5,000 cases; ⚑; A$; Mon-Fri 9-5, wkds 10.30-5.30; jazz

The first winery established in the rebirth of the Yarra Valley, and still operating in its converted chicken-shed winery. Now part of Mildara Blass, which has plans to rebuild the ornate 19th-century winery on its original site some distance away. Chardonnay and Cabernet are invariably good, plus Roussanne.

Steels Creek Estate NR
1 Sewell Road, Steels Creek, Vic 3775, ☏ (03) 5965 2448, Ⓕ (03) 5965 2448; est 1981; ♦ 400 cases; ⚑; A$; wkds & public hols 10-6
Simon Pierce has a wine science degree, and runs a 1.7-hectare estate planted between 1981 and 1994 with an eclectic choice of Colombard, Chardonnay, Shiraz and Cabernet Sauvignon, the latter producing the best results to date.

Tarrawarra Estate ☆☆☆☆½
Healesville Road, Yarra Glen, Vic 3775, ☏ (03) 5962 3311, Ⓕ (03) 5962 3887; est 1983; ♦ 16,000 cases; ⚑; A$; 7 days 10.30-4.30
Established by the clothing magnate Marc Besen and family. The winery speciality is a slowly evolving Chardonnay of great structure and complexity; robust, ageworthy Pinot Noir. The second-label, Tunnel Hill, wines are more accessible when young.

The Green Vineyards ☆☆☆☆
1 Alber Road, Upper Beaconsfield, Vic 3808, ☏ (03) 5944 4599, Ⓕ (03) 5944 4599; est 1994; ♦ 2,000 cases; ⚑; A$; wkds by appt
Sergio Carlei has come a long way in a little time, graduating from home winemaking in a suburban garage to his own winery in Upper Beaconsfield, just within the boundaries of the Yarra Valley. He has already produced a number of remarkably stylish wines, with more in the pipeline.

Wantirna Estate NR
Bushy Park Lane, Wantirna South, Vic 3152, ☏ (03) 9801 2367, Ⓕ (03) 9887 0225; est 1963; ♦ 900 cases; ⚑; A$; by appt
Solicitor Reg Egan became a pioneer of the area when he purchased Wantirna, part of a nature reserve. Not rated, in deference to Reg Egan's firmly held views, but produces very good wines, particularly Isabella Chardonnay and Lily Pinot Noir.

Warramate ☆☆☆
27 Maddens Lane, Gruyere, Vic 3770, ☏ (03) 5964 9219, Ⓕ (03) 5964 9219; est 1970; ♦ 900 cases; ⚑; A$; 7 days 10-6
Set up and still owned by the Church family which runs two hectares of Riesling, Shiraz, Cabernet Sauvignon and a little Merlot on a very distinguished site. This distinction is not always fully reflected in the wines, perhaps due to the difficulties of small-scale winemaking in a confined space.

Yarra Burn ☆☆☆☆
Settlement Road, Yarra Junction, Vic 3797, ☏ (03) 5967 1428, Ⓕ (03) 5967 1146; est 1975; ♦ 4,500 cases; ⚑; A$; 7 days 10-5; ⚑; ⇌
Acquired by BRL Hardy in 1995 and destined to become the

Yarra Edge ☆☆☆☆
PO Box 390, Yarra Glen, Vic 3775, ☎ (03) 9730 1107, ℻ (03) 9739 0135; est 1984; ❧ 2,000 cases; at Yering Station

Now leased to Yering Station, where the estate wines are made but still labelled under the Yarra Edge brand. Yering Station winemaker Tom Carson was briefly winemaker/manager at Yarra Edge, and knows the property intimately, so the rich styles of the Chardonnay and Cabernets can be expected to continue.

Yarra Ridge ☆☆☆☆ V
Glenview Road, Yarra Glen, Vic 3755, ☎ (03) 9730 1022, ℻ (03) 9730 1131; est 1983; ❧ 40,000 cases; ❢; A$; 7 days 10-5

Now under the sole ownership and control of Mildara Blass, but with the ever-affable Rob Dolan continuing to work winemaking and production miracles at a winery that is strained to its limits. Not all Yarra Ridge wines come exclusively from the Yarra Valley.

Yarra Track Wines NR
Viggers Vineyard, 518 Old Healesvile Road, Yarra Glen, Vic 3775, ☎ (03) 9730 1349, ℻ (03) 9730 1349; est 1989; ❧ 400 cases; ❢; A$; wkds & public hols 10-5; ⦿

Jim and Diana Viggers have established three hectares each of Chardonnay and Pinot Noir. Part of the grape production is sold, part contract-made for sale through the cellar door and restaurant.

Yarra Valley Hills ☆☆☆☆
Delaneys Road, Warranwood, Vic 3134, ☎ (03) 5962 4173, ℻ (03) 5962 4059; est 1989; ❧ 15,000 cases; ❢; A$; wkds & public hols 11-5; ⦿

Former schoolteacher Terry Hill has built up an empire in short order through leasing two substantial vineyards and principally acting as a grape supplier to others. A small proportion of the grapes are contract-made by a range of Yarra Valley winemakers.

Yarra Yarra ☆☆☆☆☆
239 Hunts Lane, Steels Creek, Vic 3775, ☎ (03) 5965 2380, ℻ (03) 9830 4180; est 1979; ❧ NFP; ❢; A$; by appt

Notwithstanding its tiny production, the wines of Yarra Yarra have found their way into Melbourne's best restaurants. Ian Maclean has increased the estate plantings from two hectares to over seven. The Semillon/Sauvignon Blanc and Cabernets (Bordeaux blend) have exceptional finesse, balance and longevity.

Yarra Yering ☆☆☆☆☆
Briarty Road, Coldstream, Vic 3770, ☎ (03) 5964 9267, ℻ (03) 5964 9239; est 1969; ❧ 6,000 cases; ❢; A$; Sat, public hols 10-5, Sun 12-5

Dr Bailey Carrodus makes extremely powerful, occasionally

idiosyncratic wines from his 25-year-old, low-yielding unirrigated vineyards. Both red and white wines have an exceptional depth of flavour and richness; I believe his reds to be greatest.

Yarrabank ☆☆☆☆☆
42 Melba Highway, Yarra Glen, Vic 3775, ☎ (03) 9730 2188, ⓕ (03) 9730 2189; est 1993; ❀ 2,000 cases; ♇; A$; 7 days 10-5; wine bar
Shares the same spectacular new winery facility built in 1997 by joint-venture partners Yering Station and Champagne Devaux (the owner). The sparkling wine is, in the author's view, the finest and best traditional method fizz in Australia, made from fruit sourced from the Yarra Valley and Mornington Peninsula.

Yering Farm ☆☆☆☆⚬
St Huberts Road, Yering, Vic 3770, ☎ (03) 9735 4161, ⓕ (03) 9735 4012; est 1989; ❀ 850 cases; No visitors
Alan and Louise Johns established their 12-hectare vineyard in 1989 on the site of the original Yeringa winery built by the Deschamps family in the last century. Yarra Ridge buys much of the fruit and makes very competent wines for this label.

Yering Grange Vineyard NR
14 McIntyre Lane, Coldstream, Vic 3770, ☎ (03) 9739 1172, ⓕ (03) 9739 1172; est 1989; ❀ 300 cases; ♇; A$; by appt
While some of the two hectares of Cabernet Sauvignon under vine are sold, a tiny amount of wine is made at Hanging Rock by John Ellis for the Yering Grange label and sold by mailing list.

Yering Station ☆☆☆☆⚬
Melba Highway, Yering, Vic 3770, ☎ (03) 9730 1107, ⓕ (03) 9739 0135; est 1988; ❀ 25,000 cases; ♇; A$; Thur-Sun 10-5; ❖; ⌂.
The historic Yering Station was purchased by the Rathbone family in 1996; a joint venture with Champagne Devaux has resulted in a spectacular winery, handling the Yarrabank sparkling wines, Yering Station and Yarra Edge wines. A focal points of the Yarra Valley, particularly with the historic Chateau Yering next door. Luxury accommodation and the fine dining also.

Yeringberg ☆☆☆☆☆
Maroondah Highway, Coldstream, Vic 3770, ☎ (03) 9739 1453, ⓕ (03) 9739 0048; est 1863; ❀ 1,000 cases; ♇; A$; by appt
Established by Guill de Pury's great-grandfather, Yeringberg has the only working winery from the 19th century (built in the 1880s). Superbly sited hillside vineyards produce a Marsanne/Roussanne blend that harks back to the last century, powerful Pinot Noir, and a Cabernet blend that soars in warmer vintages.

Mornington Peninsula
Traditionally the major lure for summer visitors, the ocean also plays a very important role in shaping the viticultural climate, as there are places on the peninsula that are simply too cool for commercially viable grape-growing. Site and varietal selection are

matters of financial life or death for would-be *vignerons*. Of these there are no shortage: the growth in their numbers has been every bit as great as in the Yarra Valley. Yet in stark contrast to the Yarra, most properties are relatively small, due to a deliberate life-style choice by the doctor/lawyer/banker owner, the lack of and high costs of land, and the shortage of large holdings (over 100 hectares). The largest of the local wineries is Stonier's, in which Petaluma has a 70 per cent interest.

Overall, grapes ripen on the peninsula several weeks after the Yarra. Its most successful varieties are Chardonnay, Pinot Gris and Pinot Noir, its least successful Cabernet and Merlot. Shiraz is the odd man out; a couple of producers (Merricks, Paringa Estate and Port Phillip Estate) have made striking wines in good years.

Barak Estate NR
Barak Road, Moorooduc, Vic 3933, ☏ (03) 5978 8439, Ⓕ (03) 5978 8439; est 1996; ❖ 450 cases; ❢; A$; wkds & public hols 11-5; ⊨

When James Williamson decided to plant vines on his 4-hectare property and establish a micro-winery, he knew it was far cheaper to buy wine. Undeterred, he picked the first grapes in 1993, and opened Barak Estate in 1996.

Boneo Plains NR
RMB 1400 Browns Road, South Rosebud, Vic 3939, ☏ (03) 5988 6208, Ⓕ (03) 5988 6208; est 1988; ❖ 2,500 cases; ❢; A$; by appt

A 9-hectare vineyard and winery established by the Tallarida family, which also manufactures and supplies winemaking equipment. The Chardonnay is the best of the wines so far.

Craig Avon Vineyard ☆☆☆♪
Craig Avon Lane, Merricks North, Vic 3926, ☏ (03) 5989 7465, Ⓕ (03) 5989 7615; est 1986; ❖ 1,000 cases; ❢; A$; wkds & public hols 12-5

A part-time interest for owner/winemaker Ken Lang. All the wines are sold through the cellar door and by mailing list. The wines are competently made, with clean fruit flavours.

Darling Park ☆☆☆♪
Red Hill Road, Red Hill, Vic 3937, ☏ (03) 5989 2324, Ⓕ (03) 5989 2254; est 1986; ❖ 1000 cases; ❢; A$; Jan, Feb-Dec: 7 days, wkds & hols 11-5; ❙◐❙

At the ripe young age of 70, John Sargeant took over the red wine making (prior to 1996 the wines were contract-made), and with wife Delys has opened a cellar-door-cum-restaurant. The labels are the most gloriously baroque of any to be found in Australia.

Dromana Estate ☆☆☆☆
Cnr Harrisons Road and Bittern-Dromana Road, Dromana, Vic 3936, ☏ (03) 5987 3800, Ⓕ (03) 5981 0714; est 1982; ❖ 20,000 cases; ❢; A$; 7 days 11-4; ❙◐❙; *playground*

The ever-energetic, lateral-thinking Garry Crittenden is a consultant viticulturist, winemaker and wine marketer and is well-known for his estate-grown Pinot and Chardonnay, as well as his strikingly labelled range of Italian-style wines. Fruit for the latter is sourced from many parts of Australia.

Elan Vineyard ☆☆☆ V
17 Turners Road, Bittern, Vic 3918, ☏ (03) 5983 1858, Ⓕ (03) 5983 2821; est 1980; ❖ 600 cases; ❣; A$; first wkd of month & public hols 11-5 or by appt

Selma Lowther made an impressive debut with her spicy, fresh, crisp Chardonnay. Riesling is also good, and the Gamay (one of Australia's few) is well worth a look.

Eldridge Estate NR
Red Hill Road, Red Hill, Vic 3937, ☏ (03) 5989 2644, Ⓕ (03) 5989 2644; est 1985; ❖ 700 cases; ❣; A$; Jan, wkds & public hols 11-5

David Lloyd had made wine nearly everywhere before he and wife Wendy purchased this 3.5-hectare estate, planted with seven varieties, in 1995. Vineyard improvements will pay dividends.

Elgee Park NR
Wallaces Road, Merricks North, Vic 3926, ☏ (03) 5989 7338, Ⓕ (03) 5989 7553; est 1972; ❖ 1,500 cases; ❣; A$; one day a year (Sun, Queen's Birthday wkd)

The pioneer of the Mornington Peninsula in its 20th-century resurrection, owned by Baillieu Myer and family. Since the closure of its winery, the wines are now made at Stonier's.

Ermes Estate NR
2 Godings Road, Moorooduc, Vic 3933, ☏ (03) 5978 8376; est 1989; ❖ 500 cases; ❣; A$; wkds & public hols 11-5

Ermes Zucchet, of north Italian descent, and wife Denise started planting the 2-hectare vineyard in 1989, adding Pinot Gris in 1991. In 1994 a piggery was converted to a winery and cellar-door area.

Hanns Creek Estate NR
Kentucky Road, Merricks North, Vic 3926, ☏ (03) 5989 7266, Ⓕ (03) 5989 7500; est 1987; ❖ 1,500 cases; ❣; A$; 7 days 11-5; ❢; petanque

Denise and Tony Aubrey-Slocock established this 3-hectare vineyard. After an uncertain start, Kevin McCarthy is now consulting and wine style has steadied.

Hickinbotham NR
Nepean Highway (near Wallaces Road), Dromana, Vic 3936, ☏ (03) 5981 0355, Ⓕ (03) 5981 0355; est 1981; ❖ 2,000 cases; ❣; A$; 7 days; wine education centre

Grandfather Alan Hickinbotham was a brilliant wine scientist who led world research into the role of pH in winemaking. Father Ian also contributed much, but the spark seems to have gone from this family business. Spicy/grapey Taminga is good.

Hurley Vineyard NR
101 Balnarring Road, Balnarring, Vic 3926, ☏ (03) 9608 8220, Ⓕ (03) 9608 7293; est 1998; ❖ NA; No visitors

Established by Melbourne QC Kevin Bell. The four hectares of Pinot Noir planted in 1998 have yet to come into production.

Karina Vineyard ☆☆☆☆ V
RMB 4055 Harrisons Road, Dromana, Vic 3936, ☏ (03) 5981 0137, Ⓕ (03) 5981 0137; est 1984; ♦ 1,500 cases; ⚑; A$; wkds 11-5, Jan: 7 days

Just three km from the shores of Port Phillip Bay. Immaculately tended and with picturesque gardens. Fragrant Riesling and cashew-accented Chardonnay are its best wines.

Kings Creek Winery ☆☆☆☆ V
237 Myers Road, Bittern, Vic 3918, ☏ (03) 5983 2102, Ⓕ (03) 5983 5153; est 1981; ♦ 3,000 cases; ⚑; A$; 7 days 11-5; lunches

Kings Creek is owned and operated by the Bell, Glover and Perraton families. Planting began in 1981, and the vines are now fully mature. Since 1990, the quality of the wines, particularly the Chardonnay and Pinot Noir, has been beyond reproach.

Lavender Bay NR
39 Paringa Road, Red Hill South, Vic 3937, ☏ (03) 9869 4405, Ⓕ (03) 9869 4423; est 1988; ♦ NA; No visitors

Marketing consultant Kevin Luscombe established this spectacular 4-hectare property in Red Hill South (overlooking Phillip Island) in 1988. Wines are contract-made by Dromana Estate.

Main Ridge Estate ☆☆☆☆
Lot 48 William Road, Red Hill, Vic 3937, ☏ (03) 5989 2686, Ⓕ (03) 5931 0000; est 1975; ♦ 1,000 cases; ⚑; A$; Mon-Fri 12-4, wkds 12-5; Sun lunch, gardens

Nat White pays meticulous attention to every aspect of his viticulture and winemaking, doing annual battle with one of the coolest sites on the peninsula. The same attention to detail extends to the winery and the winemaking. The Half Acre Pinot Noir is a measure of the size of the business.

Mantons Creek Vineyard NR
Tucks Road, Main Ridge, Vic 3928, ☏ (03) 5989 6264, Ⓕ (03) 5959 6060; est 1998; ♦ 2,500 cases; ⚑; A$; 7 days 10-5; ✴; ⛴

The 14-hectare vineyard, planted in 1990, includes three hectares of Tempranillo, which owner John Williams says shows great potential. Label and cellar door/restaurant were launched in 1998.

Maritime Estate NR
Tucks Road, Red Hill, Vic 3937, ☏ (03) 9848 2926, Ⓕ (03) 9882 8325; est 1988; ♦ 1,000 cases; ⚑; A$; wkds & public hols 11-5, Dec 27-Jan 26: 7 days

John and Linda Ruljancich have enjoyed great success since their first vintage in 1994. This is no doubt due in part to skilled contract-winemaking by T'Gallant, but also to the situation of their vineyard, looking across the hills and valleys of the Red Hill subregion.

Massoni Main Creek ☆☆☆☆
Mornington Flinders Road, Red Hill, Vic 3937, ☏ (03) 5989 2352, ℱ (03) 5989 2014; est 1984; ❖ 2,500 cases; ⚑; A$; by appt

Long known for the concentration and richness of its estate-grown Chardonnay and Pinot Noir. Under industry veteran Ian Home's ownership, its sights have turned to Langhorne Creek for additional grapes to provide lower-priced wines.

Merricks Estate ☆☆☆☆
Thompsons Lane, Merricks, Vic 3916, ☏ (03) 5989 8416, ℱ (03) 9627 4035; est 1977; ❖ 2,500 cases; ⚑; A$; first wkd each month 12-5

Melbourne solicitor George Kefford, with wife Jacquie, runs Merricks Estate as a weekend and holiday enterprise as a relief from professional practice. Produces distinctive, spicy, cool-climate Shiraz and pleasant Chardonnay and Pinot Noir.

Miceli NR
RMB 9230, Main Creek Road, Main Ridge, Vic 3928, ☏ (03) 5989 2755, ℱ (03) 5989 2755; est 1991; ❖ 800 cases; ⚑; A$; first wkd each mth 12-5, also Jan: every wkd and by appt

This may be a part-time labour of love for Dr Anthony Miceli, but this hasn't prevented him taking the venture very seriously. While establishing the 3-hectare vineyard, he studied wine science at University and in August 1999 won a trophy for his Pinot Noir.

Moorooduc Estate ☆☆☆☆✓
501 Derril Road, Moorooduc, Vic 3936, ☏ (03) 9696 4130, ℱ (03) 9696 2841; est 1983; ❖ 7,000 cases; ⚑; A$; first wkd each month 12-5; ℱ; ⌂

Dr Richard McIntyre regularly produces one of the richest and most complex Chardonnays in the region. Sauvignon Blanc and Pinot Noir are more elegant, but less exciting.

Morning Cloud Wines NR
15 Ocean View Avenue, Red Hill South, Vic 3937, ☏ (03) 5989 2762, ℱ (03) 5989 2700; est 1983; ❖ 500 cases; ⚑; A$; by appt

A joint venture between the Allen and Maxwell families, who pool their grape resources and use contract winemaking. The Cabernet is light and leafy; the Chardonnay medium-bodied.

Mornington Vineyards Estate ☆☆☆
Moorooduc Road, Moorooduc South, Vic 3931, ☏ (03) 5974 2097, ℱ (03) 5974 2097; est 1989; ❖ 2,500 cases; ⚑; A$; wkds & public hols 11-5

One of the largest vineyards on the peninsula, with 20 hectares under vine. The wines are contract-made at Blue Pyrenees winery in central Victoria. Could be more depth to fruit flavour.

Osborns ☆☆☆☆
RMB 5935 Ellerina Road, Merricks North, Vic 3926, ☏ (03) 5989 7417, ℱ (03) 5989 7510; est 1988; ❖ 1,600 cases; ⚑; A$; by appt

Frank and Pamela Osborn have taken the slow boat to

commercial winemaking. They began planting in 1988 and opened for business in 1997 with six vintages each of complex, nutty Chardonnay and sappy, spicy Pinot Noir, in tiny quantities.

Paringa Estate ☆☆☆☆☆
44 Paringa Road, Red Hill South, Vic 3937, ☏ (03) 5989 2669, Ⓕ (03) 5989 2669; est 1985; ❦ 2,000 cases; ⚱; A$; Mon, Wed-Fri 12-5, wkds & public hols 11-5; ¶⦿

Former schoolteacher Lindsay McCall makes wines with an unequalled depth, complexity and power. The Pinot Noir, in particular, is usually awesome, but then so are the Chardonnay and Shiraz. Only the wet, cold vintages show he is human.

Poplar Bend NR
RMB 8655 Main Creek Road, Main Ridge, Vic 3928, ☏ (03) 5989 6046, Ⓕ (03) 5989 6460; est 1988; ❦ 350 cases; ⚱; A$; wkds & public hols 10-5, also by appt

Poplar Bend was the offspring of Melbourne journalist, author and raconteur Keith Dunstan and wife Marie. They sold Poplar Bend to David Briggs on retiring in 1997. The (nude) Chloe label is as delightful as that of Darling Park.

Port Phillip Estate ☆☆☆☆☆
261 Red Hill Road, Red Hill, Vic 3937, ☏ (03) 5989 2708, Ⓕ (03) 5989 2891; est 1987; ❦ 4,000 cases; ⚱; A$; wkds & public hols 12-5

Established by leading Melbourne QC Jeffrey Sher, with Lindsay McCall of Paringa Estate as contract winemaker working similar magic here. It is hard to choose between the Reserve Pinot Noir and the Reserve Shiraz; both have extra dimensions of flavour.

Red Hill Estate ☆☆☆☆
53 Redhill Shoreham Road, Red Hill South, Vic 3937, ☏ (03) 5989 2838, Ⓕ (03) 5989 2855; est 1989; ❦ 10,000 cases; ⚱; A$; 7 days 11-5; ⚘; ¶⦿

Owned by Sir Peter Derham and family, producing taut, fine sparkling wine and bracing Chardonnay in a different style to most Mornington producers. Superb views over the 10-hectare vineyard and Phillip Island from the tasting room and restaurant.

Ryland River NR
RMB 8945 Main Creek Road, Main Ridge, Vic 3928, ☏ (03) 5989 6098, Ⓕ (03) 9899 0184; est 1986; ❦ 2,000 cases; ⚱; A$; wkds & public hols 10-5 or by appt; lunches, herb garden, trout fishing

Jack's Delight Tawny Port and 20-year-old Liqueur Muscat tell you that Ryland River is far from the average Mornington winery, happy to source much of its wine from elsewhere.

Sea Winds Vineyard NR
RMB 9020, Main Creek Road, Main Ridge, Vic 3928, ☏ (03) 5989 6204, Ⓕ (03) 5989 6204; est 1990; ❦ NA; No visitors

Ron Matson has three hectares of Sauvignon Blanc, Chardonnay and Pinot Noir. Wines made by Kevin McCarthy at T'Gallant.

Stonier's Wines ☆☆☆☆☆
362 Frankston-Flinders Road, Merricks, Vic 3916, ☏ (03) 5989 8300, ⓕ (03) 5989 8709; est 1978; ❧ 20,000 cases; ♀; A$; 7 days 12-5; ✗; lunches

The aquisition of a 70 per cent interest by Petaluma in 1998 has boosted Stonier's credibility; now its region's pre-eminent winery. Quality is led by its Reserve Chardonnay and Reserve Pinot Noir.

Stumpy Gully ☆☆☆☆
1247 Stumpy Gully Road, Moorooduc, Vic 3933, ☏ (03) 5978 8429, ⓕ (03) 5978 8429; est 1988; ❧ 2,000 cases; ♀; A$; first wkd of each month 12-5

Dutch owners/winemakers Frank and Wendy Zantvoort sell 80 per cent of production from the 11-hectare vineyard as grapes.

T'Gallant ☆☆☆☆☆
Mornington Road, Red Hill, Vic 3937, ☏ (03) 5989 6565, ⓕ (03) 5989 6577; est 1990; ❧ 12,000 cases; ♀; A$; 7 days 10-5; ⌘

The husband-and-wife team of Kathleen Quealy and Kevin McCarthy have established a major contract-winemaking business while being at the top of the mast for Australian Pinot Gris. They share a common disdain for oak in white wines.

Tanglewood Downs NR
Bulldog Creek Road, Merricks North, Vic 3926, ☏ (03) 5974 3325, ⓕ (03) 5974 4170; est 1984; ❧ 1,000 cases; ♀; A$; Sun-Mon 12-5; ⌘; playground

A smaller and lower-profile winery, with Ken Bilham quietly doing his own thing on 2.5 hectares of estate plantings.

Tuck's Ridge ☆☆☆☆ V
37 Red Hill-Shoreham Road, Red Hill South, Vic 3937, ☏ (03) 5989 8660, ⓕ (03) 5989 8579; est 1988; ❧ 10,000 cases; ♀; A$; 7 days 12-5

After an initial burst of frenetic activity following its launch in July 1993, Tuck's Ridge has slowed down a little. But, plantings have increased to over 25 hectares, making it one of the largest vineyards in this region. Fragrant Riesling is good value.

Turramurra Estate NR
RMB 4327 Wallaces Road, Dromana Vic 3926, ☏ (03) 5987 1146, ⓕ (03) 5987 1286; est 1989; ❧ 750 cases; ♀; A$; 12-5 first wkd of month or by appt

Dr David Leslie gave up his job as a medical practitioner to concentrate on developing the family's 10-hectare estate at Dromana. Wife Paula is the viticulturist, tending Sauvignon Blanc, Chardonnay, Pinot Noir, Shiraz and Cabernet Sauvignon.

Villa Primavera NR
Mornington-Flinders Road, Red Hill, Vic 3937, ☏ (03) 5989 2129; est 1984; ❧ 300 cases; ♀; A$; wkds & public hols 10-5, Jan: 7 days 10-5; ⌘; concerts

Gennaro Mazzella genially presides over an Italian-style family restaurant. It consistently wins tourism and food awards, and sells virtually all the Villa Primavera wine.

Vintina Estate NR
1282 Nepean Highway, Mount Eliza, Vic 3930, ☎ (03) 9787 8166, ℻ (03) 9775 2035; est 1985; ❖ 400 cases; ⚱; A$; 7 days 9-5
On the evidence to date, Vintina is still feeling its way. Strawberry wine and cherry 'Port' are ominous offerings.

Willow Creek ☆☆☆½
166 Balnarring Road, Merricks North, Vic 3926, ☎ (03) 5989 7448, ℻ (03) 5989 7584; est 1989; ❖ 8,000 cases; ⚱; A$; 7 days 10-5; ❧; playground
Fifteen hectares of estate Chardonnay, Cabernet Sauvignon and Pinot Noir (the best) underpin a cellar-door sales area. There are also picnic areas, barbecue facilities, trout fishing and *petanque*; lunches are served every day, and dinners by appointment.

Wyldcroft Estates NR
98 Stanleys Road, Red Hill South, Vic 3937, ☎ (03) 5989 2646, ℻ (03) 5989 2646; est 1987; ❖ 800 cases; wkds & public hols 10-5
Richard Condon and Sharon Stone (not the film star) built their own mud-brick winery and cellar door as a weekend pursuit.

Geelong

Geelong sits to the southwest of Melbourne. Like the Yarra Valley, the initial impetus for viticulture in Geelong was created by Swiss settlers, and until 1874 it seemed the two regions would vie with each other for supremacy. Then their paths diverged dramatically: *phylloxera* was discovered in Geelong, and the Victorian parliament swiftly passed controversial legislation requiring the uprooting of all the vineyards. Compensation was inadequate.

Viticulture did not return to Geelong until 1966 and the arrival of the Seftons at Idyll Vineyard. They planted Gewurztraminer, Shiraz and Cabernet Sauvignon. Chardonnay and Pinot Noir followed in due course, but not to the exclusion of later-ripening varieties such as Riesling, Shiraz and Cabernet Sauvignon.

Geelong is a windswept place, yet vineyards established in hollows or on river banks sheltered from the wind have found frost the greater of the two evils. The soils and climate are very different to those of the Yarra Valley; Chardonnay and Pinot Noir are more robust here. Then there is Shiraz. A fascinating contemporary battle is being waged over a variety that may be statistically unimportant, but is capable of great things.

Asher NR
360 Goldsworthy Road, Lovely Banks, Geelong, Vic 3231, ☎ (03) 5276 1365; est 1975; ❖ minuscule cases; ⚱; A$; Sat & public hols 10-5, Sun 12-5
Tiny, semi-home-winemaking operation in the picturesquely named town of Lovely Banks on the outskirts of Geelong.

Austin's Barrabool ☆☆☆☆ V
50 Lemins Road, Waurn Ponds, Vic 3221, ☏ (03) 5241 8114, ℻ (03) 5241 8122; est 1982; ❖ 2,500 cases; ♀; A$; by appt

Increasing amounts of wine from Pamela Austin's 10-hectare vineyard are contract-made by John Ellis (Hanging Rock). Riesling, Chardonnay and a brilliantly coloured, spicy-flavoured Reserve Shiraz are all recommended.

Bannockburn Vineyards ☆☆☆☆☆
Midland Highway, Bannockburn, Vic 3331, ☏ (03) 5281 1363, ℻ (03) 5281 1349; est 1974; ❖ 8,000 cases; No visitors

A sorry tale from Bannockburn: two vintages out of three decimated by hail, and family succession problems leading to the departure of long-serving winemaker Gary Farr. He leaves a legacy of immensely concentrated and complex Chardonnay, similarly structured Pinot Noir (both influenced by Gary's 15 years of pilgrimages to Burgundy) and a Rhône-inspired Shiraz.

Clyde Park NR
Midland Highway, Bannockburn, Vic 3331, ☏ (03) 5281 7274, ℻ (03) 5281 7274; est 1980; ❖ 2,000 cases; No visitors

Has undergone several changes of ownership since it was founded by Gary Farr. Has 12 hectares of mostly mature Chardonnay, Sauvignon Blanc, Pinot Noir, Shiraz and Cabernet Sauvignon, with Pinot Gris a recent addition.

Idyll Vineyard ☆☆☆
265 Ballan Road, Moorabool, Vic 3221, ☏ (03) 5276 1280, ℻ (03) 5276 1537; est 1966; ❖ 4,500 cases; ♀; A$; Tues-Sun & hols 10-5

The founding Sefton family sold Idyll to the Littore Group (also owners of Jindalee Wines) in June 1999. Assertive, pungent Traminer and long-vatted, powerful Shiraz and Cabernet have been the best wines.

Innisfail Vineyards NR
Cross Street, Batesford, Vic 3221, ☏ (03) 5276 1258, ℻ (03) 5221 8442; est 1980; ❖ 1,800 cases; No visitors

This 6-hectare vineyard released its first wines in 1988, made in a small on-site modern winery. Chewy, complex Chardonnay.

Jindalee Wines NR
PO Box 5146, North Geelong, Vic 3215, ☏ (03) 5277 2836, ℻ (03) 5277 2840; est 1997; ❖ 8,000 cases; No visitors

Jindalee Wines made its debut with the 1997 vintage. It is part of the Littore Group, which currently has 400 premium hectares in production and under development in the Riverland. First wines were contract-made, but a winery is planned for early 21st century.

Kilgour Estate NR
85 McAdams Lane, Bellarine, Vic 3223, ☏ (03) 5251 2223, ℻ (03) 5251 2223; est 1989; ❖ 2,000 cases; ♀; A$; Wed-Sun 10.30-6, Jan: 7 days; ⦿

Kilgour Estate has seven hectares of vines, and the wines are contract-made at Hanging Rock. Fruit-driven Pinot Noir and Chardonnay are winery specialities, each Pinot Noir having won at least one gold medal.

Mount Anakie Wines ☆☆☆

Staughton Vale Road, Anakie, Vic 3221, ☏ (03) 5284 1452, ℻ (03) 5284 1405; est 1968; ❖ 6,000 cases; ⚑; A$; Tues-Sun 11-6, ⍾

Otto Zambelli produces an eclectic range of wines, including a fruity Dolcetto and a Biancone. The 60-seat restaurant (described as 'rustic') opens for weekend lunches.

Mount Duneed ☆☆☆

Feehan's Road, Mount Duneed, Vic 3216, ☏ (03) 5264 1281, ℻ (03) 5264 1281; est 1970; ❖ 1,000 cases; ⚑; A$; wkds & public hols 11-5, or by appt

Rather idiosyncratic wines are the order of the day, some of which can develop surprisingly well in bottle; the Botrytis Noble Rot Semillon has, from time to time, been of very high quality. A significant part of the production from the 7.5 hectares of vineyards is sold.

Prince Albert ☆☆☆☆ V

100 Lemins Road, Waurn Ponds, Vic 3221, ☏ (03) 5241 8091, ℻ (03) 5241 8091; est 1975; ❖ 500 cases; ⚑; A$; by appt

Bruce Hyett re-established Prince Albert on the north-facing slope of a 19th-century vineyard, which then, as today, produced only Pinot Noir. The wine always has pure varietal character, and is on the lighter, more elegant side.

Red Rock Winery NR

RMB 5059 East West Road, Barongarook, Vic 3249, ☏ (015) 231 190, ℻ (03) 9380 9711; est 1981; ❖ NA; A$; wkds & public hols 11-5 or by appt

The former Barongvale Estate, with five hectares of Riesling, Semillon, Chardonnay, Pinot Noir, Merlot and Cabernet Sauvignon. A part-time occupation for Rohan Little, with wines sold under both the Red Rock and Ottway Vineyards labels.

Scotchmans Hill ☆☆☆☆ V

190 Scotchmans Road, Drysdale, Vic 3222, ☏ (03) 5251 3176, ℻ (03) 5253 1743; est 1982; ❖ 30,000 cases; ⚑; A$; 7 days 10.30-4.30

The Brockett family own and run two adjacent vineyards, and specialise in aromatic, fresh Chardonnay and Pinot Noir. Scotchmans has more weight than second label Spray Farm, but both are relatively understated and certainly not overoaked.

Staughton Vale Vineyard NR

20 Staughton Vale Road, Anakie, Vic 3221, ☏ (03) 5284 1229, ℻ (03) 5284 1229; est 1986; ❖ 1800 cases; ⚑; A$; Fri-Mon & public hols 10-5, or by appt

Paul Chambers has six hectares of grapes, with the accent on the classic Bordeaux mix of Cabernet Sauvignon, Merlot, Cabernet Franc and Petit Verdot, although Chardonnay and Pinot Noir are also planted. Weekend lunches are available at the Staughton Cottage Restaurant.

The Minya Winery NR
Minya Lane, Connewarre, Vic 3227, ☎ (03) 5264 1397; est 1974; ❀ 500 cases; ⚑; A$; public hols, or by appt; ⏏; ⌂
Geoff Dans first planted vines in 1974 on his family's dairy farm, followed by further plantings in 1982 and 1988. Barbecue facilities and light meals are available, as is cottage accommodation on the farm.

Waybourne NR
60 Lemins Road, Waurn Ponds, Vic 3221, ☎ (03) 5241 8477, ℻ (03) 5241 8477; est 1980; ❀ 730 cases; ⚑; A$; by appt
Owned by Tony and Kay Volpato, who have relied upon external consultants to assist with the winemaking. The last wines tasted were distinctly rough around the edges.

Macedon Ranges
The hills of the Macedon Ranges, though not the vineyards, ascend to over 700 metres above sea level. Site selection, aspect, slope and varietal selection are therefore all-important in this decidedly mountainous area, for many parts of this region tremble on the brink of commercial viability. Wind (often biting and bleak, even in summer) and frost are obvious dangers, but in the cooler, wetter vintages there may simply be insufficient sunshine hours and warmth to properly ripen the grapes.

All that said, there are some excellent producers of sparkling wines (Cope Williams and Hanging Rock) and a growing band of Chardonnay and Pinot Noir producers, of which Bindi is the brightest and most recent star. Then there are the long-established Virgin Hills and Knight Granite Hills, both of whom bypassed Pinot Noir and Chardonnay in favour of Riesling (Knight), Cabernet Sauvignon and Shiraz (both).

Ashworths Hill NR
Ashworths Road, Lancefield, Vic 3435, ☎ (03) 5429 1689, ℻ (03) 5429 1689; est 1982; ❀ 100 cases; ⚑; A$; 7 days 10-6; tea rooms
A venture still in its infancy, with 3.8 hectares of estate plantings coming into bearing. Macedon Ranges Cabernet is the estate wine; Victorian Riesling and Chardonnay are also available. Light food offered through the day by Peg and Ken Reaburn.

Bindi ☆☆☆☆☆
343 Melton Road, Gisborne, Vic 3437, ☎ (03) 5428 2564, ℻ (03) 5428 2564; est 1988; ❀ 900 cases; No visitors
This house is a relatively new arrival that has gone from strength to strength. The Chardonnay is top shelf, the ultra-concentrated Pinot Noir as remarkable (in its own idiom) as Bass Phillip, Giaconda or any of the other tiny-production icon wines.

Candlebark Hill ☆☆☆☆
Fordes Lane, Kyneton, Vic 3444, ☎ (03) 9836 2712, ⓕ (03) 9836 2712; est 1987; ❖ 500 cases; ⚜; A$; Sun 10-6 and by appt
David Forster has established a marvellously scenic 3.5-hectare vineyard, planted predominantly with Pinot Noir but also with Chardonnay, the three Bordeaux varieties, Shiraz and Malbec. The quality of the first Pinot Noir and Cabernet/Merlot blend was exemplary, promising much for the future.

Cleveland ☆☆☆☆
Shannons Road, Lancefield, Vic 3435, ☎ (03) 5429 1449, ⓕ (03) 5429 2017; est 1985; ❖ 4,000 cases; ⚜; A$; 7 days 9-6; ⦿; ⛃
The Cleveland homestead, built in 1889 in the style of a Gothic Revival manor house, had been abandoned for 40 years when purchased by the Brien family in 1983. It has since been painstakingly restored, and 3.5 hectares of surrounding vineyard established. Not surprisingly, Chardonnay and Pinot Noir are the pick, with Cabernet Sauvignon occasionally shining.

Cobaw Ridge ☆☆☆☆
Perc Boyer's Lane, East Pastoria via Kyneton, Vic 3444, ☎ (03) 5423 5227, ⓕ (03) 5423 5227; est 1985; ❖ 1,300 cases; ⚜; A$; wkds 10-5, or by appt
Nelly and Alan Cooper have established a 4-hectare vineyard at an altitude of 610 metres above Kyneton, complete with pole-framed mud-brick house and winery. Chardonnay and Shiraz do very well in warm vintages, and have been joined by the rare northern Italian grape, Lagrein.

Cope-Williams ☆☆☆☆ V
Glenfern Road, Romsey, Vic 3434, ☎ (03) 5429 5428, ⓕ (03) 5429 5655; est 1977; ❖ 7,000 cases; ⚜; A$; 7 days 11-5; ⦿; ⛃, cricket, royal tennis
Anyone with a penchant for cricket must visit this gloriously situated property (it has its own village-green cricket ground for hire). While architect Gordon Cope-Williams and wife Judy are the driving forces of the tourism aspect, son Michael makes excellent sparkling wines, plus a diverse range of table wines using fruit drawn from elsewhere.

Glen Erin Vineyard Retreat NR
Woodend Road, Lancefield, Vic 3435, ☎ (03) 5429 1041, ⓕ (03) 5429 2053; est 1993; ❖ 1,000 cases; ⚜; A$; wkds & public hols 10-6; ⦿; ⛃
Brian Scales acquired the former Lancefield Winery and renamed it Glen Erin; the wines are contract-made using grapes from Macedon and other regions. The conference and function facilities are supported by 24 rooms.

Hanging Rock Winery ☆☆☆☆ V
The Jim Jim, Jim Road, Newham, Vic 3442, ☎ (03) 5427 0542, ⓕ (03) 5427 0310; est 1982; ❖ 15,000 cases; ⚜; A$; 7 days 10-5; ⛃

Takes its name from a celebrated rock formation which can be seen from the vineyard. John Ellis, veteran winemaker of 25 years, standing, makes Australia's most complex sparkling wine, Macedon Cuvée, in the style of Bollinger. Local zesty Jim Jim Sauvignon Blanc and opulent Heathcote Shiraz are quality leaders, while Picnic White and Picnic Red are bargains.

Knight Granite Hills ☆☆☆↓ V
Burke and Wills Track, Baynton RSD 391, Kyneton, Vic 3444,
☎ *(03) 5423 7264,* ℻ *(03) 5423 7288; est 1970;* ❖ *6,000 cases;*
♀; *A$; Mon-Sat 10-6, Sun 12-6*
This was Macedon's pace-setter for cool-climate, spicy Shiraz and intense limey, citrous Riesling. Renewed efforts in a buoyant market to raise its profile, and the introduction of the lesser-priced Mica range, have resulted in greater activity. Plantings remain at nine hectares of mature, low-yielding vineyards.

Mawarra NR
69 Short Road, Gisborne, Vic 3437, ☎ *(03) 5428 2228,*
℻ *(03) 9621 1413; est 1978;* ❖ *NA;* ♀; *A$; by appt*
Bob Nixon has a little under three hectares of Semillon, Chardonnay and Pinot Noir, and the wines are made for him by Macedon specialist John Ellis (of Hanging Rock).

Mount Charlie Winery NR
Mount Charlie Road, Riddells Creek, Vic 3431, ☎ *(03) 5428 6946,*
℻ *(03) 5428 6946; est 1991;* ❖ *700 cases; No visitors*
The wines are sold through mail order (no cellar-door sales) and selected restaurants.

Mount Gisborne Wines NR
5 Waterson Road, Gisborne, Vic 3437, ☎ *(03) 5428 2834,*
℻ *(03) 5428 2834; est 1987;* ❖ *1,200 cases;* ♀; *A$; by appt*
This is a weekend and holiday occupation for proprietor David Ell. He makes the Chardonnay and Pinot Noir from his 6-hectare vineyard under the watchful and skilled eye of industry veteran Stuart Anderson (the Balgownie founder), who now lives in semi-retirement high in the Macedon Hills.

Mount Macedon NR
Bawden Road, Mount Macedon, Vic 3441, ☎ *(03) 5427 2735,*
℻ *(03) 5427 1071; est 1989;* ❖ *1,500 cases;* ♀; *A$; 7 days 10-6;* ⑩
Don and Pam Ludbey have established a substantial operation at Mount Macedon, drawing upon two separate vineyards, Mount Macedon and Hay Hill. In all, they have 12.5 hectares under vine, and also run a weekend-only restaurant.

Mount William Winery ☆☆☆ V
Mount William Road, Tantaraboo, Vic 3764, ☎ *(03) 5429 1595,*
℻ *(03) 5429 1998; est 1987;* ❖ *1,500 cases;* ♀; *A$; 7 days 11-5*
Adrienne and Murray Cousins established six hectares of vineyards between 1987 and 1992, planted with Pinot Noir,

Cabernet Franc, Semillon and Chardonnay. They also buy Riesling. The wines are made under contract (Cope-Williams), and are sold through a stone-built tasting room and cellar-door facility which was completed in 1992.

Portree ☆☆☆☆ ¶
Powells Track via Mount William Road, Lancefield, Vic 3455,
☎ *(03) 5429 1422,* ℻ *(03) 5429 2205; est 1983;* ❖ *1,500 cases;*
▼*; A$; wkds & public hols at Antique Centre, Lancefield 11-5*

All the wines show distinct cool-climate characteristics, the Quarry Red having similarities to the wines of Chinon in the Loire Valley. But it is with its principal wine, the multi-layered and multi-faceted Chardonnay, that Portree has done best.

Rochford ☆☆☆☆ ¶
Romsey Park, Rochford, Vic 3442, ☎ *(03) 5429 1428,* ℻ *(03) 5429 1066; est 1983;* ❖ *2,500 cases;* ▼*; A$; by appt*

In 1998 Helmut Konecsny and Yvonne Lodoco-Konecsny acquired Rochford, with David Creed continuing as winemaker. It is the Konecsnys' intention to leave the wine style unchanged, with the emphasis on Chardonnay and Pinot Noir, while gradually increasing production.

Sandy Farm Vineyard NR
RMB 3734 Sandy Farm Road, Denver via Daylesford, Vic 3641,
☎ *(03) 5348 7610; est 1988;* ❖ *800 cases;* ▼*; A$; wkds 10-5,*
or by appt

Peter Covell has a small, basic winery in which he makes preservative-free Cabernet Sauvignon, Merlot and Pinot Noir, which have a loyal local following.

Straws Lane NR
Cnr Mount Macedon Road and Straws Lane, Hesket, Vic 3442, ☎
(03) 9654 9380, ℻ *(03) 9663 6300; est 1987;* ❖ *1,000 cases; No visitors*

Stuart Anderson guides the making of the Pinot Noir, Hanging Rock Winery handles the Gewurztraminer and the sparkling wine base, and Cope-Williams looks after the second fermentation and maturation of the sparkling wine. It's good to have cooperative neighbours.

Trio Station NR
1721 Piper Street, Kyneton, Vic 3444, ☎ *(03) 5423 2755,* ℻ *(03) 5423 2756; est 1996;* ❖ *NA;* ▼*; A$; 7 days 10-6*

Trio Station is one of the businesses of Vincorp Wineries (other important winery is Virgin Hills). Situated in an historic building in the heart of Kyneton, it has 40 hectares at the Glenhope Vineyard in the Macedon Ranges and a further 28-hectare vineyard in Western Australia. Still finding its direction.

Virgin Hills ☆☆☆☆☆
Salisbury Road, Lauriston West via Kyneton, Vic 3444, ☎ *(03) 5422 7444,* ℻ *(03) 5422 7400; est 1968;* ❖ *4,000 cases;* ▼*; A$; by appt*

Now part of Vincorp/Trio Station, with Mark Sheppard returning to the role he had as winemaker for many years. Between 1996 and 1998 the single wine (Cabernet/Shiraz/Merlot blend) was made organically (without sulphur). This requires enormous skill, and compounds the challenge of growing late-ripening varieties in an obviously cool region. Disappointing '96 vintage was withdrawn from sale, small amounts of SO_2 will be used.

Woodend Winery NR
82 Mahoneys Road, Woodend, Vic 3442, ☏ (03) 5427 2183, ⓕ (03) 5427 4007; est 1983; ❖ 600 cases; ♀; A$; wkds 10-6
Howard Bradfield has two hectares of mature Chardonnay, Pinot Noir and Cabernet Franc, but the Woodend label is a very recent arrival on the scene.

Sunbury

Sunbury has gentle hills that rise from dead-flat country to the south and west. The nearest region to Melbourne, it has a great history, much of it miraculously preserved. In 1858 one-time Victorian premier James Francis Goodall planted the first vines at Goona Warra. James S Johnstone followed on quickly, establishing Craiglee in 1864. In 1872 he made a Shiraz that I have been lucky enough to taste (found in the 1950s). A powerful testament to the suitability of Sunbury for the production of long-lived Shiraz. However, Shiraz by no means dominates the plantings in this unambiguously cool region; Chardonnay, Semillon, Pinot Noir and the Bordeaux varieties are all grown here.

Craiglee ☆☆☆☆☆ V
Sunbury Road, Sunbury, Vic 3429, ☏ (03) 9744 4489, ⓕ (03) 9744 4489; est 1976; ❖ 2,000 cases; ♀; A$; Sun & public hols 10-5, or by appt
An historic winery with a proud 19th-century record, which reopened for winemaking in 1976 after a prolonged hiatus. Pat Carmody produces one of the finest cool-climate Shirazes in Australia, redolent of cherry, liquorice and spice in the better (ie warmer) vintages, lighter-bodied in the cooler ones. Maturing vines and improved viticulture have yielded more consistent (and even better) wines over the past ten years or so.

Diggers Rest NR
205 Old Vineyard Road, Sunbury, Vic 3429, ☏ (03) 9740 1660, ⓕ (03) 9740 1660; est 1987; ❖ 1,000 cases; ♀; A$; by appt
Purchased from founders Frank and Judith Hogan in July 1998. New owners Elias and Joseph Obeid intend to expand the vineyards and, by that means, significantly increase production.

Goona Warra Vineyard ☆☆☆✦
Sunbury Road, Sunbury, Vic 3429, ☏ (03) 9740 7766, ⓕ (03) 9744 7648; est 1863; ❖ 2,500 cases; ♀; A$; 7 days 10-5; ⑩
Historic stone winery, with excellent tasting facilities. Outstanding venue for celebrations. Chardonnay and Cabernet Franc can excel.

Kennedys Keilor Valley NR
Lot 3 Overnewton Road, Keilor, Vic 3036, ☎ (03) 9311 6246, ℻ (03) 9331 6246; est 1994; ♦ 300 cases; ?; A$; by appt
Newly established, estate-based Chardonnay specialist, producing its only wine from 1.8 hectares of relatively young vineyards.

Longview Creek Vineyard NR
150 Palmer Road, Sunbury, Vic 3429, ☎ (03) 9744 1050, ℻ (03) 9744 1050; est 1988; ♦ 150 cases; ?; A$; Sun 11-5
A relatively new arrival in the Sunbury region, owned by Ron and Joan Parker. Has 5.3 hectares of Chardonnay, Pinot Noir, Chenin Blanc and Shiraz.

Ray-Monde ☆☆☆✓
250 Dalrymple Road, Sunbury, Vic 3429, ☎ (03) 5428 2657, ℻ (03) 5428 3390; est 1988; ♦ 770 cases; ?; A$; Sun, or by appt
The Lakey family has established a little under four hectares of Pinot Noir on its 230-hectare grazing property, at an altitude of 400 metres. Initially the grapes were sold to Domaine Chandon, but in 1994 son John, a Pinot-fanatic, started making the wine, and very competently.

Wildwood Vineyards ☆☆☆✓
St John's Lane, Wildwood, Bulla, Vic 3428, ☎ (03) 9307 1118, ℻ (03) 9331 1590; est 1983; ♦ 2,000 cases; ?; A$; 7 days 10-6
Situated four km past Melbourne airport in the Oaklands Valley. Plastic surgeon Wayne Stott has taken what is very much a part-time activity rather more seriously than most by completing the Wine Science degree at Charles Sturt University. He produced a glorious Shiraz in 1997.

Grampians

For old-timers, this region remains known as Great Western. The reasons for the change need not detain us, but some are due to the imperatives of the GI legislation. The history of the Grampians is inextricably woven with the discovery of gold in 1851. When the gold started to run out, Joseph Best employed the out-of-work miners to dig underground tunnels for his winery. His brother Henry also established a vineyard, near Concongella Creek, in 1866; it is now is the jewel in the crown of Best's Wines. There has never been any doubt that the region is ideally suited to Shiraz. The three leading exponents are Seppelt, Best's and Mount Langi Ghiran. While Shiraz is the outstanding variety, Riesling, too, does particularly well, while Chardonnay and Cabernet Sauvignon are good.

Armstrong Vineyards NR
Lot 1 Military Road, Armstrong, Vic 3381, ☎ (08) 8277 6073, ℻ (08) 8277 6035; est 1989; ♦ 1,000 cases; No visitors
The brain-child of Tony Royal, former Seppelt Great Western winemaker who now runs the Australian arm of Seguin Moreau (French coopers). His 6.5 hectares of Shiraz make lush wine.

Best's Wines ☆☆☆☆↓
1 km off Western Highway, Great Western, Vic 3377,
☎ (03) 5356 2250, Ⓕ (03) 5356 2430; est 1866; ❖ 30,000 cases;
℥; A$; Fri-Sat 10-5, Sun by appt; ✗

Historic winery, owning some priceless vineyards planted as long ago as 1867. Consistently produces elegant, supple wines that deserve far greater recognition than they receive. The Shiraz is a classic; the deluxe Thomson Family Shiraz is magnificent.

Cathcart Ridge Estate NR
Moyston Road, Cathcart via Ararat, Vic 3377, ☎ (03) 5352 1997,
Ⓕ (03) 5352 1558; est 1977; ❖ 2,000 cases; ℥; A$; 7 days 10-5

Now owned and operated by the Farnhill family, it remains to be seen whether the high reputation Cathcart Ridge enjoyed in the early 1980s can be restored. The most recent releases tasted are ambivalent, with their potential still to be realised.

Donovan ☆☆↓ V
Main Street, Great Western, Vic 3377, ☎ (03) 5356 2288; est 1977;
❖ 2,000 cases; ℥; A$; Mon-Sat 10-5.30, Sun 12-5; Devonshire teas, cheese platters

Donovan quietly makes some attractively fragrant Riesling and concentrated, powerful Shiraz, most of which is sold with considerable bottle-age via cellar door and by mail order.

Garden Gully Vineyards ☆☆☆↓ V
Garden Gully, Great Western, Vic 3377, ☎ (03) 5356 2400,
Ⓕ (03) 5356 2400; est 1987; ❖ 2,000 cases; ℥; A$; Mon-Fri 10.30-5.30, wkds 10-5.30

Brian Fletcher and Warren Randall, former Seppelt winemakers, use their intimate knowledge of the Grampians to guide the fortunes of Garden Gully from afar. Both Riesling and Shiraz are excellent, as are the offerings of Sparkling Burgundy, Sparkling Chardonnay and Sparkling Pinot Noir.

Kimbarra Wines NR
422 Barkly Street, Ararat, Vic 3377, ☎ (03) 5352 2238,
Ⓕ (03) 5352 1950; est 1990; ❖ 3,500 cases; ℥; A$; Mon-Fri 9-5

Peter and David Leeke have established 14 hectares of Riesling, Shiraz and Cabernet Sauvignon, the three varieties to have proven best suited to the Grampians region.

Montara ☆☆☆ V
Chalambar Road, Ararat, Vic 3377, ☎ (03) 5352 3868,
Ⓕ (03) 5352 4968; est 1970; ❖ NFP; ℥; A$; Mon-Sat 9.30-5, Sun 12-4

Achieved considerable attention for its Pinot Noirs during the 1980s. Nowadays the wines have a fragrance and elegance, yet lack richness and concentration. Prices and labels are attractive.

Mount Langi Ghiran Vineyards ☆☆☆☆☆
Warrak Road, Buangor, Vic 3375, ☎ (03) 5354 3207, Ⓕ (03) 5354 3277; est 1969; ❖ 25,000 cases; ℥; A$; Mon-Fri 9-5, wkds 12-5

The Shiraz leads the way for cool-climate examples of this variety: weight, texture and spicy, fruity richness. Now owned by Trevor Mast and German wine-entrepreneur Riquet Hess, the most tangible sign of the partnership has been the erection of a new, state-of-the-art winery and vineyard expansion to 70 hectares.

Seppelt Great Western ☆☆☆☆☆ V
Moyston Road, Great Western, Vic 3377, ☎ (03) 5361 2239, ℱ (03) 5361 2200; est 1865; ♦ NFP; ₮; A$; 7 days 10-5; ✗, playground

Australia's best-known producer of sparkling wine. Seppelt also makes Australia's best Sparkling Shirazes and excellent Grampians-sourced table wines. Victorian-based Sheoak Riesling, Corella Ridge Chardonnay and Sunday Creek Pinot Noir are ludicrously underpriced given their quality.

The Gap NR
Pomonal Road, Halls Gap, Vic 3381, ☎ (03) 5356 4252, ℱ (03) 5356 4645; est 1969; ♦ 2,000 cases; ₮; A$; Wed-Sun 10-5, 7 days during school hols

The former Boroka winery purchased by Mount Langi Ghiran in 1998 boasts a spectacular vineyard site near the famous Halls Gap. Former indifferent wine quality is improving exponentially.

Pyrenees

The Australian Pyrenees is a quiet region, like many wine areas on the road to nowhere in particular. While viticulture played a role between 1848 and 1945, it was a minor one. Then in 1963 the French brandy producer Rémy Martin arrived. It believed the region was particularly suited for the production of good quality Australian brandy. The large Chateau Remy vineyard was accordingly planted with Trebbiano. When the brandy market was destroyed by federal excise taxation, Chateau Remy moved from spirits to sparkling wine production. Over the years, Chardonnay and Pinot Noir have replaced the Trebbiano.

Meanwhile, other wineries in the region, like Dalwhinnie, Redbank and Taltarni, set out to prove that the Pyrenees is an excellent region for the production of full-bodied reds, based primarily on Shiraz, Cabernet Sauvignon and Merlot.

Blue Pyrenees Estate ☆☆☆
Vinoca Road, Avoca, Vic 3467, ☎ (03) 5465 3202, ℱ (03) 5465 3529; est 1963; ♦ 80,000 cases; ₮; A$; Mon-Fri 10-4.30, wkds & public hols 10-5; meals at wkds

Founded by Rémy Martin as Chateau Remy, this estate is increasing its focus on table wines under the premium Blue Pyrenees label and second label Fiddlers Creek. The latter uses grapes and wine sourced from across southeast Australia. Lots of dollars, lots of sweat, but you have to wonder why.

Dalwhinnie ☆☆☆☆☆
Taltarni Road, Moonambel, Vic 3478, ☎ (03) 5467 2388, ℱ (03) 5467 2237; est 1976; ♦ 4,500 cases; ₮; A$; 7 days 10-5

The wines all show tremendous depth of fruit flavour, reflecting the relatively low-yielding, well-maintained 33 hectares of estate vineyards. It is hard to say whether the Chardonnay or the Shiraz is the more distinguished; the Pinot Noir (made with help from Rick Kinzbrunner) makes quite a startling entrance.

Kara Kara Vineyard ☆☆☆
Sunraysia Highway, St Arnaud, Vic 3478 (10 km south of St Arnaud), ☏ *(03) 5496 3294,* ⓕ *(03) 5496 3294; est 1977;* ❖ *2,500 cases;* ⚲*; A$; Mon-Fri 10.30-6, wkds 9-6*

Hungarian-born Steve Zsigmond comes from a long line of *vignerons*, and sees Kara Kara as the eventual retirement occupation for himself and wife Marlene. There are nine hectares of estate plantings, and the wine is competently contract-made at Hanging Rock.

Laanecoorie ☆☆☆
Bendigo Road, Betley, Vic 3472, ☏ *(03) 5468 7260,* ⓕ *(03) 5468 7388; est 1982;* ❖ *1,500 cases; No visitors*

John McQuilten's 7.5-hectare vineyard, divided equally into Cabernet Sauvignon, Cabernet Franc and Merlot (designed to make a single wine), produces grapes of consistent quality. Contract-winemaking at Hanging Rock has done the rest.

Mount Avoca Vineyard ☆☆☆☆
Moates Lane, Avoca, Vic 3467, ☏ *(03) 5465 3282,* ⓕ *(03) 5465 3544; est 1970;* ❖ *17,000 cases;* ⚲*; A$; Mon-Fri 9-5, wkds 10-5; cheese platters, petanque*

The Barry family runs a substantial winery, which has for long been one of the stalwarts of the Pyrenees region. It is steadily growing, with 24 hectares of vineyards. A significant refinement in the style of the red wines has occurred over the past few years.

Mountain Creek Wines ☆☆☆
Mountain Creek Road, Moonambel, Vic 3478, ☏ *(03) 5467 2230,* ⓕ *(03) 5467 2230; est 1973;* ❖ *500 cases;* ⚲*; A$; wkds & hols 10-7*

Brian Cherry acquired the this estate in 1975 and has extended it to a total of 13 hectares. Chiefly a grape-growing business, but some wine is made under contract and shows the substance and weight for which the district is renowned.

Peerick Vineyard NR
Wild Dog Track, Moonambel, Vic 3478, ☏ *(03) 9817 1611,* ⓕ *(03) 9817 1611; est 1990;* ❖ *3,000 cases;* ⚲*; A$; wkds & public hols 10-4*

The venture of Melbourne lawyer Chris Jessup and wife Meryl. Despite rationalisation of the plantings, they still manage to grow Cabernet Sauvignon, Shiraz, Cabernet Franc, Merlot, Sauvignon Blanc and Viognier in the six hectares under vine.

Redbank Winery ☆☆☆☆
Sunraysia Highway, Redbank, Vic 3467, ☏ *(03) 5467 7255,* ⓕ *(03) 5467 7248; est 1973;* ❖ *58,000 cases;* ⚲*; A$; Mon-Sat 9-5, Sun 10-5*

Neill and Sally Robb might seem laid back in best Aussie style, but they have built a thriving business, ranging from the estate-grown flagship Sally's Paddock (a Cabernet/Shiraz/Malbec) and, at the other end, the export-oriented, budget-priced Long Paddock wines, made for them elsewhere.

Summerfield ☆☆☆☆ V
Main Road, Moonambel, Vic 3478, ☏ (03) 5467 2264, Ⓕ (03) 5467 2380; est 1979; ♦ 2,300 cases; ₹; A$; 7 days 9-6; ⌘; airstrip
Ian and Mark Summerfield are specialist red wine producers, their particular forté Shiraz. Since 1988 the wines have been consistently excellent, luscious, full-bodied and fruit-driven, yet with a slice of vanilla oak to top them off.

Taltarni ☆☆☆☆ ½ V
Taltarni Road, Moonambel, Vic 3478, ☏ (03) 5467 2218, Ⓕ (03) 5467 2306; est 1972; ♦ 70,000 cases; ₹; A$; 7 days 10-5, winter school hols only
In the shadow of the departure (on the best of terms) of long-serving winemaker and chief executive Dominique Portet, Taltarni has backed off the high levels of tannin and extract evident in the older vintage wines. This ought to be a step in the right direction, but perversely seems to have robbed the red wines of some of their formidable character. A rock and a hard place, it seems.

Warrenmang Vineyard ☆☆☆☆ ½
Mountain Creek Road, Moonambel, Vic 3478, ☏ (03) 5467 2233, Ⓕ (03) 5467 2309; est 1974; ♦ 4,000 cases; ₹; A$; 7 days 9-5; ⍟; resort
The focus of a superb accomodation and restaurant complex created by former restaurateur Luigi Bazzani and wife Athalie, which is in much demand as a conference centre as well as for weekend tourism. Wine quality has fluctuated, but is in the ascendant, especially the Luigi Riserva.

Far South West
This is a remote corner of Victoria that might be far better known were it not for the arbitrary placement of the state border with South Australia. It lies a relatively few kilometres east of some of Australia's well-known wine regions, including Coonawarra and Padthaway. As it is, Drumborg is the only significant wine district in Victoria's Far South West, and Seppelt the only substantial vine-grower. The soil and the plentiful supply of underground water are links in common with those regions over the border to the west. That said, the climate of Drumborg is significantly cooler. Pinot Noir and Chardonnay are tailor-made for fine sparkling wine in the cooler vintages, but not table wine. Riesling produces a fragrant yet steely wine in most years, and in the warmer vintages intense Pinot Noir, Cabernet Sauvignon and Merlot come to the fore. Overall, the Far South West remains one of the last frontiers. When the next wave of viticulture comes in ten or 20 years time, it must surely sweep over this region.

Barretts Wines NR
Portland-Nelson Highway, Portland, Vic 3305, ☏ (03) 5526 5251; est 1983; ❖ 1,000 cases; ♀; A$; 7 days 11-5

The second (and newer) winery in the Portland region. The initial releases were made at Best's, but since 1992 the Riesling, Traminer, Pinot Noir and Cabernet Sauvignon have been made on the property by Rod Barrett.

Crawford River Wines ☆☆☆☆☆
Hotspur Upper Road, Condah, Vic 3303, ☏ (03) 5578 2267, Ⓕ (03) 5578 2240; est 1975; ❖ 3,500 cases; ♀; A$; 7 days 10-4

Full-time grazier, part-time winemaker John Thomson clearly has the winemaker's equivalent of the gardener's 'green fingers'. He makes exemplary wines right across the range. The Riesling and Semillon/Sauvignon Blanc are consistently outstanding, the Cabernet-based wines excellent in warmer vintages.

Kingsley ☆☆☆ V
6 Kingsley Court, Portland, Vic 3305, ☏ (03) 5523 1864, Ⓕ (03) 5523 1644; est 1983; ❖ 1,900 cases; ♀; A$; 7 days 1-4

Only a small part of the ten hectares is held back for the Kingsley label; the rest is sold as grapes. Older vintages are usually available at cellar door, often offered at low prices.

St Gregory's NR
Bringalbert South Road, Bringalbert South via Apsley, Vic 3319, ☏ (03) 5586 5225; est 1983; ❖ NFP; ♀; A$; by appt

Gregory Flynn's operation sells its limited production of fortified wines (port-style only) direct to enthusiasts by mailing list.

Ballarat

Phylloxera struck Ballarat and Bendigo in the 1890s, putting a sudden and savage end to grape-growing and winemaking. Given the cool climate of Ballarat (far colder than that of Bendigo), it is probable that the level of winemaking would have decreased and possibly ceased in any event, but we shall never know. In 1971 Melbourne businessman and *bon vivant* Ian Home established Yellowglen. By 1975 he had planted Cabernet and Shiraz. It did not take all that long for the realise that this region was far too cold for these red varieties. Those who have arrived since focus instead on developing Chardonnay, Pinot Noir and Pinot Meunier.

Dulcinea ☆☆☆☆
Jubilee Road, Sulky, Ballarat, Vic 3352, ☏ (03) 5334 6440, Ⓕ (03) 5334 6828; est 1983; ❖ 800 cases; ♀; A$; 7 days 9-5

Rod Stott is a part-time but passionate grape-grower. With winemaking help from various sources, he has produced a series of very interesting and often complex wines.

Eastern Peake NR
Clunes Road, Coghills Creek, Vic 3364, ☏ (03) 5343 4245, Ⓕ (03) 5343 4365; est 1983; ❖ 1,500 cases; ♀; A$; 7 days 10-5

Over 15 years ago Norm Latta and Di Pym established 4.5 hectares of Chardonnay and Pinot Noir. Originally grape-growers, they now make relatively austere, cool-climate wines.

Mount Beckworth ☆☆☆½
RMB 915 Learmonth Road, Tourello via Ballarat, Vic 3363,
☎ *(03) 5343 4207,* ℻ *(03) 5343 4207; est 1984;* ❧ *630 cases;*
❡*; A$; wkds 10-6 and by appt; petanque*
This place has a near-identical history to Eastern Peake, moving from grape-growing to winemaking (at Best's) and, again like Eastern Peake, producing quite lean wines.

Whitehorse Wines NR
4 Reid Park Road, Mount Clear, Vic 3350, ☎ *(03) 5330 1719,*
℻ *(03) 5330 1288; est 1981;* ❧ *900 cases;* ❡*; A$; wkds 11-5*
The Myers family is yet another to move from grape-growing to winemaking, using fruit grown on its the attractive hillside vineyard. Four hectares of vines are in production, with Pinot Noir and Chardonnay the principal varieties.

Yellowglen ☆☆☆☆
Whites Road, Smythesdale, Vic 3551, ☎ *(03) 5342 8617,* ℻ *(03) 5333 7102; est 1975;* ❧ *100,000 cases;* ❡*; A$; Mon-Fri 10-5, wkds 11-5*
Ballarat was the original viticultural home of Yellowglen and is still the (nominal) headquarters. It produces utterly reliable sparkling wines at all price points, using base wines from all over Australia.

Bendigo

By 1864 there were more than 40 vineyards in the Bendigo region. By 1880, 216 hectares supported over 100 wineries (one must suppose this number included lean-tos at the back of the house). *Phylloxera* heralded a brutal end to winemaking when it arrived in 1893, but no doubt the bank crash of the same year and the move to fortified wines also played their role in the cessation of winemaking in the region. A gap of over 60 years followed, until Bendigo pharmacist Stuart Anderson planted vines at Balgownie in 1969, making startling red wines. Ron and Elva Laughton followed, establishing Jasper Hill in 1975. In 1999 the Chapoutier brothers from the northern Rhône Valley entered into a joint venture with the Laughtons to develop an adjoining property. If you are content to follow the slow road and bypass the need for irrigation water (as the Laughtons were, and are), there is much exceptional vineyard country around.

Balgownie Estate ☆☆☆☆☆½ V
Hermitage Road, Maiden Gully, Vic 3551, ☎ *(03) 5449 6222,*
℻ *(03) 5449 6506; est 1969;* ❧ *12,000 cases;* ❡*; A$; Mon-Sat 10.30-5*
In mid-1999 Mildara Blass sold Balgownie Estate to the Forrester family of Queensland. Long-serving winemaker Lindsay Ross remains in charge and will continue to make the truly excellent rich, full-bodied Shiraz and Cabernet Sauvignon of recent years.

Barnadown Run NR

390 Cornella Road, Toolleen, Vic 3551, ☎ (03) 5433 6376,
℻ (03) 5433 6386; est 1994; ❦ NA; ♀; A$; 7 days 10-5

Five hectares of Chardonnay, Merlot, Malbec, Shiraz, Cabernet Franc and Cabernet Sauvignon have been planted, and Andrew Millis has established a small winery on site.

BlackJack Vineyards ☆☆☆♪

Cnr Blackjack Road and Calder Highway, Harcourt, Vic 3453,
☎ (03) 5474 2355, ℻ (03) 5474 2355; est 1987; ❦ 2,000 cases;
♀; A$; wkds & public hols 11-5

Ian McKenzie (no relation to Seppelt's eponymous chief winemaker) and Ken Pollock make full-blooded, sometimes rustic, red wines from a vineyard established on an old apple and pear orchard in the Harcourt Valley.

Blanche Barkly Wines NR

Rheola Road, Kingower, Vic 3517, ☎ (03) 5443 3664; est 1972;
❦ NFP; ♀; A$; wkds & public hols 10-5

A long-established but low-profile winery owned by David Reimers, producing earthy, concentrated wines from low-yielding, unirrigated vineyards. All the wine is sold at the cellar door.

Charlotte Plains NR

The Grange, RMB 3180, Dooleys Road, Maryborough, Vic 3465,
☎ (03) 5361 3137; est 1990; ❦ 80 cases; ♀; A$; by appt

A classic example of miniature production comes from a close-planted vineyard which is only 0.3 hectares in size. One quarter is Shiraz, the remainder Sauvignon Blanc. The tiny production is sold solely through the mailing list and by phone.

Chateau Dor NR

Mandurang Road, via Bendigo, Vic 3551, ☎ (03) 5439 5278;
est 1860; ❦ 1,000 cases; ♀; A$; Tues-Sun 10-6

Chateau Dor has been in the ownership of the Gross family since 1860; the winery buildings date from 1860 and 1893. A priceless heirloom, which is grossly under-utilised, its production is small, the quality decidedly modest.

Chateau Leamon ☆☆☆

5528 Calder Highway, Bendigo, Vic 3550, ☎ (03) 5447 7995,
℻ (03) 5447 0855; est 1973; ❦ 1,500 cases; ♀; A$; Wed-Mon 10-5

After a period of uncertainty, Chateau Leamon is returning to some of its former glory. Ian Leamon uses locally grown grapes, but also looks to the Strathbogie Ranges (now known as the Central Victorian High Country) for fruit for other wines, including Pinot Noir. Limited retail distribution.

Connor Park Winery NR

59 Connors Road, Leichardt, Vic 3516, ☎ (03) 5437 5234,
℻ (03) 5437 5204; est 1994; ❦ 2,000 cases; ♀; A$; 7 days 10-6

The vineyard dates back to the mid-1960s, and to the uncle of the present owners, a man who had plans for designing an automatic grape harvester. When the present owners purchased the property in 1985, the vineyard had run wild. Since then it has been expanded to ten hectares, and winemaking has commenced.

Cooperage Estate NR New
15 Markovitch Lane, Junortoun, Vic 3551, ☎ 0418 544 743, ℻ (03) 5449 3681; est 1995; ❖ NA; No visitors

The Gregurek family has established 2.2. hectares of Shiraz and Cabernet Sauvignon on its vineyard in the southern outskirts of the town of Bendigo. As the name suggests, there is also a cooperage on site.

Eppalock Ridge NR
633 North Redesdale Road, Redesdale, Vic 3444, ☎ (03) 5425 3135, ℻ (03) 5425 3135; est 1979; ❖ 1,000 cases; ☐; A$; 7 days 10-6 by appt

Long-term winemaker/proprieter Rod Hourigan runs a low-key operation, and now focuses solely on estate-grown Shiraz.

Harcourt Valley Vineyards ☆☆☆✦
Calder Highway, Harcourt, Vic 3453, ☎ (03) 5474 2223, ℻ (03) 5474 2293; est 1976; ❖ 2,000 cases; ☐; A$; 7 days 10-6

A picturesque setting where the granite cellars, hewn from local rock, are set among river gums. New owner John Livingstone continues to make the flagship Barbara's Shiraz in its rich, full-bodied regional style; also Chardonnay, Riesling and Cabernet.

Heathcote Winery ☆☆☆✦
183-185 High Street, Heathcote, Vic 3523, ☎ (03) 5433 2595, ℻ (03) 5433 3081; est 1978; ❖ 5,000 cases; ☐; A$; summer: 7 days 10-6, rest of year: 11-5

After a period in the doldrums, Heathcote was purchased by a small syndicate of wine-loving businessmen. They immediately injected life into the business, winning a trophy at the Adelaide Wine Show for an excellent Seventh Horse Bendigo-Padthaway Shiraz. A mature vineyard planting of Viognier adds interest.

Huntleigh Vineyards ☆☆☆✦ V
Tunnecliffes Lane, Heathcote, Vic 3523, ☎ (03) 5433 2795; est 1975; ❖ 425 cases; ☐; A$; 7 days 10-5.30

Leigh Hunt's wines are decidedly rustic, but the five hectares of low-yielding estate vineyards are a rich resource, and prices are from another decade.

Jasper Hill ☆☆☆☆☆
Drummonds Lane, Heathcote, Vic 3523, ☎ (03) 5433 2528, ℻ (03) 5433 3143; est 1975; ❖ 3,000 cases; ☐; A$; by appt

Ron and Elva Laughton, together with daughters Georgia and Emily, make some of Australia's greatest Shiraz. Georgia's Paddock (9.5 hectares) is 100 per cent Shiraz; Emily's Paddock (3.2 hectares) has a dash of Cabernet Franc to accompany the Shiraz.

Kangderaar Vineyard NR
Melvilles Caves Road, Rheola, Vic 3517, ☎ *(03) 5438 8292,*
℻ *(03) 5438 8292; est 1980;* ❖ *500 cases;* ♇; *A$; Mon-Sat 9-5, Sun 10-5*
The 4.5-hectare vineyard owned by James and Christine Nealy is situated at Rheola, surrounded by the Kooyoora State Park.

Langanook Wines NR
Faraday Road RSD 1, Castlemaine, Vic 3450, ☎ *(03) 5474 8250,*
℻ *(03) 5474 8250; est 1985;* ❖ *600 cases; No visitors*
The Langanook vineyard was established back in 1985 on the slopes of Mount Alexander, at an altitude of 450 metres. The wines, which followed much later, are available through a mailing list and limited retail distribution.

McIvor Creek NR
Costerfield Road, Heathcote, Vic 3523, ☎ *(03) 5433 3000,* ℻ *(03) 5433 3456; est 1973;* ❖ *5,000 cases;* ♇; *A$; 7 days 10-5.30; local crafts*
The beautifully situated McIvor Creek winery is well worth a visit, offering wines of diverse styles, of which the reds are the most regional. Peter Turley has five hectares of Cabernet Sauvignon, and 2.5 of Cabernet Franc and Merlot. He supplements his intake with grapes from other growers.

Mount Alexander Vineyard ☆☆
Calder Highway, North Harcourt, Vic 3453, ☎ *(03) 5474 2262,*
℻ *(03) 5474 2553; est 1984;* ❖ *6,000 cases;* ♇; *A$; 7 days 10-5.30*
This is a substantial operation with large vineyards, of which 17 hectares are planted to all the best-suited varieties.

Mount Ida ☆☆☆☆ V
Northern Highway, (vineyard only) Heathcote, Vic 3253;
est 1978; ❖ *3,000 cases; No visitors*
Planted by the famous Australian artist Leonard French and Dr James Munro, Mount Ida was acquired by Tisdall, itself in turn swallowed up by Mildara Blass. Consistently sumptuous Shiraz, in typical Heathcote style, sells out rapidly each year.

Munari Wines ☆☆☆☆
1129 Northern Highway, Heathcote, Vic 3523, ☎ *(03) 5433 3366,*
℻ *(03) 5433 3095; est 1993;* ❖ *1,000 cases;* ♇; *A$; 7 days 10-5*
Adrian and Deborah Munari have made a singularly impressive entry onto the winemaking scene. Each of their 1997 vintage wines have won various medals. With a little over four hectares of estate vines, production will be limited. Worth seeking out.

Newstead Winery NR
Tivey Street, Newstead, Vic 3462, ☎ *(03) 5476 2733,* ℻ *(03) 5476 2536; est 1994;* ❖ *900 cases;* ♇; *A$; by appt*
The winery is established in the old Newstead Butter Factory, drawing upon two distinct vineyards at Welshman's Reef (near Maldon) and Burnt Acre Vineyard at Marong, west of Bendigo. Vineyard designations are used for each of the wines.

Nuggetty Ranges Winery NR
Maldon-Shelbourne Road, Nuggetty, Vic 3463, ☏ (03) 5475 1347, ⓕ (03) 5475 1647; est 1993; ❖ 500 cases; ⚑; A$; Apr-Nov: wkds 10-4, or by appt

Draws upon five hectares of estate plantings, with production through mailing list and cellar door.

Passing Clouds ☆☆☆☆⚐
RMB 440 Kurting Road, Kingower, Vic 3517, ☏ (03) 5438 8257, ⓕ (03) 5438 8246; est 1974; ❖ 3,000 cases; ⚑; A$; 7 days 12-5 by appt

Graeme Leith is one of the great personalities of the industry, with a superb sense of humour. He makes lovely regional reds, packed with cassis, berry and minty fruit.

Paul Osicka ☆☆☆⚐
Majors Creek Vineyard at Graytown, Vic 3608, ☏ (03) 5794 9235, ⓕ (03) 5794 9288; est 1955; ❖ NFP; ⚑; A$; Mon-Sat 10-5, Sun 12-5

A low-profile producer but reliable, particularly when it comes to its smooth but rich Shiraz. Has the distinction of being the only winery open for business in Victoria between 1930 and '63.

Red Edge ☆☆☆☆⚐ V
Golden Fully Road, Heathcote, Vic 3523, ☏ (03) 9370 9565, ⓕ (03) 9370 9565; est 1971; ❖ 300 cases; No visitors

Red Edge is a new name, but the vineyard dates back to 1971 and the renaissance of the Victorian wine industry. In the early 1980s, it yielded the wonderful wines of Flynn & Williams. Peter and Judy Dredge have now revived the estate and produced two quite lovely wines in their first two vintages ('97 and '98).

Sandhurst Ridge ☆☆☆ New
156 Forest Drive, Marong, Vic 3515, ☏ (03) 5435 2534, ⓕ (03) 5435 2548; est 1990; ❖ 1,200 cases; ⚑; A$; wkds 12-5

With their complementary background skills, the four Greblo brothers have established a 6.6-hectare vineyard (principally Cabernet Sauvignon and Shiraz) and built a full-scale winery in 1996. Wine quality is good.

Tannery Lane Vineyard NR
174 Tannery Lane, Mandurang, Vic 3551, ☏ (03) 5439 5011, ⓕ (03) 5439 5891; est 1990; ❖ 200 cases; ⚑; A$; by appt

Ray and Anne Moore established their tiny vineyard in 1990, gradually establishing a total of two hectares of Shiraz, Cabernet Sauvignon, Cabernet Franc, Sangiovese (only such wine coming from this region), Merlot and Nebbiolo. The micro-production is sold through cellar door only.

Tipperary Hill Estate NR
Alma-Bowendale Road, Alma via Maryborough, Vic 3465, ☏ (03) 5461 3312, ⓕ (03) 5461 3312; est 1986; ❖ 300 cases; ⚑; A$; wkds 10-5, or by appt; ⊙; petanque

Winemaker Paul Flowers built the rough-cut pine winery and

the bluestone cottage next door with the help of friends. Wine production, he says 'depends on the frost, wind and birds'.

Water Wheel ☆☆☆✓ V
Bridgewater-on-Loddon, Bridgewater, Vic 3516, ☎ (03) 5437 3060, Ⓕ (03) 5437 3082; est 1972; ❖ 25,000 cases; ⚲; A$; Mon-Sat 9-5, Sun 12-5
Peter Cumming quietly goes about the business of making competitively priced, unfailingly honest, smooth and varietally distinctive wines, of which the Chardonnay, Shiraz and Cabernet Sauvignon are the best.

Whispering Hills NR
54 Gibbs Road, Majorca, Vic 3465, ☎ (03) 5964 6070, Ⓕ (03) 5964 6231; est 1994; ❖ 200 cases; No visitors
The minuscule production of Whispering Hills is limited to one wine (a Cabernet Sauvignon), which is sold by mail order and word of mouth by owner Murray Lyons.

Wild Duck Creek Estate NR
Spring Flat Road, Heathcote, Vic 3523, ☎ (03) 5433 3133, Ⓕ (03) 5433 3133; est 1980; ❖ 500 cases; ⚲; A$; by appt
David and Diana Anderson slowly built the tiny, part-time vineyard and winery between 1980 and 1993. All the effort was worthwhile as their 1996 Shiraz was the public's choice as Best Red Wine at the 1997 Victorian Winemakers Exhibition.

Zuber Estate NR
Northern Highway, Heathcote, Vic 3523, ☎ (03) 5433 2142; est 1971; ❖ 450 cases; ⚲; A$; 7 days 9-6
A somewhat erratic winery, quite capable of producing the style of Shiraz for which Bendigo is famous; not always achieving it.

Goulburn Valley
This region is divided into two subregions: the Upper Goulburn Valley was a major viticultural centre as long ago as 1860. It is a logical place to grow grapes, as it is as warm as the Barossa Valley, and has ample underground (and river) water off-setting the dry, low-humidity summers. Noted for long-lived Shiraz, Cabernet and Marsanne. The Lower Goulburn Valley runs along the southern side of the Murray River, and the overall focus switches from red to white. The climate is warmer again, and drier, but water is even more freely available. Yields are even higher than the already generous crops of the Upper Goulburn. The key wineries for both regions are Chateau Tahbilk and Mitchelton. There are few wineries in the world with such charm as Tahbilk's. Mitchelton was built 100 or so years later, but also in grand style.

12 Acres ☆☆✓
NagambieRushworth Road, Bailieston, Vic 3608, ☎ (03) 5794 2020, Ⓕ (03) 5794 2020; est 1994; ❖ 650 cases; ⚲; A$; Thurs-Mon 10-6, July: wkds only

The charmingly named 12 Acres is a red wine specialist. Peter and Jana Prygodicz make the wines on site in a tiny winery. The wines could benefit from renewal of the oak in which they are matured, for they are all quite astringent.

Burramurra ☆☆☆✓
Barwood Park, Nagambie, Vic 3608, ☏ (03) 5794 2181, Ⓕ (03) 5794 2755; est 1988; ❀ 800 cases; No visitors
Burramurra is the relatively low-profile vineyard operation of the Deputy Premier of Victoria, the Honourable Pat McNamara. Most of the grapes are sold to Mitchelton; a small amount is contract-made for the Burramurra label.

Chateau Tahbilk ☆☆☆☆ V
Goulburn Valley Highway, Tabilk, Vic 3607, ☏ (03) 5794 2555, Ⓕ (03) 5794 2360; est 1860; ❀ 100,000 cases; ☖; A$; Mon-Sat 9-5, Sun 11-5
A winery steeped in tradition (with high National Trust classification) and which makes wines in keeping with that tradition. The Marsanne ages wonderfully, but the essence of its heritage is the tiny quantities of a special Shiraz made entirely from vines planted in 1860.

Dalfarras ☆☆☆☆
PO Box 123, Nagambie, Vic 3608, ☏ (03) 5794 2637, Ⓕ (03) 5794 2360; est 1991; ❀ 35,000 cases; No visitors
The personal project of Alister Purbrick (of Chateau Tahbilk) and artist-wife Rosa (née) Dalfarra, whose paintings adorn the labels of the wines. It has its own 37 hectares of vines and, to use Alister's words, 'It allows me to expand my winemaking horizons and mould wines in styles different to Chateau Tahbilk.'

David Traeger ☆☆☆
139 High Street, Nagambie, Vic 3608, ☏ (03) 5794 2514, Ⓕ (03) 5794 1776; est 1986; ❀ 8,000 cases; ☖; A$; 7 days 10-5
David Traeger learned much during his years as assistant winemaker at Mitchelton, and knows Central Victoria well. The red wines are solidly crafted, the Verdelho interesting but more variable in quality.

Fyffe Field ☆☆☆✓
Murray Valley Highway, Yarrawonga, Vic 3730, ☏ (03) 5748 4282, Ⓕ (03) 5748 4284; est 1993; ❀ 1,300 cases; ☖; A$; 7 days 10-5; playground
Graeme and Liz Diamond seek to attract tourists to their mud-brick and leaded-light tasting room opposite an historic homestead. A more unusual highlight is the ornamental pig collection on display (set up long before 'Babe' was born).

Hankin Estate NR
Johnsons Lane, Northwood via Seymour, Vic 3660, ☏ (03) 5792 2396, Ⓕ (03) 9353 2927; est 1975; ❀ 600 cases; ☖; A$; wkds 10-5

The principal retirement occupation of Dr Max Hankin, who has left full-time medical practice. He has had to contend with *phylloxera*; the replanting process is still underway.

Hayward's Whitehead Creek NR
Lot 18A Hall Lane, Seymour, Vic 3660, ☏ (03) 5792 3050; est 1975; ❦ 600 cases; ♀; A$; Mon-Sat 9-6, Sun 10-6
Five hectares of low-yielding vineyards planted with Riesling, Shiraz, Cabernet and Malbec produce somewhat rustic but full-flavoured wines seldom seen outside the cellar door.

Heritage Farm Wines NR
RMB 1005 Murray Valley Highway, Cobram, Vic 3655, ☏ (03) 5872 2376; est 1987; ❦ 5,000 cases; ♀; A$; 7 days 9-5; bottle collection, horse-drawn farm equipment
Claims to be the only vineyard and orchard in Australia still using horsepower, with Clydesdales used for most of the general farm work. The winery and cellar-door area boast a large range of restored horse-drawn farm machinery and a bottle collection.

Longleat ☆☆☆ V
Old Weir Road, Murchison, Vic 3610, ☏ (03) 5826 2294, ℱ (03) 5826 2510; est 1975; ❦ 1,500 cases; ♀; A$; 7 days 10-5
Longleat has long had a working relationship with Chateau Tahbilk, which makes the Longleat wines under contract. Tahbilk also buys significant quantities of grapes, surplus to Longleat's requirements, from the 30 hectares of vines. The wines are always honest and full-flavoured, if rather tannic.

Mitchelton ☆☆☆☆☆ V
Mitchellstown via Nagambie, Vic 3608, ☏ (03) 5794 2710, ℱ (03) 5794 2615; est 1969; ❦ 200,000 cases; ♀; A$; 7 days 10-5; 🍴; gallery, river cruises
Acquired by Petaluma in 1994, Mitchelton boasts an impressive array of wines across a broad spectrum of style and price, all carefully aimed at a market niche. Exemplary Blackwood Park Riesling, Goulburn Valley Marsanne and Print Label Shiraz.

Monichino Wines ☆☆☆
1820 Berrys Road, Katunga, Vic 3640, ☏ (03) 5864 6452, ℱ (03) 5864 6538; est 1962; ❦ 14,000 cases; ♀; A$; Mon-Sat 9-5, Sun 10-5
Carlo and Terry Monichino have for many years quietly made clean, fresh wines in which the fruit character is carefully preserved. Both table wines and fortified wines are produced.

Strathkellar ☆☆☆ V
Murray Valley Highway, Cobram, Vic 3644, ☏ (03) 5873 5274, ℱ (03) 5873 5270; est 1990; ❦ 2,500 cases; ♀; A$; 7 days 10-6
Dick Parkes planted his 5.5-hectare vineyard with Chardonnay, Shiraz and Chenin Blanc in 1990, and has the wine contract-made at Chateau Tahbilk by Alister Purbrick. The wines are as unpretentious as they are honest.

Central Victorian High Country

Another region to be renamed under the GI legislation, and still more familiar to most by its previous name of Strathbogie Ranges. This region boasts many well-known vineyards. Foremost among them are Delatite and Mount Helen. It is relatively large, but is unified by its elevation and by the hilly topography. Most of the vineyards are planted between 300-500 metres. Overall, this is a premium to super-premium wine-producing area. Elevation, which varies considerably, is a key factor in determining style. Yields are significantly lower than, for example, those of the King Valley, and the cool climate produces generally fine wines.

Antcliff's Chase ☆☆
RMB 4510, Caveat via Seymour, Vic 3660, ☏ (03) 5790 4333, ℻ (03) 5790 4333; est 1982; ♦ 800 cases; ♀; A$; wkds 10-5

A scarecrow on the label tells its own story of the problems caused by birds in small, remote vineyards. The grapes from the four hectares are principally sold; a small amount is vinified under the Antcliff's Chase label.

Delatite ☆☆☆☆
Stoneys Road, Mansfield, Vic 3722, ☏ (03) 5775 2922, ℻ (03) 5775 2911; est 1982; ♦ 14,000 cases; ♀; A$; 7 days 10-4

Rosaland Ritchie (and family) run this acclaimed winery. With its sweeping views across to the snow-clad peaks, this is an uncompromisingly cool-climate viticultural enterprise and the wines naturally reflect the climate. Light but intense Riesling and spicy Traminer flower with a year or two in bottle, and in the warmer vintages, the red wines achieve flavour and texture, albeit with a distinctive mintiness.

Henke ☆☆⁄
175 Henke Lane, Yarck, Vic 3719, ☏ (03) 5797 6277, ℻ (03) 5797 6277; est 1974; ♦ 250 cases; ♀; A$; by appt

Produces tiny quantities of deep-coloured, full-flavoured, minty red wines known only to a chosen few. Typically, a range of back vintages with up to five years of age is available at the cellar door.

Lost Valley Winery NR
35 Yamby Road, Strath Creek, Vic 3141, ☏ (03) 5797 0212, ℻ (03) 9351 2005; est 1995; ♦ 1,600 cases; No visitors

Dr Robert Ippaso owns a 3-hectare vineyard at 450 metres above sealevel on the slopes of Mount Tallarook. It is planted with Shiraz, Merlot, Verdelho and Cortese. The latter is the only planting of this variety in Australia and pays homage to Dr Ippaso's birthplace in the Savoie, in the Franco-Italian Alps, where the grape flourishes.

Murrindindi ☆☆☆☆
Cummins Lane, Murrindindi, Vic 3717, ☏ (03) 5797 8217, ℻ (03) 5797 8422; est 1979; ♦ 2,000 cases; No visitors

Remote from any other winery, owned and run by the

Cuthbertson family (Hugh is a senior executive with Mildara Blass). Its unequivocally cool climate means that special care has to be taken in the vineyard to produce ripe fruit. Hard work is rewarded with elegant Chardonnay and Cabernet/Merlot.

Plunkett ☆☆☆ V
Lambing Gully Road, Avenell, Vic 3664, ☎ (03) 5796 2150, ℻ (03) 5796 2147; est 1980; ❖ 10,000 cases; ♀; A$; 7 days 11-5; ⦿
Grape-growers since 1980, turning part-winemakers in 1992, the Plunkett family has 100 hectares under vine. Pleasant, light Riesling, Sauvignon Blanc and Chardonnay are sensibly priced.

Rutherglen

Rutherglen has a character and personality second to none. It is steeped in history and legend. As in so much of Victoria, gold and wine remained intertwined during the boom years from 1860 to 1893. It was an environment in which vast winery and vineyard enterprises flourished. There was Mount Ophir, with 280 hectares and way-out architecture; Fairfield, home to the Morris family and the largest winery in the southern hemisphere, and Graham's, owner of 250 hectares. This region's decline resulted as exports to the UK fell and the domestic market's taste shifted from fortified wines to table wines. Happily, all was not lost. Production of the sublime Muscats and Tokays, virtually without parallel elsewhere in the world, continues, drawing on base wines aged in a *solera*-style system that extends back to the turn of the century. The Winery Walkabout, held on the long weekend of the queen's birthday at the start of June, rivals the Barossa Vintage Festival in popularity. This is one of the truly great wine tourism destinations.

All Saints ☆☆☆☆ǃ
All Saints Road, Wahgunyah, Vic 3687, ☎ (02) 6033 1922, ℻ (02) 6033 3515; est 1864; ❖ NFP; Mon-Sat 9-5.30, Sun 10-5.30; ⦿
One of the great, if whimsical, landmarks on the Australian scene. This castellated, red-brick Scottish castle, acquired by Peter Brown (of Brown Brothers) after it suffered a period of financial instability, offers good table wines, great fortified Tokay and Muscat, and an excellent restaurant.

Anderson NR
Lot 12 Chiltern Road, Rutherglen, Vic 3685, ☎ (02) 6032 8111; est 1993; ❖ 1,000 cases; ♀; A$; 7 days 10-5
With a winemaking career spanning 30 years, including a stint at Seppelt Great Western, Howard Anderson and family have started their own winery. The ultimate intention is to specialise in sparkling wine made entirely on site.

Bullers Calliope ☆☆☆☆ǃ V
Three Chain Road, Rutherglen, Vic 3685, ☎ (02) 6032 9660, ℻ (02) 6032 8005; est 1921; ❖ 5,000 cases; ♀; A$; Mon-Sat 9-5, Sun 10-5
The winery rating is very much influenced by the recent superb releases of Rare Liqueur Muscat and Rare Liqueur Tokay,

dazzlingly beautiful examples of their style. Limited releases of Calliope Shiraz and Shiraz Mondeuse can also be extremely good.

Campbells ☆☆☆☆
Murray Valley Highway, Rutherglen, Vic 3685, ☏ (02) 6032 9458, Ⓕ (02) 6032 9870; est 1870; ❖ 35,000 cases; ♇; A$; Mon-Sat 9-5, Sun 10-5

Offers a wide range of table and fortified wines of ascending quality and price, which are always honest. As so often happens in this part of the world, the fortified wines are the best, with the extremely elegant Isabella Tokay and Merchant Prince Muscat at the top of the tree.

Chambers Rosewood ☆☆☆☆☆
Barkley Street, Rutherglen, Vic 3685, ☏ (02) 6032 8641 , Ⓕ (02) 6032 8101; est 1858; ❖ 10,000 cases; ♇; A$; Mon-Sat 9-5, Sun 11-5; playground

The rating is given for the tiny quantities of Special Old Liqueur Muscat and Special Old Liqueur Tokay, which Bill Chambers grudgingly hands out. He tends to raise the price every time someone has the temerity to buy these classics.

Cofield ☆☆☆☽ V
Distillery Road, Wahgunyah, Vic 3687, ☏ (02) 6033 3798, Ⓕ (02) 6033 3798; est 1990; ❖ 5,000 cases; ♇; A$; Mon-Sat 9-5, Sun 10-5; gourmet barbecue packs

District veteran Max Cofield, together with wife Karen and sons Damien, Ben and Andrew, is developing a strong cellar-door sales base by staging winery functions with guest chefs, and also providing a large barbecue and picnic area. The quality of the red wines, in particular, is good, and improving all the time.

Fairfield Vineyard ☆☆☽ V
Murray Valley Highway, Browns Plains via Rutherglen, Vic 3685, ☏ (02) 6032 9381; est 1959; ❖ 4,200 cases; ♇; A$; Mon-Sat 10-5, some Suns 12-5

Specialist in red and fortified wines made using 19th-century wine equipment in the grounds of the historic Fairfield Mansion. A must for wine tourists. Offers a wide range of old vintages.

Gehrig Estate ☆☆☆ V
Cnr Murray Valley Highway. and Howlong Road, Barnawartha, Vic 3688, ☏ (02) 6026 7296, Ⓕ (02) 6026 7424; est 1858; ❖ 5,000 cases; ♇; A$; Mon-Sat 9-5, Sun 10-5; ⌘; playground

This historic winery (and adjacent house) are superb legacies of the last century. Fifth-generation Brian Gehrig has modernised the winery, significantly lifting the quality of the white and red table wines without imperilling the fortifieds.

Jones Winery NR
Jones Road, Rutherglen, Vic 3685, ☏ (02) 6032 8496, Ⓕ (02) 6032 8495; est 1864; ❖ 7,000 cases; ♇; A$; Fri-Sat 10-5, Sun & hols 10-4

Late in 1998, the winery was purchased from Les Jones by Leanne Schoen and Mandy and Arthur Jones (nieces and nephew of Les). They plan to redevelop the property over the next few years, and concentrate on Shiraz and fortified wines. Mandy has been winemaking in Europe for a number of years.

Morris ☆☆☆☆☆ V
Mia Mia Road, Rutherglen, Vic 3685, ☎ (02) 6026 7303,
℻ (02) 6026 7445; est 1859; ❖ NFP; ♀; A$; Mon-Sat 9-5, Sun 10-5
One of the greatest, some would say *the* greatest, of the fortified winemakers. To test that view, try the Old Premium Muscat and Old Premium Tokay, the reasons for the winery rating. They are absolute bargains given their age and quality. Table wines are dependable – white wines made by owner Orlando-Wyndham.

Mount Prior Vineyard ☆☆☆½ V
Cnr River Road and Popes Lane, Rutherglen, Vic 3685,
☎ (02) 6026 5591, ℻ (02) 6026 7456; est 1860; ❖ 15,000 cases;
♀; A$; 7 days 9-5; ⇌, ❡; gift shop
Yet another great legacy of the 1800s. The element of surprise can come with its wines, such as a superb 1998 Chardonnay.

Pfeiffer ☆☆☆
Distillery Road, Wahgunyah, Vic 3687, ☎ (02) 6033 2805,
℻ (02) 6033 3158; est 1984; ❖ 12,000 cases; ♀; A$; Mon-Sat 9-5,
Sun 11-4; playground
Ex-Lindemans fortified winemaker Chris Pfeiffer occupies one of the historic wineries (built in 1880) that abound in North East Victoria. Worth a visit on this score alone. The fortified wines are good, and the table wines have improved considerably over recent vintages, drawing upon 21 hectares of estate plantings.

St Leonards ☆☆☆½ V
Wahgunyah, Vic 3687, ☎ (02) 6033 1004, ℻ (02) 6033 3636;
est 1860; ❖ NFP; ♀; A$; Thurs-Sun & hols 11-3; ❡; wkd barbecues
An old favourite on the banks of the Murray, relaunched in late 1997 with a range of three premium wines (Chardonnay, Shiraz, Ruby Cabernet) cleverly marketed at the cellar door and bistro.

Stanton & Killeen Wines ☆☆☆☆½ V
Jacks Road, Murray Valley Highway, Rutherglen, Vic 3685,
☎ (02) 6032 9457, ℻ (02) 6032 8018; est 1875; ❖ 20,000 cases;
♀; A$; Mon-Sat 9-5, Sun 10-5
Chris Killeen has skilfully expanded the portfolio here, but without in any way compromising its reputation as a traditional maker of smooth, rich reds, and attractive, fruity Muscats and Tokay. His great 'Vintage Ports' equal the very best in Australia.

Sutherland Smith Wines NR
Cnr Falkners Road and Murray Valley Highway, Rutherglen, Vic 3685, ☎ (03) 6032 8177, ℻ (03) 6032 8177; est 1993; ❖ 1,000 cases; ♀; A$; wkds 10-5, or by appt

George Sutherland Smith, for decades head of All Saints, has opened up his own small business in Rutherglen. He makes wine in the refurbished 1850s Emu Plains winery, drawing on fruit grown in a leased vineyard at Glenrowan and also from grapes grown in the King Valley.

Warrabilla ☆☆☆☆ V
Murray Valley Highway, Rutherglen, Vic 3685, ☏ (02) 6035 7242, ⓕ (02) 6035 7242; est 1986; ❖ 4,500 cases; ♀; A$; 7 days 10-5
Former All Saints winemaker Andrew Sutherland-Smith has leased a small winery at Corowa to make the Warrabilla wines from a 4-hectare vineyard developed by himself and Carol Smith in the Indigo Valley. The reds, and in particular the Shiraz, have reached cult status, selling out well before the release of the following vintage.

Glenrowan

The advent of the GI legislation has seen the division of North East Victoria into four regions: Rutherglen and Glenrowan, the King Valley and the Ovens Valley. The first two walk together (as do the latter two), for Glenrowan is every bit as famous for its Muscats and its Tokays as Rutherglen. It is no less renowned for its red wine. The special features of Glenrowan, which do legitimately differentiate it from Rutherglen, are the deep red friable soils, and the tempering climatic influence of Lake Mokoan. The key Glenrowan producer is Baileys, a somewhat ill-fitting outpost of the Mildara Blass wine empire (in near identical fashion to Morris's place in the Orlando-Wyndham group). In each case their corporate masters have, by and large, left well alone.

Auldstone ☆☆☆½
Booths Road, Taminick via Glenrowan, Vic 3675, ☏ (03) 5766 2237; est 1987; ❖ 2500 cases; ♀; A$; Thur-Sun 9-5; lunches
Michael and Nancy Reid have restored the century-old stone winery and replanted the largely abandoned 24-hectare vineyard that surrounds it. Gourmet lunches are available at weekends to accompany a wide range of table and fortified wines.

Baileys of Glenrowan ☆☆☆☆☆
Cnr Taminick Gap Road. and Upper Taminick Road., Glenrowan, Vic 3675, ☏ (03) 5766 2392, ⓕ (03) 5766 2596; est 1870; ❖ 5,000 cases; ♀; A$; Mon-Fri 9-5, wkds 10-5
Part of the Mildara Blass empire, but thankfully left pretty much to its own devices. Ripe black-cherry 1920s Block Shiraz impressively heads the table wines, but it is the Old Liqueur Tokay and Old Liqueur Muscat which are truly the nectar of the gods.

Booth's Taminick Cellars ☆☆½
Taminick via Glenrowan, Vic 3675, ☏ (03) 5766 2282,
ⓕ (03) 5766 2151; est 1904; ❖ 4,000 cases; ♀; A$; Mon-Sat 9-5, Sun 10-5
An ultra-conservative producer of massively flavoured and concentrated red wines, usually with more than a few rough

edges, which time may or may not smooth over. Part of the production from the old 21-hectare vineyard is sold.

HJT Vineyards NR
Keenan Road, Glenrowan, Vic 3675, ☎ (03) 5766 2252, Ⓕ (03) 5765 3260; est 1979; ❦ 1,200 cases; ♀; A$; Fri-Sat 10-5, Sun during school hols

Founded by the late Harry Tinson after he left Baileys, following a long and illustrious stewardship. It is now run by his daughter Wendy Tinson, with the tiny production from the 2-hectare estate all sold from the cellar door.

King Valley

Vineyard altitudes range from 150 to 630 metres, creating a spread of climate ranging from very warm (similar to Rutherglen) to very cool (similar to Macedon). It is a beautiful region, blessed by its deep, rich soils. In 1970 two farmers (of Anglo Saxon descent) decided to diversify into grape production: John Levigny at Meadow Creek, and Guy Darling at Koombahla. Thereafter, the number of grape-growers (mainly Italian) grew exponentially until 1989, as did tonnage. Yet there was only one purchaser: Brown Brothers had made the area its fiefdom. The informal exclusivity broke in 1989 and now King Valley grapes are used in wines made as far afield as the Hunter and Barossa Valleys. Two large wineries were built at the end of the 1990s, one by Miranda, the other by a group of investors.

Chardonnay and Riesling are the most widely planted white grapes, and Cabernet Sauvignon heads a contingent of all the main red varieties. The two areas in which the King Valley can excel are with sparkling wines and the principal Italian varieties: Nebbiolo, Sangiovese and Barbera. With the qualified exception of sparkling wine, the best results will come from growers who take steps to control the usually prolific yields. They cannot afford to become mountain cousins of the traditional Riverland growers.

Avalon Vineyard ☆☆❦
RMB 9556 Whitfield Road, Wangaratta, Vic 3678, ☎ (03) 5729 3629, Ⓕ (03) 5729 3635; est 1981; ❦ 1,000 cases; ♀; A$; 7 days 10-5

Much of the production from the 10-hectare vineyard is sold, with limited quantities made by Doug Groom, a graduate of Roseworthy, and one of Avalon's owners.

Brown Brothers ☆☆☆☆ V
Snow Road, Milawa, Vic 3678, ☎ (03) 5720 5500, Ⓕ (03) 5720 5511; est 1885; ❦ 300,000 cases; ♀; A$; 7 days 9-5; epicurean centre, playground

Deservedly one of the most successful family wineries in Australia, drawing on vineyards spread throughout a range of climates, varying according to altitude from very warm to very cool. It is also known for the diversity of grape varieties with which it works, and the wines always represent excellent value for money.

Ciavarella ☆☆ⅾ
Evans Lane, Oxley, Vic 3678, ☎ (03) 5727 3384, ℉ (03) 5727 3384; est 1978; ❖ 2,000 cases; ⛾; A$; Mon-Sat 9-6, Sun 10-6

The Ciavarellas have been grape-growers in the King Valley for almost 20 years, selling their grapes to others. Since 1994 slackening demand has encouraged them to make limited quantities of wines that are pleasant, albeit light-bodied, in a rustic, Italian-influenced style.

Dal Zotto Wines NR
Edi Road, Cheshunt, Vic 3678, ☎ (03) 5729 8321, ℉ (03) 5729 8490; est 1987; ❖ 1,500 cases; ⛾; A$; by appt

Remains primarily a contract grape-grower, with almost 26 hectares of vineyards (predominantly Chardonnay, Cabernet Sauvignon and Merlot, but with trial plantings of Sangiovese, Barbera and Marzemino), but does make a small amount of wine for local sale (and by mail order).

Darling Estate ☆☆☆
Whitfield Road, Cheshunt, Vic 3678, ☎ (03) 5729 8396, ℉ (03) 5729 8396; est 1990; ❖ 400 cases; ⛾; A$; by appt

Guy Darling was one of the pioneers of the King Valley when he planted his first vines in 1970. For many years, the entire production was purchased by Brown Brothers for its well-known Koombahla Estate label. Since 1991, however, Guy has retained some of the estate's output to produce a full range of wines under the Darling Estate label.

John Gehrig Wines ☆☆ⅾ
OxleyMilawa Road, Oxley, Vic 3678, ☎ (03) 5727 3395, ℉ (03) 5727 3699; est 1976; ❖ 5,600 cases; ⛾; A$; 7 days 9-5

Honest wines, seldom exciting. Occasional Chardonnay, Pinot Noir, Merlot and Cabernet/Merlot have risen above their station.

La Cantina King Valley NR
Honeys Lane, King Valley, Vic 3678 ☎ (03) 5729 3615; est 1996; ❖ NA; ⛾; A$; wkds & hols 10-5 and by appt

Gino and Peter Corsini have 20 hectares of Chardonnay, Riesling, Shiraz and Cabernet Sauvignon. They sell most of the fruit, but make a small amount on site in a traditional Tuscan-style winery. The wines are organic, made without the use of SO_2.

Markwood Estate ☆☆
Morris Lane, Markwood, Vic 3678, ☎ (03) 5727 0361, ℉ (03) 5727 0361; est 1971; ❖ 900 cases; ⛾; A$; 7 days 9-5

A member of the famous Morris family, Rick Morris shuns publicity, and relies almost exclusively on cellar-door sales for his small range. Both table and great fortified wines are made.

Michelini Wines ☆☆ⅾ
Great Alpine Road, Myrtleford, Vic 3737, ☎ (03) 5751 1990, ℉ (03) 5751 1990; est 1982; ❖ 3,000 cases; ⛾; A$; Thurs-Mon 10-5

Italian-born tobacco farmers-turned-grape-growers, the Michelinis have 42 hectares of vineyard established on *terra rossa* soil. Most of the production is sold, but since 1996 a large (1,000-tonne) on-site winery has seen the first wines made under the Michelini label. The initial releases were pleasant but lacked concentration.

Miranda (King Valley) ☆☆☆ V
Corner Snow and Whitfield Roads, Oxley, Vic 3768, ☎ (02) 6960 3016, ℻ (02) 6964 4135; est 1998; ❖ 45,000 cases; No visitors
Miranda now has three quite separate winemaking entities. The original (and largest) is in Griffith; the next in the Barossa Valley, and the most recent in the King Valley. It is here that the High Country range is made, using fruit from 35 hectares of estate vineyards and supplemented by purchased grapes.

Pizzini ☆☆☆☆ V
King Valley Road, Wangaratta, Vic 3768, ☎ (03) 5729 8278, ℻ (03) 5729 8495; est 1980; ❖ 4,000 cases; ♖; A$; 7 days 10-4; ⌑
Fred and Katrina Pizzini have been grape-growers in the King Valley for over 20 years, cultivating over 60 hectares of vineyard. Grape-growing still continues to be the major focus of activity, but their move into winemaking has been particularly successful, notably with Sangiovese.

Reads ☆☆
Evans Lane, Oxley, Vic 3678, ☎ (03) 5727 3386, ℻ (03) 5727 3559; est 1972; ❖ 1,900 cases; ♖; A$; Mon-Sat 9-5, Sun 10-6
Kenneth Read has eight hectares of vineyard, including a recent planting of Viognier. The vineyard slopes down to the King River, which provides secluded picnic areas. No recent tastings.

Victorian Alps Wine Co NR
Great Alpine Road, Gapsted, Vic 3737, ☎ (03) 5751 1992, ℻ (03) 5751 1368; est 1996; ❖ 15,000 cases; ♖; A$; by appt
This very large winery processes grapes from over 320 hectares spread through the King Valley and adjacent Alpine areas. Mainly a bulk producer, but the Gapstead label exports to the UK.

Wood Park ☆☆☆
RMB 1139 Bobinawarrah-Whorouly Road, Milawa, Vic 3678, ☎ (03) 5727 3367, ℻ (03) 5727 3682; est 1989; ❖ 1,800 cases; ♖; A$; by appt
Grazier and farmer John Stokes diversified into grape-growing in 1989. He sells most of the grapes but makes a Chardonnay and Shiraz/Cabernet with the assistance of the exceptionally talented Rick Kinzbrunner. The results include wines of show quality.

Ovens Valley
The region consists of four river basins or valleys and takes in the more elevated Beechworth subregion in its northwestern corner. This range of togography explains the climate: quite warm at the lowest elevation of around 150 metres, and distinctly cool at its

higher points at over 300 metres. Gold was discovered nearby in 1852, and four years later the first vines were planted at Beechworth. By 1891 the area under vine had reached 660 hectares, but by the end of the First World War all the vineyards had disappeared, felled by the grim reaper, *phylloxera*. Between 1945 and 1969 vines made a tentative reappearance, spreading more steadily in the 1970s; in the 1980s the wineries of today made their first appearance. Of these, the icon winery Giaconda is by far the most illustrious.

Boynton's of Bright ☆☆☆⚹
Ovens Valley Highway, Bright, Vic 3747, ☏ *(03) 5756 2356,*
℻ *(03) 5756 2610; est 1987;* ❦ *15,000 cases;* ♀; *A$; 7 days 10-5;* ⦿;
⛊; *playground*

Kel Boynton has a beautiful 16-hectare vineyard, framed by Mount Buffalo rising into the skies above it. Overall, the red wines have always outshone the whites. The initial very strong American oak input has been softened in more recent vintages to give a better fruit/oak balance.

Giaconda ☆☆☆☆☆
McClay Road, Beechworth, Vic 3747, ☏ *(03) 5727 0246,*
℻ *(03) 5727 0246; est 1985;* ❦ *1,000 cases; by appt*

Rick Kinzbrunner makes wines that command a super-cult status. Given the tiny production, this makes them extremely difficult to find; they are sold chiefly through restaurants and mail order. All have a cosmopolitan edge, as befits Kinzbrunner's international winemaking experience. The Chardonnay and Pinot Noir are made in contrasting styles: the Chardonnay tight and reserved, the Pinot Noir usually opulent and ripe.

Park Wines NR
RMB 6291, Sanatorium Road, Allan's Flat, Yackandandah, Vic 3691, ☏ *(02) 6027 1564,* ℻ *(02) 6027 1561; est 1995;* ❦ *NA;* ♀; *A$; wkds & public hols 10-5*

Rod and Julia Park have a 6-hectare vineyard set in beautiful hill country. Part of the vineyard – planted with Riesling, Chardonnay, Merlot, Cabernet Franc and Cabernet Sauvignon – is still coming into bearing, and the business is still in its infancy.

Pennyweight Winery NR
Pennyweight Lane, Beechworth, Vic 3747, ☏ *(03) 5728 1747,*
℻ *(03) 5728 1704; est 1982;* ❦ *1,000 cases;* ♀; *A$; Thur-Tues 10-5*

Established by Stephen Morris (and wife Elizabeth), great-grandson of GF Morris, founder of Morris Wines. The three hectares of vines are not irrigated, and are moving towards organic certification. 'It's a perfect world,' says Elizabeth Morris.

Rosewhite Vineyards ☆☆⚹ V
Happy Valley Road, Rosewhite via Myrtleford, Vic 3737,
☏ *(03) 5752 1077; est 1983;* ❦ *700 cases;* ♀; *A$; wkds & public hols 10-5, Jan: 7 days*

After a career with the Victorian Department of Agriculture, agricultural scientists Ron and Joan Mullett began establishing two hectares of vineyards at an altitude of 300 metres. The wines are extraordinarily inexpensive.

Sorrenberg ☆☆☆½
Alma Road, Beechworth, Vic 3747, ☏ (03) 5728 2278, ℻ (03) 5728 2278; est 1986; ❧ 1,200 cases; ⚑; A$; Mon-Fri by appt, most wkds 1-5 (phone first)
Barry and Jan Morey made their first wines in 1989 from the 2.5-hectare vineyard on the outskirts of Beechworth. Wine quality has steadily improved since the early days, with a particular following for the Chardonnay and Gamay. Some, indeed, would accord it a higher rating.

Tawonga Vineyards NR
2 Drummond Street, Tawonga, Vic 3697, ☏ (03) 5754 4945, ℻ (03) 5754 4945; est 1994; ❧ 350 cases; ⚑; A$; by appt
Diz and John Adams made their first wine in 1995, but it was not until 1998 that they finally received their producer's license to sell their wines. Production will not exceed 650 cases per year.

Gippsland

This is one of the most far-flung and climatically diverse of all Victoria's Regions. Indeed, it is both a Zone and Region, and it seems only a matter of time before it divides itself into subregions. Phillip Jones of Bass Phillip believes there are six climatically distinct subregions, but most content themselves with three: east, west and south. South Gippsland is the coolest and wettest, similar to Burgundy and the Loire Valley. It has proved itself absolutely ideal for Pinot Noir and excellent for Chardonnay. West Gippsland is drier and a little warmer than either the south or east, and periodic droughts make irrigation essential. East Gippsland has a more Mediterranean climate, with lower rainfall again making irrigation highly desirable. Its weather patterns are complex, some coming from the north, others moving in from the west. It is capable of producing spectacularly rich Chardonnay from its generally low-yielding vineyards, provided botrytis is kept at bay.

Although centred on Pinot Noir and Chardonnay, the Gippsland wines extend across the full range of styles from Sauvignon Blanc to Bordeaux blends. The regional style is one of richness and robustness, with the exception of some elegant and fine Pinot Noirs.

Ada River ☆☆☆
Main Road, Neerim South, Vic 3831, ☏ (03) 5628 1221, ℻ (03) 5466 2333; est 1983; ❧ 1,000 cases; ⚑; A$; 10-6 wkds & public hols
The Kelliher family has established two vineyards in Gippsland, and taken a long-term lease of a third in the Yarra Valley. Two streams of wine come from these vineyards, both delicate rather than robust.

Bass Phillip ☆☆☆☆☆
Tosch's Road, Leongatha South, Vic 3953, ☏ (03) 5664 3341,
⨍ (03) 5664 3209; est 1979; ❦ 700 cases; ⚑; A$; 7 days 11-6
summer and autumn

Phillip Jones has retired from the Melbourne rat-race to hand-craft tiny quantities of superlative Pinot Noir, which, at its finest, has no equal in Australia. Painstaking site selection, ultra-close vine spacing and the very, very cool climate of south Gippsland are the keys to the magic of Bass Phillip and its eerily Burgundian Pinots.

Briagolong Estate ☆☆❧
Valencia Briagolong Road, Briagolong, Vic 3860, ☏ (03) 5147 2322, ⨍ (03) 5147 2400; est 1979; ❦ 300 cases; ⚑; A$; by appt

This is a weekend hobby for medical practitioner Gordon McIntosh, who, with mixed success, nonetheless tries hard to invest his wines with Burgundian complexity. Dr McIntosh must have established an all-time record with the 15.4 per cent alcohol in the '92 Pinot Noir.

Dargo Valley Winery ☆☆
Lower Dargo Road, Dargo, Vic 3682, ☏ (03) 5140 1228,
⨍ (03) 5140 1388; est 1985; ❦ 200 cases; ⚑; A$; Mon-Thur 12-8,
wkds & hols 10-8; ⦿; wine bar; ⌭

Hermann Bila has 2.5 hectares of mountain vineyard looking towards the Bogong National Park. The white wines tend to be rustic, the sappy/earthy/cherryish Pinot Noir the pick of the red wines. The restaurant is handy, given the remote location.

Djinta Djinta Winery ☆☆
10 Stevens Road, Kardella South, Vic 3950, ☏ (03) 5658 1163,
⨍ (03) 5658 1863; est 1991; ❦ 170 cases; ⚑; A$; wkds & public hols 10-5 or by appt

A vineyard with a short but convoluted history. Peter Harley has completed the wine science degree at Charles Sturt University, and together with wife Helen is endeavouring to run an organic-oriented vineyard and winery. High natural acidity in the wines helps stability, but it can be fierce on the palate. Early days; worth watching.

Ensay Winery NR
Great Alpine Road, Ensay, Vic 3895, ☏ (03) 5157 3203; est 1992;
❦ NA; ⚑; A$; public & school hols 11-5, or by appt

A weekend and holiday business for the Coy family, headed by David Coy, tending three hectares of Chardonnay, Pinot Noir, Merlot, Shiraz and Cabernet Sauvignon.

Jinks Creek Winery NR
Tonimbuk Road, Tonimbuk, Vic 3815, ☏ (03) 5629 8502,
⨍ (03) 5629 8551; est 1981; ❦ NA; ⚑; A$; by appt

The 2.5-hectare vineyard borders on the evocatively named Bunyip State Park. Andrew Clarke completed the on-site winery in 1992, making wines from estate-grown fruit only. The 'sold out' sign goes up each year.

Kongwak Hills Winery NR
1030 Korumburra-Wonthaggi Road, Kongwak, Vic 3951,
☎ (03) 5657 3267; est 1989; ❦ 350 cases; ❢; A$; wkds & public hols 10-5

Peter and Jenny Kimmer began developing their vineyard in 1989, and now have 0.5 hectares each of Cabernet Sauvignon, Shiraz and Pinot Noir, together with lesser quantities of Malbec, Merlot and Riesling. Most of the wines are sold through the cellar door.

Lyre Bird Hill ☆☆☆
Inverloch Road, Koonwarra, Vic 3954, ☎ (03) 5664 3204,
℻ (03) 5664 3206; est 1986; ❦ 1,000 cases; ❢; A$; wkds & hols 10-5 or by appt; ⊨

Former Melbourne professionals Owen and Robyn Schmidt run a combined winemaking and bed-and-breakfast business. Shiraz has been the most successful wine to date, although the Pinot Noir has pronounced varietal character in a sappy/tomato style that will appeal to some. The Cabernet Sauvignon is also a pleasant, well-made wine.

Mair's Coalville ☆☆☆
Moe South Road, Moe South, Vic 3825, ☎ (03) 5127 4229,
℻ (03) 5127 2148; est 1985; ❦ 250 cases; ❢; A$; by appt

Dr Stewart Mair makes one wine, Coalville Red, a Cabernet Sauvignon with a little Cabernet Franc, Malbec and Merlot blended in. It has been remarkably consistent; a little on the lean side, perhaps, but with the elegance that comes from very cool-grown fruit.

McAlister Vineyards NR
Golden Beach Road, Longford, Vic 3851, ☎ (03) 5149 7229,
℻ (03) 5149 7229; est 1975; ❦ 550 cases; ❢; A$; by appt

Another producer of a single wine, a blend of Cabernet Sauvignon, Cabernet Franc and Merlot called The McAlister. Winemaker Peter Edwards actively shuns publicity, which, on the basis of prior tastings, is a pity.

Narkoojee ☆☆☆☆ V
1110 Francis Road, Glengarry, Vic 3854, ☎ (03) 5192 4257, ℻ (03) 5192 4257; est 1981; ❦ 700 cases; ❢; A$; by appt; picnic hampers

The 4-hectare vineyard is near the old gold-mining town of Walhalla. Harry Friend was an amateur winemaker of note before turning to commercial winemaking with Narkoojee. His skills show through in the elegant, well-balanced Chardonnay, Merlot and Cabernets.

Nicholson River ☆☆☆☆
Liddells Road, Nicholson, Vic 3882, ☎ (03) 5156 8241, ℻ (03) 5156 8433; est 1978; ❦ 2,000 cases; ❢; A$; 7 days 10-4; playground

The fierce commitment to quality in the face of the temperamental Gippsland climate and frustratingly small production has been handsomely repaid by some stupendous Chardonnays. Ken Eckersley does not refer to these as white wines, but as gold wines, and you understand why.

Paradise Enough NR
Stewarts Road, Kongwak, Vic 3951, ☏ *(03) 5657 4241,*
℻ *(03) 5657 4229; est 1987;* ❧ *600 cases;* ⚑*; A$; Sun & public hols 12-5*
Phillip Jones of Bass Phillip persuaded John Bell and Sue Armstrong to establish their small vineyard on a substantial dairy and beef cattle property. The focus is on powerfully-hewn Chardonnay, Pinot Noir, plus sparkling wine made from these two varieties.

Phillip Island Vineyard ☆☆☆☆ V
Berrys Beach Road, Phillip Island, Vic, ☏ *(03) 5956 8465,*
℻ *(03) 5956 8465; est 1993;* ❧ *2,500 cases;* ⚑*; A$; Nov-March: 7 days 11-7, April-Oct: 7 days 11-5; lunch platters*
When the Lance family (of Diamond Valley Vineyards in the Yarra Valley) planted the first vines on Phillip Island, it was well known for its penguins and motor-bike races. Now there is the remarkable sight of a permanently enclosed 2.5-hectare vineyard. The netting provides protection against both wind and birds. Sauvignon Blanc, Chardonnay, Pinot Noir, Merlot and Cabernet Sauvignon are all delicately refined but impressive.

Sarsfield Estate ☆☆½
345 Duncan Road, Sarsfield, Vic 3875, ☏ *(03) 5156 8962,*
℻ *(03) 5156 8970; est 1995;* ❧ *300 cases; No visitors*
Owned by Swiss-born Peter Albrecht and Suzanne Rutschmann, who has a PhD in chemistry, a diploma in horticulture, and is in year four of the Charles Sturt University BSc (wine science) course. The first vintage made at the winery was 1998, the grapes being sold in previous years to others.

Tarwin Ridge NR
Wintles Road, Leongatha South, Vic 3953, ☏ *(03) 5664 3211,*
℻ *(03) 5664 3211; est 1983;* ❧ *700 cases;* ⚑*; A$; wkds & hols 10-5*
For the time being Brian Anstee is making his wines at Nicholson River under the gaze of fellow social worker Ken Eckersley. The wines come from two hectares of estate-grown Pinot and half a hectare each of Cabernet and Sauvignon Blanc.

The Gurdies ☆☆½
St Helier Road, The Gurdies, Vic 3984, ☏ *(03) 5997 6208,*
℻ *(03) 5997 6511; est 1991;* ❧ *1,000 cases;* ⚑*; A$; 7 days 10-5*
It took Peter Kozik ten years before he harvested the first grapes from his vineyard on the slopes of The Gurdies, overlooking Westernport Bay. His perseverance has been repaid with a striking, peppery Shiraz, and he has plans to expand the vineyard and ultimately build a restaurant.

Wa-De-Lock ☆☆☆
Stratford Road, Maffra, Vic, ☏ (03) 5147 3244, Ⓕ (03) 5147 3132; est 1987; ❧ 2,500 cases; ⚐; A$; Thur-Tues 10-5

Graeme Little started his vineyard conventionally enough in 1987 with Pinot Noir, Cabernet Sauvignon and Sauvignon Blanc, but has now ventured out with experimental plantings of Nebbiolo and Durif, as well as the safe Chardonnay, Shiraz and Merlot. A 12-hectare 'Joseph's coat' is the result, and equally interesting wines.

Wild Dog NR
South Road, Warragul, Vic 3820, ☏ (03) 5623 1117, Ⓕ (03) 5623 6402; est 1982; ❧ 2,500 cases; ⚐; A$; 7 days 10-5

An aptly named winery, which produces somewhat rustic wines from the 11.5 hectares of estate vineyards. Even winemaker John Farrington says that the Shiraz comes 'with a bite', also pointing out that there is minimal handling, fining and filtration. Be warned.

Windy Ridge Vineyard NR
Foster Fish Creek Road, Foster, Vic 3960, ☏ (03) 5682 2035; est 1978; ❧ 350 cases; ⚐; A$; holiday wkds 10-5

Graeme Wilson makes Traminer, long-vatted Pinot Noir and Cabernet/Malbec. These are what one might expect, but not Vintage Port, George's Liqueur Pinot Noir and Graeme's Late Bottled Vintage Port; after all, this is claimed to be the most southerly vineyard in mainland Australia.

Wyanga Park ☆☆☆
Baades Road, Lakes Entrance, Vic 3909, ☏ (03) 5155 1508, Ⓕ (03) 5155 1443; est 1970; ❧ 6,000 cases; ⚐; A$; 7 days 9-5; ⑃; boat cruises

Offers a broad range of wines of diverse provenance directed at the tourist trade; one of the Chardonnays and the Cabernet Sauvignon are estate-grown. Winery cruises are scheduled four days a week.

Murray Darling and Swan Hill

The Murray River, Australia's answer to the Mississippi, is the umbilical cord that joins the largest vineyard plantings of New South Wales, Victoria and South Australia in an area often called the Riverlands.

The water of the Murray River has transformed the parched red sand and stunted growth of this region. Viticulture is an important, but by no means dominant, part of this miraculously transformed landscape. The Murray Darling and Swan Hill regions together form a vast area extending from Mildura in the east and Swan Hill in the east. Together they are responsible for growing almost 40 per cent of the annual Australian grape crush. This is the industrial face of winemaking, efficient and economical. The vineyards are vast, the wineries more like refineries; costs are kept under rigid control. As the new Millennium unfolds, so does a major challenge to the economy of the Riverlands. Only 15 years ago, two-thirds of the grapes used to make Australia's wine were multi-purpose – for winemaking, drying (sultanas) or fresh table grapes. Obviously, a large volume of the grapes then went to winemaking. Even by 1999, when the proportion had fallen from 66 per cent to under 20 per cent, 200,000 tonnes of multi-purpose grapes were still used for winemaking. However, by the year 2002, it seems highly unlikely that more than a few thousand tonnes will be so used. This is simply because of the avalanche of premium Chardonnay, Shiraz and Cabernet Sauvignon (and the other classic vinifera varieties) to come from the 40,000 hectares of new vineyard plantings in Australia between 1995 and 2000. It remains to be seen how the Riverlands adapts both its viticultural and agricultural means of income to this changing scene.

Ashwood Grove NR
Wood Wood, Swan Hill, Vic 3585, ☎ (03) 5030 5291, ℱ (03) 5030 5605; est 1995; ❧ 50,000 cases; ℞; A$; by appt

The Peace family has been a major Swan Hill grape-grower since 1980, and moved into winemaking with the opening of a A$3,000,000 winery in 1997. The modestly priced wines are aimed at supermarkets around the world.

Bullers Beverford ☆☆☆
Murray Valley Highway, Beverford (Swan Hill), Vic 3590, ☎ (03) 5037 6305, ℱ (03) 5037 6803; est 1952; ❧ 50,000 cases; ℞; A$; Mon-Sat 9-5

Traditional wines that, in the final analysis, reflect both their Riverland origin and a fairly low-key approach to style in the winery. Red wine quality is on the ascendant, however.

Capogreco Estate NR
Riverside Avenue, Mildura (Murray Darling), Vic 3500, ☎ (03) 5023 3060; est 1976; ❧ NFP; ℞; A$; Mon-Sat 10-6

Italian-owned and run, making wines that are a blend of Italian and Riverlands. Herb-infused Rosso Dolce is a good example.

Deakin Estate ☆☆☆☆ V
Kulkyne Way, via Red Cliffs (Murray Darling), Vic 3496, ☎ (03) 5029 1666, ℱ (03) 5024 3316; est 1980; ❧ 200,000 cases; No visitors

This is the sharp end of the wine empire, owned by feuding members of the Yunghanns clan. Shareholder disagreements do not stop Deakin Estate from consistently producing excellent Chardonnay, Shiraz and Cabernet Sauvignon at two price and quality levels (Alfred is best); both offer outstanding value.

Lindemans (Karadoc) ☆☆☆☆ V
Edey Road, Karadoc via Mildura (Murray Darling), Vic 3496, ☎ (03) 5051 3333, ℱ (03) 5051 3390; est 1974; ❧ 10,000,000 cases; ℞; A$; Mon-Sun 10-4.30

This is the home of the world's largest-selling Chardonnay brand,

Lindemans Bin 65, viewed by many around the world as the best-value Chardonnay. It is also the production centre for much of the Southcorp group's white wine output. Clever landscaping and a friendly cellar door make it an enjoyable place to visit.

Roberts Estate Wines NR
Game Street, Merbein (Murray Darling), Vic 3505, ☏ *(03) 5024 2944,* ℻ *(03) 5024 2877; est 1998;* ❧ *NA; No visitors*

A very large winery acting as a processing point for grapes grown up and down the Murray River. Over 10,000 tonnes are crushed each vintage. Much of the wine is sold in bulk to others, but some is exported under the Denbeigh and Kombacy labels.

Robinvale ☆☆❧
Sea Lake Road, Robinvale (Murray Darling), Vic 3549,
☏ *(03) 5026 3955,* ℻ *(03) 5026 1123; est 1976;* ❧ *15,000 cases;*
🍷*; A$; Mon-Fri 9-6, Sun 1-6; playground*

Claims to be the only winery in Australia to be fully accredited with the Biodynamic Agricultural Association of Australia. Most, but not all, of the wines are produced from organically-grown grapes, some are preservative-free. Production has increased dramatically, reflecting the interest in organic and biodynamic viticulture and winemaking.

Salisbury Estate ☆☆☆ V
Campbell Avenue, Irymple (Murray Darling), Vic 3498,
☏ *(03) 5024 6800,* ℻ *(03) 5024 6605; est 1977;* ❧ *385,000 cases;*
🍷*; A$; Mon-Sat 10-4.30*

Salisbury Estate, Milburn Park and Castle Crossing are three of the principal brands of Australian Premium Wines; it has an even larger bulk-wine production of around 5,000,000 litres.

South Australia

1994   27,447 hectares   40.93 per cent of total plantings
1998   43,916 hectares   44.61 per cent of total plantings
South Australia is reasserting itself as the 'Wine State'; and if grape tonnage for winemaking is the measure, it did in fact produce over 52 per cent of the national grape crush in 1998.

Barossa Valley

The Barossa Valley continues to beat at the heart of Australia's wine industry. Past, present and future are inextricably bound here. The essence of the valley is all around you. There are the patches of bush-pruned vines, many over 100 years old; the 140-year-old granite and bluestone buildings are as immoveable as the day they were built (mid-19th century). Then there are the wonderful smoked meats, sausages and breads found nowhere else in Australia. And, of course, the wine.

More wine is now made in the Barossa each year than in any other single region. A large amount is certainly trucked in as grapes, must or juice from elsewhere in South Australia, as many of Australia's largest wine companies have their headquarters here. (Only BRL Hardy, based in McLaren Vale, is missing).

As a viticultural region in its own right, the Barossa has more than recovered from the decline it suffered in the 1970s and early 1980s. It is first and foremost a red wine region. Shiraz is its first grape; Cabernet Sauvignon, too, is an important part of the viticultural scene, and rapidly increasing prices reflect the demand for the old plantings of Grenache and Mourvedre. The style of these red wines is unfailingly rich, ripe and generous, and lends itself to the influence of vanilla-flavoured American oak.

Statistics tell you there is almost as much white wine as there is red made from Barossa Valley grapes. What they do not tell you is that, with the qualified exception of Riesling, the white wines are decidedly inferior to the red wines. If ever the criticism of clumsy, oaky, phenolic white wines is to be justly levelled, it is at Barossa Semillon and Chardonnay.

Little more than an hour's drive from Adelaide, the Barossa Valley is the first place wine tourists wish to visit. It's hardly surprising, given its rich viticultural history and the wineries, large and small, now to be visited. The Barossa also has an abundance of good restaurants and guest houses, including an ever-increasing number of bed-and-breakfast places that are by far the best in Australia.

Barossa Ridge Wine Estate NR
Light Pass Road, Tanunda, SA 5352, ☎ *(08) 8563 2811,*
℻ *(08) 8563 2811; est 1987;* ❖ *1,000 cases;* ⚑*; A$; by appt*

Marco Litterini is a grape grower-turned-winemaker. His Valley of Vines is the only Merlot/Cabernet Franc/Cabernet Sauvignon/Petit Verdot blend in the Barossa; he also offers a varietal Cabernet Franc, a rare beast in Australia.

South Australia 111

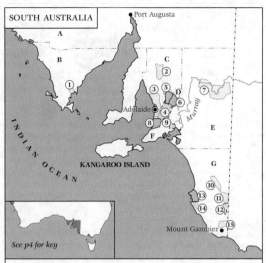

A *Far North*	**1** *Port Lincoln*	**9** *Langhorne Creek*
B *The Peninsulas*	**2** *Clare Valley*	**10** *Padthaway*
C *Mt Lofty Ranges and Adelaide*	**3** *Adelaide Plains*	**11** *Koppamurra*
	4 *Adelaide Hills*	**12** *Coonawarra*
D *Barossa*	**5** *Barossa Valley*	**13** *Mount Benson*
E *Lower Murray*	**6** *Eden Valley*	**14** *Robe*
F *Fleurieu*	**7** *Riverland*	**15** *Mount Gambier*
G *Limestone Coast*	**8** *McLaren Vale*	

Barossa Settlers ☆☆☆
Trial Hill Road, Lyndoch, SA 5351, ℡ *(08) 8524 4017,* ℻ *(08) 8524 4519; est 1983;* ❦ *500 cases;* ⚑; *A$; Mon-Sat 10-4, Sun 11-4*

A beautifully situated 31-hectare hillside vineyard owned by the Haese family. Part of the production is sold, the rest vinified; Gully Winds Riesling is very good.

Basedow ☆☆☆☆ ⌀
161-165 Murray Street, Tanunda, SA 5352, ℡ *(08) 8563 3666,* ℻ *(08) 8563 3597; est 1896;* ❦ *100,000 cases;* ⚑; *A$; Mon-Fri 10-5, wkds & public hols 11-5*

An old and well-regarded winery which has undergone several changes of ownership in the '90s. Full-bodied, oaky Semillon (once called White Burgundy) is its best-known, albeit slighty old-fashioned, wine.

Bethany Wines ☆☆☆☆
Bethany Road, Bethany via Tanunda, SA 5352, ℡ *(08) 8563 2086,* ℻ *(08) 8563 0046; est 1977;* ❦ *25,000 cases;* ⚑; *A$; Mon-Sat 10-5, Sun 1-5*

112 Wines of Australia

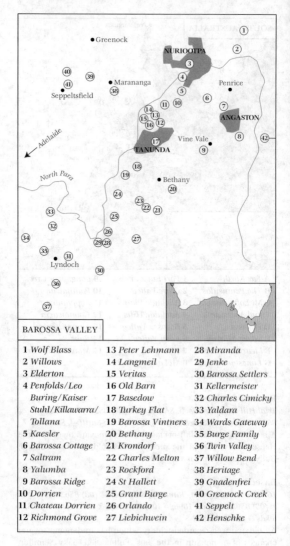

BAROSSA VALLEY

1 *Wolf Blass*
2 *Willows*
3 *Elderton*
4 *Penfolds/Leo Buring/Kaiser Stuhl/Killawarra/Tollana*
5 *Kaesler*
6 *Barossa Cottage*
7 *Saltram*
8 *Yalumba*
9 *Barossa Ridge*
10 *Dorrien*
11 *Chateau Dorrien*
12 *Richmond Grove*
13 *Peter Lehmann*
14 *Langmeil*
15 *Veritas*
16 *Old Barn*
17 *Basedow*
18 *Turkey Flat*
19 *Barossa Vintners*
20 *Bethany*
21 *Krondorf*
22 *Charles Melton*
23 *Rockford*
24 *St Hallett*
25 *Grant Burge*
26 *Orlando*
27 *Liebichwein*
28 *Miranda*
29 *Jenke*
30 *Barossa Settlers*
31 *Kellermeister*
32 *Charles Cimicky*
33 *Yaldara*
34 *Wards Gateway*
35 *Burge Family*
36 *Twin Valley*
37 *Willow Bend*
38 *Heritage*
39 *Gnadenfrei*
40 *Greenock Creek*
41 *Seppelt*
42 *Henschke*

The Schrapel family has been growing grapes for 140 years, and making wine since 1977. The peacock packaging is a little strident, but the wine is good, especially the opulent Shiraz.

Branson Wines NR
Seppeltsfield Road, Greenock, SA 5360, ☎ (08) 8562 8085, ℻ (08) 8562 8085; est 1997; ❖ 1,000 cases; ☷; A$; Wed-Mon 10.30-5

Malcolm Aspden and family purchased this property at the gateway to the Barossa Valley in 1990 and began planting five hectares of Shiraz and one each of Semillon, Cabernet Sauvignon and Chardonnay. The cellar door opened in 1997.

Burge Family Winemakers ☆☆☆☆
Barossa Way, Lyndoch, SA 5351, ☎ *(08) 8524 4644,* ⓕ *(08) 8524 4444; est 1928;* ✤ *3,500 cases;* ⛾; *A$; 7 days 10-5*
An arm of the Burge winemaking dynasty, with invaluable vineyards. Look out for the Old Vines Grenache/Shiraz and Draycott Shiraz (especially the Reserve), built to last on a foundation of richly concentrated fruit.

Charles Cimicky ☆☆☆☆
Gomersal Road, Lyndoch, SA 5351, ☎ *(08) 8524 4025,* ⓕ *(08) 8524 4772; est 1972;* ✤ *15,000 cases;* ⛾; *A$; Tues-Sat 10.30-4.30*
A quixotic combination of conservatism and adventurousness, this winery is best known within South Australia. Intense Sauvignon Blanc and richly flavoured vanilla/cherry Signature Shiraz lead the way.

Charles Melton ☆☆☆☆☆
Krondorf Road, Tanunda, SA 5352, ☎ *(08) 8563 3606,* ⓕ *(08) 8563 3422; est 1984;* ✤ *7,500 cases;* ⛾; *A$; 7 days 11-5*
Diminutive dynamo Graeme (Charlie) Melton has taken his Nine Popes red (a blend of Shiraz, Grenache and Mourvèdre from old vines) to icon status in short order. It, the Shiraz and Cabernet Sauvignon are all beautifully crafted and balanced. His little wooden winery is a pleasure to visit.

Chateau Dorrien NR
Cnr Seppeltsfield Road. and Barossa Valley Way, Dorrien, SA 5352, ☎ *(08) 8562 2850,* ⓕ *(08) 8562 1416; est 1983;* ✤ *2,000 cases;* ⛾; *A$; 7 days 10-5*
Unashamedly and successfully directed at the tourist trade with a range of dry, semi-sweet and sweet table and fortified wines.

Dorrien Estate ☆☆☆☆
Cnr Barossa Valley Way/Siegersdorf Road, Tanunda, SA 5352, ☎ *(08) 8561 2200,* ⓕ *(08) 8561 2299; est 1982;* ✤ *750,000 cases; No visitors*
The base of Cellarmaster, the largest direct-mail organisation in Australia, acquired by Mildara Blass in 1997. Produces a plethora of wines and labels, some bought in bulk, but all well made and keenly priced.

Elderton ☆☆☆☆
3 Tanunda Road, Nuriootpa, SA 5355, ☎ *(08) 8562 1058,* ⓕ *(08) 8562 2844; est 1984;* ✤ *32,000 cases;* ⛾; *A$; Mon-Fri 8.30-5, wkds & hols 11-4*
The core of this substantial business is old, high-quality vineyards on the valley floor. Shiraz, Cabernet Sauvignon and

blends are best, led by a fleshy, vanilla Command Shiraz much admired by the redoubtable Robert Parker.

Glaetzer Wines NR
34 Barossa Valley Way, Tanunda, SA 5352, ☎ (08) 8563 0288, ℻ (08) 8563 0218; est 1995; ♦ 3,000 cases; ᵂ; A$; Mon-Sat 10.30-4.30, Sun & public hols 11.30-4.30
Colin and Ben Glaetzer come from a very well-known wine family. They purchase grapes from Barossa Valley growers, and make an array of traditional Barossa styles.

Gnadenfrei Estate NR
Seppeltsfield Road, Marananga via Nuriootpa, SA 5355, ☎ (08) 8562 2522, ℻ (08) 8562 3470; est 1979; ♦ 1,500 cases; ᵂ; A$; Tues-Sun 10-5.30; ⑩
Malcolm Seppelt did his own thing (as a separate venture from the main Seppelt company) with this small estate-based winery and restaurant.

Grant Burge ☆☆☆☆✓
Jacobs Creek, Tanunda, SA 5352, ☎ (08) 8563 3700, ℻ (08) 8563 2807; est 1988; ♦ 108,000 cases; ᵂ; A$; 7 days 10-5
Astute, energetic winemaker-cum-marketer Grant Burge has amassed a vineyard empire and hugely successful winemaking enterprise. Meshach Shiraz, Shadrach Cabernet Sauvignon and Holy Trinity (a Grenache/Shiraz/Mourvedre blend) are as bold as Burge himself.

Greenock Creek Cellars NR
Radford Road, Seppeltsfield, SA 5360, ☎ (08) 8562 8103, ℻ (08) 8562 8259; est 1978; ♦ 1,500 cases; ᵂ; A$; Wed-Mon 11-5; ⌂
This is one of the first wineries you will see driving up to the Barossa Valley, where stonemason Michael Waugh and wife Annabel make cult wines that sell rapidly at their cellar door.

Haan Wines ☆☆☆☆
Siegersdorf Road, Tanunda, SA 5352, ☎ (08) 8562 2122, ℻ (08) 8562 3034; est 1993; ♦ 4,000 cases; No visitors
Hans and Fransien Haan have a 16-hectare vineyard near Tanunda, successfully focusing on supple, chocolate-and-mulberry Merlot, speciality of contract winemaker James Irvine.

Heritage Wines ☆☆☆☆✓
106a Seppeltsfield Road, Marananga, SA 5355, ☎ (08) 8562 2880, ℻ (08) 8562 2692; est 1984; ♦ 6,000 cases; ᵂ; A$; 7 days 11-5
A little-known winery that deserves a far wider audience, for Stephen Hoff is apt to produce some startlingly good Chardonnay, Riesling and Shiraz.

Jenke Vineyards ☆☆☆☆
Barossa Valley Way, Rowland Flat, SA 5352, ☎ (08) 8524 4154, ℻ (08) 8524 5044; est 1989; ♦ 7,000 cases; ᵂ; A$; 7 days 10-4.30

The Jenkes have been grape-growers since 1854, but only since 1989 have they made wines from a small part of their production. Shiraz and dark berry/bitter chocolate Old Vine Mourvedre are profoundly impressive.

Kaesler ☆☆☆
Barossa Valley Way, Nuriootpa, SA 5355, ☏ (08) 8562 2711, ⓕ (08) 8562 2788; est 1990; ❖ 3,000 cases; ☙; A$; 7 days 10-5; ¶❘; ⇌
The Hueppauffs run this as a small winery, restaurant and accommodation business on the 12-hectare Kaesler Farm they acquired in 1985. Specialities are Bush Vine Grenache and Old Vine Shiraz.

Kaiser Stuhl ☆☆⚘
Tanunda Road, Nuriootpa, SA 5355, ☏ (08) 8560 9389, ⓕ (08) 8562 1669; est 1931; ❖ 1,300,000 cases; ☙; A$; Mon-Sat 10-5, Sun 1-5
A once huge cooperative now entirely absorbed into the Southcorp group, and producing wines at the cheapest end of the market.

Kellermeister ☆☆☆
Barossa Valley Highway, Lyndoch, SA 5351, ☏ (08) 8524 4303, ⓕ (08) 8524 4880; est 1970; ❖ 8,000 cases; ☙; A$; 7 days 9-6
An unusual operation offering multiple vintages of a multitude of traditionally styled wines at enticing prices, made by industry veteran Trevor Jones.

Killawarra ☆☆☆☆
Tanunda Road, Nuriootpa, SA 5355, ☏ (08) 8560 9389, ⓕ (08) 8562 1669; est 1975; ❖ 205,000 cases; No visitors
In reality this is purely a Southcorp sparkling wine brand. The Killawarra label offers ultra-consistent quality and value for money, using Chardonnay and Pinot Noir grown everywhere other than the Barossa Valley.

Krondorf ☆☆☆⚘
Krondorf Road, Tanunda, SA 5352, ☏ (08) 8563 2145, ⓕ (08) 8562 3055; est 1978; ❖ 30,000 cases; ☙; A$; 7 days 10-5
A tumultuous history, with a razzle-dazzle rise under Grant Burge and the late Ian Wilson before its acquisition by Mildara Blass. Now a comfortable, motherly figure producing well-behaved, conformist wines of most hues.

Langmeil Winery ☆☆☆⚘
Cnr Para and Langmeil Roads, Tanunda, SA 5352, ☏ (08) 8563 2595, ⓕ (08) 8563 3622; est 1996; ❖ 6,000 cases; ☙; A$; 7 days 10-5
This winery has had a convoluted Barossa-Deutsch lineage since the 1840s, with various ownership and direction changes. Following the most recent upheaval in 1996, Langmeil now produces luscious red wines from a 5-hectare vineyard planted entirely with Shiraz.

Leo Buring ☆☆☆☆
Tanunda Road, Nuriootpa, SA 5355, ☎ *(08) 8563 2184,* Ⓕ *(08) 8563 2804; est 1931;* ❦ *23,000 cases;* ⛾; *A$; Mon-Sat 10-5, Sun 1-5*

An arm of the Southcorp octopus, with a great lineage of superb, long-lived Rieslings formerly made by genius John Vickery. Super-premium Rieslings, variously from the Clare or Eden Valleys, are now released under the Leonay label. Its other wines are reliably utilitarian.

Liebich Wein NR
Steingarten Road, Rowland Flat, SA 5352, ☎ *(08) 8524 4543,* Ⓕ *(08) 8524 4543; est 1992;* ❦ *600 cases;* ⛾; *A$; wkds 11-5, Mon-Fri by appt*

Barossa-Deutsch for 'I love wine', this is a small venture into winemaking by long-term grape-grower and local character Ron Darky Liebich, who has been making wine for others since 1969.

Miranda Rovalley Estate ☆☆☆⍟
Barossa Highway, Rowland Flat, SA 5352, ☎ *(08) 8524 4537,* Ⓕ *(08) 8524 4066; est 1919;* ❦ *NA;* ⛾; *A$; 7 days 9-4.30;* 🍴

An offshoot of the large Riverina-based Miranda winery, producing mainstream Barossa styles at affordable prices. The Old Vine Shiraz stands out as a wine of real stature.

Old Barn NR
Langmeil Road, Tanunda, SA 5352, ☎ *(08) 8563 0111; est 1990;* ❦ *2,200 cases;* ⛾; *A$; Mon-Fri 9-5, wkds 10-5*

Takes its name from the stone barn built in 1861, and which now acts as the cellar door where all the wines, contract-made by the ubiquitous Trevor Jones, are sold to tourists.

Orlando ☆☆☆☆⍟
Barossa Valley Way, Rowland Flat, SA 5352, ☎ *(08) 8521 3111,* Ⓕ *(08) 8521 3100; est 1847;* ❦ *NFP;* ⛾; *A$; Mon-Fri 10-5, wkds 10-4; gift shop*

Owned by Pernod Ricard and known around the world for its mega-brand, Jacob's Creek. In recent times it has made a concerted effort to improve and expand its range of super-premium and premium wines. These include Centenary Hill Shiraz, Lawsons Shiraz and Jacaranda Ridge Cabernet Sauvignon, and special-release Jacobs Creek wines.

Penfolds ☆☆☆☆☆
Tanunda Road, Nuriootpa, SA 5355, ☎ *(08) 8560 9389,* Ⓕ *(08) 8562 2494; est 1844;* ❦ *1,100,000 cases;* ⛾; *A$; 7 days 10.30-4.30*

Heads the Southcorp wine group, the ninth largest in the world and Australia's largest vineyard owner. Justifiably famous for Grange, the peerless and (almost) ageless Shiraz created by the late Max Schubert, but also for a pyramid of red wines of great depth of flavour and structure, sold at all price points. The recently launched Yattarna Chardonnay signals a determination to make an equal impact with its white wines.

Peter Lehmann ☆☆☆⚹
Para Road, Tanunda, SA 5352, ☎ (08) 8563 2500, ⓕ (08) 8563 3402; est 1979; ❖ 200,000 cases; ⚏; A$; Mon-Fri 9.30-5, wkds & hols 10.30-4.30

The godfather of the Barossa now heads up a flourishing company listed on the Stock Exchange. Resolutely using only Barossa and Eden Valley grapes, the style is as honest as the day is long. The Mentor and Stonewell Shiraz, both marrying sweet vanilla oak with ripe and luscious fruit, are rather special.

Queen Adelaide ☆☆⚹
Sturt Highway, Waikerie, SA 5330, ☎ (08) 8541 2588, ⓕ (08) 8541 3877; est 1858; ❖ 700,000 cases; No visitors

The bargain basement of Southcorp's bottled wine empire. Price is the driving force, the elegant and historic label an anomaly.

Richmond Grove ☆☆☆☆
Para Road, Tanunda, SA 5352, ☎ (08) 8563 2184, ⓕ (08) 8563 2804; est 1977; ❖ NFP; ⚏; A$; Mon-Fri 10-5, wkds 10-4; jazz concerts

Once Chateau Leonay of Leo Buring, now renamed and owned by Orlando Wyndham. In fairytale fashion, John Vickery (formerly of Leo Buring) became winemaker and produces glorious limy, minerally Rieslings, particularly from Clare Valley (Watervale) grapes.

Rockford ☆☆☆☆⚹
*Krondorf Road, Tanunda, SA 5352, ☎ (08) 8563 2720,
ⓕ (08) 8563 3787; est 1984; ❖ 19,500 cases; ⚏; A$; Mon-Sat 11-5*

Robert (Rocky) O'Callaghan is a richly bearded, larger-than-life passionate defender of old-style, handmade wines from old, low-yielding vines. Velvety sparkling Black Shiraz is diamond-scarce and Basket Press Shiraz almost as rare. All ooze character.

Saltram ☆☆☆☆
*Angaston Road, Angaston, SA 5353, ☎ (08) 8564 3355,
ⓕ (08) 8564 2209; est 1859; ❖ 50,000 cases; ⚏; A$; 7 days 10-5; ⚑*

Now part of the Mildara Blass empire, but winemaker Nigel Dolan has breathed new life and credibility into Saltram as a true Barossa winery, making concentrated, rich but balanced Shiraz and Cabernet Sauvignon.

Schmidts Tarchalice NR
*Research Road, Vine Vale via Tanunda, SA 5352, ☎ (08) 8563 3005, ⓕ (08) 8563 0667; est 1984; ❖ 1,500 cases; ⚏; A$;
Mon-Sat 10-5, Sun 12-5*

Typically has a large range of low-priced wines (on last tasting rather rustic) sold through the cellar door.

Seppelt ☆☆☆☆☆
*Seppeltsfield via Nuriootpa, SA 5355, ☎ (08) 8568 6200,
ⓕ (08) 8562 8333; est 1851; ❖ NFP; ⚏; A$; Mon-Fri 10-5,
Sat 10.30-4.30, Sun 11-4*

This gloriously historic winery is the focal point for a dazzling array of fortified wines made by James Godrey. The wines range from a fresh manzanilla sherry-style Fino (exported as Palomino), to an unctuous 100-year-old Para Liqueur (port style) that is bottled each year on its centenary. Top Dorrien Cabernet Sauvignon is also very good.

St Hallett ☆☆☆☆½
St Halletts Road, Tanunda, SA 5352, ☏ (08) 8563 2319,
Ⓕ (08) 8563 2901; est 1944; ❦ 65,000 cases; ❦; A$; 7 days 10-4
Unstoppable Sir Lunchalot Bob McLean's marketing brilliance and Stuart Blackwell's winemaking skills have created Old Block Shiraz, Blackwell Shiraz, Faith Shiraz etc, plus natty wines like Poacher's Blend white.

Stanley Brothers ☆☆☆
Barossa Valley Way, Tanunda, SA 5352, ☏ (08) 8563 3375,
Ⓕ (08) 8563 3758; est 1994; ❦ 6,000 cases; ❦; A$; 7 days 9-5
Industry veteran Lindsay Stanley purchased his 21-hectare Kroemer Estate in 1994 and is now doing his own thing, producing the Barossa's only Sylvaner and soft, oaky reds.

Tait Wines NR
Yaldara Drive, Lyndoch, SA 5351, ☏ (08) 8524 5000, Ⓕ (08) 8524 5220; est 1994; ❦ 500 cases; ❦; A$; wkds 10-5 and by appt; cooperage display
Coopers for over 100 years, the Tait family ventured into wine in 1994 with immediate success for its bold, voluptuous wines, especially peachy Chardonnay.

The Willows ☆☆☆
Light Pass Road, Light Pass, Barossa Valley, SA 5355,
☏ (08) 8562 1080, Ⓕ (08) 8562 3447; est 1989; ❦ 4,000 cases;
❦; A$; 7 days 10.30-4.30
Successive generations of the Scholz family have grown grapes. Now Peter and Michael Scholz are making smooth, balanced and flavoursome wines. Shiraz and Cabernet Sauvignon are best.

Tollana ☆☆☆☆
Tanunda Road, Nuriootpa, SA 5355, ☏ (08) 8560 9389, Ⓕ (08) 8562 2494; est 1888; ❦ 19,000 cases; ❦; A$; Mon-Sat 10-5, Sun 1-5
Part of Southcorp, drawing most of its grapes from its long-established Eden Valley Woodbury Vineyard. Makes citrous Riesling, stylish, tangy Chardonnay and smooth but substantial Shiraz and Bin TR222 Cabernet Sauvignon.

Torbreck Vintners ☆☆☆☆½
Roenfeldt Road, Marananga, SA 5352, ☏ (08) 8562 4155,
Ⓕ (08) 8562 4195; est 1994; ❦ 400 cases; No visitors
The Powell family has had immediate and outstanding success with The Steading (Grenache/Mourvedre/Shiraz) and RunRig (Shiraz/Viognier), both crammed to the gills with luscious fruit.

Trevor Jones ☆☆☆☆ V
Barossa Valley Highway, Lyndoch, SA 5351, ☏ (08) 8524 4303, ℻ (08) 8524 4880; est 1996; ❖ 2,000 cases; ♀; A$; 7 days 9-6
Industry veteran Trevor Jones has finally introduced his own label (itself strikingly designed), offering Riesling, Virgin Chardonnay, Dry-Grown Shiraz and Cabernet/Merlot.

Turkey Flat ☆☆☆☆¹⁄
Bethany Road, Tanunda, SA 5352, ☏ (08) 8563 2851, ℻ (08) 8563 3610; est 1990; ❖ 10,000 cases; ♀; A$; 7 days 11-5
Another Barossa dynasty of grape-growers (since 1870)-turned winemakers. Peter Schulz makes delectable rosé and highly regarded Shiraz from a precious patch of 145-year-old vines.

Twin Valley Estate NR
Hoffnungsthal Road, Lyndoch, SA 5351, ☏ (08) 8524 4584, ℻ (08) 8524 4978; est 1990; ❖ 3,500 cases; ♀; A$; wkds 10-5
Like Chateau Dorrien, this is owned by Fernando Martin and clearly directed at the general tourist. Still, wines such as the spicy, limy Frontignac Spätlese are praiseworthy.

Veritas ☆☆☆¹⁄
94 Langmeil Road, Tanunda, SA 5352, ☏ (08) 8563 2330, ℻ (08) 8563 3158; est 1955; ❖ 14,000 cases; ♀; A$; on-Fri 9-5, wkds 11-5; ⛺
Rolf Binder celebrates his Hungarian heritage with Binder's Bull's Blood, but also makes an array of neatly turned, conventional white and red wines.

Wards Gateway ☆☆¹⁄
Barossa Valley Highway, Lyndoch, SA 5351, ☏ (08) 8524 4138; est 1979; ❖ 600 cases; ♀; A$; 7 days 9-5.30
As its name implies, this is the first winery visitors reach on entering the valley. Old estate vines produce the best wines, which are made without frills or new oak.

Willow Bend ☆☆☆¹⁄
Lyndoch Valley Road (PO Box 107), Lyndoch, SA 5351, ☏ (08) 8524 4169, ℻ (08) 8524 4169; est 1990; ❖ 600 cases; No visitors
Ken Semmler heads yet another leading Barossa grape-growing family, with nephew Wayne Dutschke returning from Australia-wide experience as winemaker. Smooth and stylish wines sell out quickly.

Wolf Blass ☆☆☆☆¹⁄
Bilyara Vineyards, Sturt Highway, Nuriootpa, SA 5355, ☏ (08) 8562 1955, ℻ (08) 8562 4127; est 1966; ❖ 150,000 cases; ♀; A$; Mon-Fri 9.15-4.30, wkds 10-4.30
The cheerful, impassioned mangling of the English language by Mr Wolf Blass remains as prominent as his brightest bow-tie. Executive winemaking is in the hands of kids, including Wendy Stuckey (Riesling and white wines of exceptional finesse) and Caroline Dunn (red wines).

Yaldara Wines ☆☆☆
Gomersal Road, Lyndoch, SA 5351, ☎ (08) 8524 4200, Ⓕ (08) 8524 4678; est 1947; ❖ 650,000 cases; ⚑; A$; ⚔ 7 days 9-5; ⦿⦁

An ultra-ornate chateau offering a range of wines that vary from the banal to the baroque, cheap to expensive. It was offered for sale in 1999, however, so things may change.

Yalumba ☆☆☆☆⚡
Eden Valley Road, Angaston, SA 5353, ☎ (08) 8561 3200, Ⓕ (08) 8561 3393; est 1849; ❖ 55,000 cases; ⚑; A$; Mon-Fri 8.30-5, Sat 10-5, Sun 12-5

The surviving Anglo-Australian aristocracy lorded over by actor Jeremy Irons' alter-ego Robert Hill-Smith. Languidly changing hats with just a ghost of a crooked smile, Hill-Smith runs the very complex winemaking, importing and exporting business of the Yalumba stable and other producers. Committed to quality, Yalumba is a particularly serious player at the top end of full-bodied Australian reds. Striking Eden Valley Riesling is one of several wines made under separate brand-names.

Yunbar Estate NR
Light Pass Road, Vine Vale, SA 5352, ☎ (08) 8564 0114, Ⓕ (08) 8564 0164; est 1998; ❖ 2,000 cases; ⚑; A$; 7 days 10-4.30

The intriguingly named Sinner's Shiraz, the Merlot, Semillon and Chardonnay are produced from a total of eight hectares of estate-grown grapes; the Eden Riesling is made from contract-grown grapes.

Eden Valley

The Eden Valley is a windswept series of often bare hills, more an elevated plateau than anything else. There are magic spots – none more so than the 150-year-old Hill of Grace Vineyard, with its stone church directly across the road, and the groves of white-trunked gums. Eden Valley is primarily a grape-growing region. It is the mirror reverse, if you like, of the Barossa Valley. Here, just two producers represent Eden Valley's major winery action. They are Henschke, the most highly regarded family winery in Australia, and the well-known Mountadam estate.

Eden Valley produces Shiraz of outstanding quality, but its chief claim to fame is its great Rieslings. These are wines that literally blossom with ten to 15 years' bottle age, and have a lime-citrous character and caressing texture that give them greater appeal in their youth than those of the Clare Valley.

It was the quality of Eden Valley's Riesling that led Yalumba to progressively establish its Pewsey Vale, Heggies and Hill-Smith vineyards (and brands) here, and to forsake its sources of Barossa Valley Riesling.

Craneford NR
Main Street, Springton, SA 5235, ☎ (08) 8568 2220, Ⓕ (08) 8568 2538; est 1978; ❖ 2,400 cases; ⚑; A$; Wed-Mon 11-5

A change of ownership may herald a revival in the fortunes of

Craneford, which had suffered from a range of winemaking problems over the past five years or so.

Eden Valley Wines NR
Main Street, Eden Valley, SA 5235, ☎ (08) 8564 1111, ℻ (08) 8564 1110; est 1994; ❦ 4,000 cases; ⛾; A$; 7 days 10-5; ⛾

Eden Valley Wines has waxed and waned over the years, but now seems very much in the ascendant, with 30 hectares each of recently planted Riesling, Cabernet Sauvignon and Shiraz, and five hectares of much older Mourvedre. A major part of the production is sold as grapes; the wines currently on sale have varied (non-estate) backgrounds.

Heggies Vineyard ☆☆☆☆
Heggies Range Road, Eden Valley, SA 5235, ☎ (08) 8565 3203, ℻ (08) 8565 3380; est 1971; ❦ 12,500 cases; No visitors

Heggies was the horseman pictured on the striking label – a classic after 20 years. The vineyard, established in 1973, lies at 570 metres. While owned by Yalumba, Heggies strives to keep its identity quite separate. Overall, the Riesling (soft toast, lime and kerosene flavours with a few years' bottle age) is best, Viognier the most interesting.

Henschke ☆☆☆☆☆
Henschke Road, Keyneton, SA 5353, ☎ (08) 8564 8223, ℻ (08) 8564 8294; est 1868; ❦ 40,000 cases; ⛾; A$; Mon-Fri 9-4.30, Sat 9-12, public hols 10-3

Winemaker Stephen Henschke and viticulturist wife Prue have taken Henschke to the pinnacle of small(ish) Australian wineries since taking over from father Cyril in 1978. The 135-year-old Shiraz vines at the Hill of Grace Vineyard produce a wine second only to Penfolds Grange in price, and even more eagerly sought after. Mount Edelstone is another great classic Shiraz. A scintillating array of white and red wines of diverse styles but consistent quality make up an outstanding portfolio of wines.

Hill-Smith Estate ☆☆☆☆
c/o Yalumba Winery, Angaston, SA 5353, ☎ (08) 8561 3200, ℻ (08) 8561 3393; est 1973; ❦ 6,000 cases; No visitors

Also part of the Yalumba Estate, with 23 hectares of Chardonnay and Sauvignon Blanc yielding two estate wines. Quality varies considerably with vintage; the rating is a compromise between best and least.

Irvine ☆☆☆☆½
Roeslers Road, Eden Valley, SA 5235, ☎ (08) 8564 1046, ℻ (08) 8564 1046; est 1980; ❦ 4,000 cases; No visitors

Industry veteran Jim Irvine successfully guided the destiny of several substantial South Australian wineries while quietly setting up his own vineyard and brand, which has focused on silky, cedary Merlot (Grand Merlot) chiefly sold abroad.

Karl Seppelt ☆☆☆☆

Ross Dewells Road, Springton, SA 5235, ☏ (08) 8568 2378,
Ⓕ (08) 8568 2799; est 1981; ❖ 2,500 cases; ♀; A$; 7 days 10-5

The squeaky Australian twang in Karl Seppelt's voice should not deceive you: this former marketing director of B Seppelt & Sons made the major decisions leading to the pioneering of the Drumborg (Western Victoria) and Padthaway regions. His own vineyard virtually straddles the Adelaide Hills-Eden Valley boundary, and (with contract winemaking) produces solidly flavoured, ultra-consistent sparkling, white and red wines.

Mountadam ☆☆☆☆☆

High Eden Road, High Eden Ridge, SA 5235, ☏ (08) 8564 1101,
Ⓕ (08) 8361 3400; est 1972; ❖ 12,000 cases; ♀; A$; 7 days 11-4

Established by the late David Wynn (of Wynns Coonawarra fame) for son Adam, who has long since assumed command. A complex, structured and not overoaked Chardonnay is the pick of the bunch, but a curiously named Merlot/Cabernet blend, The Red, has recently picked up pace. The David Wynn range is also good, especially the Patriarch Shiraz.

Pewsey Vale ☆☆☆☆

Brownes Road, Pewsey Vale, SA (vineyard only), ☏ (08) 8561 3200; est 1961; ❖ 30,000 cases; ♀; A$; at Yalumba

The first of the Hill-Smith/Yalumba ventures into the hills of the Eden Valley, overnight proving that this indeed was a superior region for producing Riesling. Quality wobbled a bit after a brilliant start in the late '60s, but has recently showed signs of getting back on track.

Clare Valley

It was Mick Knappstein who once observed, 'There are only two kinds of people: those who were born in Clare, and those who wish they had been.' I fall unashamedly in the latter category. The topography of the Clare Valley has seemingly acted as a bulwark against the intrusion of the 20th century. This illusion is heightened by the abundance of stone buildings and wineries as precious as the Jesuit-run Sevenhill and Wendouree, to name but two among many. Most of the wineries are small, family-owned and -run, which adds to the feeling of intimacy. And once you have set up shop here, it is hard not to make wines with equally strongly defined character.

Clare Rieslings, shy and minerally/chalky in their youth, slowly and majestically reveal their core of honey, lightly browned toast and balancing twist of lemony acidity as they age sometimes for 30 years or more. The Shiraz, Cabernet Sauvignon and Malbec are awesome. Some makers quite legitimately choose to partially tame them; others are content to give them free play, while yet others encourage and build on that power with new oak and prolonged fermentations. And how wonderful it is to find that the Clare Valley is one of the few places on this planet not to have welcomed Chardonnay.

Barletta Bros NR
Polish Hill River Estate, Sevenhill, SA 7453, ☎ (08) 8342 3395, ℻ (08) 8344 2180; est 1993; ❖ 2,000 cases; ⚑; A$; by appt

Former wine retailer Mario Barletta has turned winemaker. He presently houses his winemaking equipment at Pikes (*qv*), but intends ultimately to establish his own winery and vineyards.

Brian Barry Wines ☆☆☆✓
PO Box 128, Stepney, SA 5069, ☎ (08) 8363 6211, ℻ (08) 8362 0498; est 1977; ❖ 10,000 cases; No visitors

Brian Barry is an industry veteran with a wealth of winemaking and show-judging experience. He sells a substantial part of the production from this vineyard-only enterprise, and contract-makes some wine (under his supervision) at various wineries. They offer, as one would expect, reliably good quality.

Clos Clare NR
Government Road, Watervale, SA 5452, ☎ (08) 8843 0161, ℻ (08) 8843 0161; est 1993; ❖ 1,000 cases; ⚑; A$; wkds & public hols 10-5

Clos Clare is based on a small (1.5-hectare) unirrigated section of the original Florita Vineyard once owned by Leo Buring. It produces Riesling of extraordinary concentration and power.

Crabtree of Watervale ☆☆☆
North Terrace, Watervale SA 5452, ☎ (08) 8843 0069, ℻ (08) 8843 0144; est 1979; ❖ 4,000 cases; ⚑; 7 days 10-5

The gently eccentric Robert Crabtree and wife Elizabeth are once again very much part of the Watervale business, making full-flavoured, classic Clare wines, with Riesling and Cabernet Sauvignon to the fore.

Duncan Estate ☆☆☆
Spring Gully Road, Clare, SA 5453, ☎ (08) 8843 4335, ℻ (08) 8843 4335; est 1968; ❖ 2,500 cases; ⚑; A$; 7 days 10-4

A recent change of ownership may result in a higher profile for this estate, which first produced wines from its 7.4 hectares of vineyards in 1984. Over the years, some attractive wines have been made; the Cabernet/Merlot and Shiraz are usually good.

Eldredge ☆☆☆✓
Spring Gully Road, Clare, SA 5453, ☎ (08) 8842 3086, ℻ (08) 8842 3086; est 1993; ❖ 4,000 cases; ⚑; A$; 7 days 11-5; ❖

Leigh and Karen Eldredge have established their cellar-door facility at an altitude of 500 metres in the Sevenhill Ranges. Overnight success came with a trophy for Best Cabernet Sauvignon at the 1997 Adelaide Wine Show for their powerful savoury, blackberry-flavoured wine.

Emerald Estate NR
Main North Road, Stanley Flat, SA 5453, ☎ (08) 8842 3296, ℻ (08) 8842 2220; est 1990; ❖ 1,670 cases; ⚑; A$; Mon, Tues, Thurs, Fri 11-5, wkds 10-5

Don and Gwen Carroll purchased a 33-hectare property at Stanley Flat in 1990. A small existing vineyard was pulled up, since when 20 hectares of vines have been established. Most of the production is sold to leading wineries in the region, a portion being retained for the Emerald Estate wine label.

Grosset ☆☆☆☆☆
King Street, Auburn, SA 5451, ☏ (08) 8849 2175, ℻ (08) 8849 2292; est 1981; ❧ 8,000 cases; ⚑; A$; Wed-Sun 10-5 from first week of Sept for approx 6 weeks

Jeffrey Grosset is best known for his supremely elegant Rieslings from the Watervale and Polish Hill River areas, but his Bordeaux blend, Gaia, is equally superb. His winemaking skills do not stop there: he also makes a brilliant Semillon-Sauvignon Blanc (Clare Semillon, Adelaide Hills Sauvignon Blanc), and an even better Adelaide Hills Chardonnay (intense but harmonious) and Reserve Pinot Noir (in minuscule quantities but of awesome quality).

Howarths Pycnantha Hill NR
Benbournie Road, Clare, SA 5453, ☏ (08) 8842 2137, ℻ (08) 8842 2137; est 1997; ❧ 600 cases; No visitors

The Howarth family has established two hectares of vineyard since 1987, making its first commercial vintage ten years thereafter. It was a natural choice to name their vineyards after *acacia pycnantha* (a golden wattle growing wild over the farm.)

Jeanneret Wines NR
Jeanneret Road, Sevenhill, SA 5453, ☏ (08) 8843 4308, ℻ (08) 8843 4251; est 1992; ❧ 5,000 cases; ⚑; A$; Mon-Fri 11-5, wkds & public hols 10-5

The Jeanneret winery has a most attractive outdoor tasting area and equally charming picnic facilities on the edge of a small lake, surrounded by bushland. The wines have already established a loyal following.

Jim Barry Wines ☆☆☆☆
Main North Road, Clare, SA 5453, ☏ (08) 8842 2261, ℻ (08) 8842 3752; est 1959; ❧ 50,000 cases; ⚑; A$; Mon-Fri 9-5, wkds & hols 9-4

The irrepressibly Irish Barry family owns 160 hectares of mature vineyards, including most of the great Florita Riesling vineyard. Another provides the superlative Shiraz for The Armagh, a pretender to the Grange throne, and the McRae Wood duo of Shiraz and Cabernet/Malbec.

Kilikanoon NR
Penna Lane, Skillogalee Valley, Penwortham, SA 5453, ☏ (08) 8843 4377, ℻ (08) 8843 4377; est 1997; ❧ 2,500 cases; ⚑; A$; Thurs-Sun & public hols 11-5; 🍴

Kilikanoon has six hectares of estate vineyards at Leasingham and Penwortham. It also has a restaurant that was set up in a restored 1880s cottage.

South Australia 125

Knappstein Wines ☆☆☆☆¼
2 Pioneer Avenue, Clare, SA 5453, ☏ (08) 8842 2600, Ⓕ (08) 8842 3831; est 1976; ✦ 40,000 cases; ♀; A$; Mon-Fri 9-5, Sat 11-5, Sun & public hols 11-4

The King is dead; long live the King. Tim Knappstein has sold the winery he founded to Petaluma and moved to Lenswood in the Adelaide Hills. Back at Knappstein, Andrew Hardy has tailored a seamless transition in winemaking and wine style; Riesling, Enterprise Reserve Shiraz and Cabernet are best.

Leasingham ☆☆☆☆¼
7 Dominic Street, Clare, SA 5453, ☏ (08) 8842 2555, Ⓕ (08) 8842 3293; est 1893; ✦ 95,000 cases; ♀; A$; Mon-Fri 8.30-5.30, wkds 10-4

Successive big-company ownerships and various peregrinations in labelling and branding have not caused any permanent loss of identity or quality. With a core of high-quality vineyards planted with old vines to draw on, Leasingham is in fact going from strength to strength under BRL Hardy's direction. The stentorian red wines take no prisoners, compacting densely rich fruit and layer upon layer of oak into every long-lived bottle.

Mintaro Cellars NR
Leasingham Road, Mintaro, SA 5415, ☏ (08) 8843 9046, Ⓕ (08) 8843 9050; est 1984; ✦ 4,000 cases; ♀; A$; 7 days 9-5

Peter Houldsworth has produced some impressive Riesling over the years that develops particularly well in bottle. The red wines are formidable, massive in body and extract, and built for the long haul.

Mount Horrocks ☆☆☆☆
The Old Railway Station, Curling Street, Auburn, SA 5451, ☏ (08) 8849 2243, Ⓕ (08) 8849 2243; est 1982; ✦ 5,000 cases; ♀; A$; wkds & public hols 11-5

Mount Horrocks was established by the Ackland brothers as an adjunct to their large grape-growing business. Purchased some years ago by the feisty Stephanie Toole, the wine style is uncomplicated, the undoubted quality coming from the excellent and mature estate vineyards.

Old Station Vineyard ☆☆☆☆
St Vincent Street, Watervale, SA 5452, ☏ 0414 441 925, Ⓕ (02) 9144 1925; est 1926; ✦ 4,000 cases; No visitors

Former leading Sydney wine retailers Bill and Noel Ireland purchased a 6-hectare vineyard planted with seven-year-old vines in 1995 and, with skilled contract winemaking, hauled in a bag full of gold, silver and bronze medals.

Olssens of Watervale NR
Government Road, Watervale, SA 5452, ☏ (08) 8843 0065, Ⓕ (08) 8843 0065; est 1994; ✦ 1,000 cases; ♀; A$; 7 days 11-5 or by appt

Within two weeks of their first visit to the Clare Valley in December 1986, Kevin and Helen Olssen decided to sell their

Adelaide home and purchase a 5-hectare vineyard in a small, isolated valley near Watervale. Until 1993 they sold the grapes, but since then have had their powerful, at times slightly rustic, wines made at Mitchell.

Paulett ☆☆☆☆
Polish Hill Road, Polish Hill River, SA 5453, ☎ (08) 8843 4328, Ⓕ (08) 8843 4202; est 1983; ❖ 14,000 cases; ❣; A$; 7 days 10-5
Former Hunter Valley winemaker Neil Paulett and wife Alison purchased their 47-hectare property in 1982. The next summer their patch of old vines and the house in a grove of old trees were destroyed in the terrible bushfires of 1983. Undeterred, they have gone on to build a beautifully situated winery and to craft wines that are never less than good, and sometimes quite brilliant.

Pearson Vineyards NR
Main North Road, Penwortham, SA 5453, ☎ (08) 8843 4234, Ⓕ (08) 8843 4141; est 1993; ❖ 800 cases; ❣; A$; Mon-Fri 11-5, wkds 10-5
Jim Pearson makes his Pearson Vineyard wines at Mintaro Cellars from the 1.5 hectares of estate vines that surround the classic stone cottage-cum-cellar door.

Penwortham Wines NR
Government Road, Penwortham, SA 5453, ☎ (08) 8843 4345; est 1985; ❖ 1,500 cases; ❣; A$; Sat 10-5, Sun, hols 10-4; bed & breakfast
Richard Hughes has progressively established 12 hectares of Riesling, Semillon, Verdelho, Shiraz and Cabernet Sauvignon, selling most of the grapes and making small quantities of wine from the remainder.

Pikes ☆☆☆☆
Polish Hill River Road, Sevenhill, SA 5453, ☎ (08) 8843 4370, Ⓕ (08) 8843 4353; est 1984; ❖ 30,000 cases; ❣; A$; 7 days 10-4
Owned by the energetic Pike brothers. Until 1998 Andrew was chief viticulturist for Southcorp, while Neil was the winemaker at Mitchell. Both are now focused on this thriving business, producing powerful, complex wines (especially Reserve Riesling and Reserve Shiraz) in mainstream Clare style.

Quelltaler ☆☆☆☆
Main North Road, Watervale, SA 5452, ☎ (08) 8843 0003, Ⓕ (08) 8843 0096; est 1856; ❖ 150,000 cases; ❣; A$; Mon-Fri 8.30-5, wkds 11-4
Winemaking ceased at this marvellously historic winery in 1999, 143 years after it was built. It was an economically pragmatic decision by its brewery owner that both saddened and enraged the Clare Valley winemaking community. The excellent Annie's Lane range will henceforth be made in the Barossa Valley from Quelltaler Vineyard grapes.

Reillys Wines NR

Cnr Hill and Burra Streets, Mintaro, SA 5415, ☎ (08) 8843 9013, ⓕ (08) 8337 4111; est 1994; ❖ 5,000 cases; ⚑; A$; 7 days 10-5; ⚐; ⛨

Justin and Julie Ardill are new arrivals, with just a handful of vintages under their belt. An interesting sideline is the production of olive oil made from wild olive trees scattered around Mintaro.

Sevenhill Cellars ☆☆☆☆

College Road, Sevenhill via Clare, SA 5453, ☎ (08) 8843 4222, ⓕ (08) 8843 4382; est 1851; ❖ 24,000 cases; ⚑; A$; Mon-Fri 8.30-4.30, Sat & public hols 9-4

Sevenhill is one of the historical treasures of Australia, whose oft-photographed stone wine cellars are the oldest in the Clare Valley. Winemaking is still carried out under the direction of the Jesuitical Manresa Society, in particular by Brother John May. Quality is very good, particularly that of the powerful Shiraz, and all the wines reflect the character of the estate-grown old-vine grapes.

Skillogalee ☆☆☆☆

Off Hughes Park Road, Sevenhill via Clare, SA 5453, ☎ (08) 8843 4311, ⓕ (08) 8843 4343; est 1970; ❖ 7,000 cases; ⚑; A$; 7 days 10-5; ⚐

Owned by David and Diana Palmer since the late 1980s. The 30-year-old terraced hillside vines produce intensely rich, lime-juice Riesling, and opulently structured Shiraz (black cherry and mint) and Cabernet Sauvignon (blackberry and vanilla).

Stephen John Wines ☆☆☆

Government Road, Watervale, SA 5452, ☎ (08) 8843 0105, ⓕ (08) 8843 0105; est 1994; ❖ 4,000 cases; ⚑; A$; 7 days 11-5

The John family has been at the heart of winemaking (and barrel-making) in the Barossa and Clare Valleys for over 100 years. Former Quelltaler chief winemaker Stephen John (and wife Rita) now run a family business with the cellar door housed in an old converted stone stable.

Stringy Brae NR

Sawmill Road, Sevenhill, SA 5453, ☎ (08) 8843 4313, ⓕ (08) 8843 4313; est 1991; ❖ 1,800 cases; ⚑; A$; wkds & public hols 10-5 or by appt; ⛨

Donald and Sally Willson have established over eight hectares of vineyards, and since the 1996 vintage they have provided all the fruit for their wines; previously they sourced grapes from Langhorne Creek.

Taylors ☆☆☆

Taylors Road, Auburn, SA 5451, ☎ (08) 8849 2008, ⓕ (08) 8849 2240; est 1972; ❖ 250,000 cases; ⚑; A$; Mon-Fri 9-5, Sat & public hols 10-5, Sun 10-4

With 500 hectares of estate vineyards, this is by far the largest producer in the Clare Valley. After building a very successful

Tim Adams ☆☆☆☆
Warenda Road, Clare, SA 5453, ☎ (08) 8842 2429, Ⓕ (08) 8842 3550; est 1986; ❖ 15,000 cases; ⚲; A$; Mon-Fri 10.30-5, wkds 11-5
Former Leasingham winemaker Tim Adams runs a thriving contract winemaking business alongside that of his own wines. These are invariably full-bodied and full-flavoured, the Semillon often oaky but appealing, the reds (especially Aberfeldy Shiraz) crammed with ripe cherry, mulberry and plum fruit.

Tim Gramp ☆☆☆☆
Mintaro Road, Watervale, SA 5452, ☎ (08) 8431 3338, Ⓕ (08) 8431 3229; est 1990; ❖ 5,000 cases; ⚲; A$; wkds & hols 10.30-4.30
Tim Gramp has built a solid reputation and business, buying grapes from others in the Clare Valley and McLaren Vale. Watervale Riesling (powerful lemon/citrous and mineral) and McLaren Vale Shiraz (dark chocolate and black cherry) are best.

Waninga ☆☆☆☆
Hughes Park Road, Sevenhill via Clare, SA 5453, ☎ (08) 8843 4395, Ⓕ (08) 8843 4395; est 1989; ❖ 1,500 cases; ⚲; A$; 7 days 10-5; ⌂
The 25-year-old vineyards and skilled contract-making of part of the production results in a diverse portfolio. Skilly Hills Riesling and a richly layered Reserve Shiraz lead the way.

Wendouree ☆☆☆☆☆
Wendouree Road, Clare, SA 5453, ☎ (08) 8842 2896; est 1895; ❖ 2,500 cases; ⚲; A$; by appt
An 'iron fist in a velvet glove' is the best description for these extraordinary wines. They are fashioned with passion and yet precision from a very old vineyard, with a unique *terroir*, by Tony and Lita Brady, who rightly see themselves as custodians of a priceless treasure. The 100-year-old stone winery is virtually unchanged from the day it was built.

Wilson Vineyard ☆☆☆☆
Polish Hill River, Sevenhill via Clare, SA 5453, ☎ (08) 8843 4310; est 1974; ❖ 4,500 cases; ⚲; A$; May-Oct: wkds 10-4
Dr John Wilson is a tireless ambassador for the Clare Valley and for wine and its beneficial effect on health. When still in charge of winemaking the mantle has now passed to his son (Daniel) he created wines that could occasionally be idiosyncratic, but in recent years have been most impressive.

Adelaide Hills

Visitors to the Adelaide Hills, particularly in the autumn season, could be forgiven for thinking they were in England, with the blaze of orange, golden and red leaves on the exotic deciduous trees and the little towns and hamlets. Although only 30 minutes drive from the centre of Adelaide, the climate in the Hills is radically different. The 400- to 500-metre altitude is one of the principal factors, and often leads to a 10°C temperature differential at noon on a summer's day. Site selection (aspect, degree of slope, location) is critical. South, between Lenswood and Piccadilly, only Chardonnay and Pinot Noir can be relied upon to ripen fully, although Riesling and Sauvignon Blanc usually make racy, elegant wines. Shiraz and Cabernet have really only flourished in the north, on west-facing slopes, but some recent plantings of Shiraz in the south have resulted in striking Rhône-style wines.

The Adelaide Hills region is an ultra-sensitive water-catchment area for the city, and there are consequently exceptionally stringent controls on the building of wineries. As a result, there is much contract winemaking in shared facilities, which has aided rather than impaired wine quality. Petaluma and Glenara were the first and, for a long time the only wineries. Nepenthe is a recent arrival, investing considerable capital and high-tech, expensive waste-removal systems. Bridgewater Mill (of Petaluma) is a Mecca in a beautiful and easily accessible region.

Arranmore Vineyard NR
Rangeview Road, Carey Gully, SA 5144, ☎ (08) 8390 3034,
℻ (08) 8390 3034; est 1998; ❧ 120 cases; ♀; A$; by appt

One of the tiny operations that are appearing all over the beautiful Adelaide Hills. The two-hectare vineyard is planted with Pinot Noir, Chardonnay and Sauvignon Blanc, and the wines are basically sold through word of mouth and mail order.

Ashton Hills ☆☆☆☆½
Tregarthen Road, Ashton, SA 5137, ☎ (08) 8390 1243,
℻ (08) 8390 1243; est 1982; ❧ 1,750 cases; ♀; A$; wkds 11-5.30;
pottery sales

Stephen George is a modern-day Renaissance man. He seems to effortlessly produce fragrant lime-and-mineral Riesling, slow-developing Chardonnay and intense yet delicate Pinot Noir at this, his family-owned vineyard. He also makes the brooding, dark Wendouree Clare Valley red wines.

Barratt ☆☆☆☆☆
PO Box 204, Summertown, SA 5141, ☎ (08) 8390 1788,
℻ (08) 8390 1788; est 1993; ❧ 1,000 cases; ♀; A$; by appt;
small wine and food events

Lindsay and Carolyn Barratt own this excellent 5.2-hectare vineyard, which they share-farm with Jeffrey Grosset. Grosset takes part of the production, and makes the remainder for the Barratt label. Ultra-complex, burgundian-accented Chardonnay and heart-stopping silky, plummy Pinot Noir are the result.

Basket Range Wines NR
c/o PO Basket Range, SA 5138, ☎ (08) 9390 1515; est 1980;
❧ 500 cases; No visitors

The delightful and slightly eccentric Aboriginal rights lawyer Phillip Broderick makes 500 cases a year of a single Bordeaux blend, which is sold by word of mouth to his many friends.

Birdwood Estate ☆☆☆¼
Mannum Road, Birdwood, SA 5234, ☎ (08) 8263 0986,
Ⓕ (08) 8263 0986; est 1990; ❖ 700 cases; No visitors
Draws upon five hectares of estate vineyards progressively established since 1990. The quality of the Chardonnay and Riesling has impressed.

Bridgewater Mill ☆☆☆☆
Mount Barker Road, Bridgewater, SA 5155, ☎ (08) 8339 3422,
Ⓕ (08) 8339 5253; est 1986; ❖ 20,000 cases; ?; A$; Mon-Fri 9.30-5, wkds 10-5; ¶
Petaluma's second label, which sometimes lives in the shadow of its parent. Immaculately crafted Sauvignon Blanc, Chardonnay, Shiraz and Cabernet/Malbec. Good restaurant.

Chain of Ponds ☆☆☆☆¼
Adelaide Road, Gumeracha, SA 5233, ☎ (08) 8389 1415, Ⓕ (08) 8389 1877; est 1993; ❖ 8,000 cases; ?; A$; 7 days 10.30-4.30; ⌂
The largest grape-grower in the Adelaide Hills, owned by Caj and Genny Amadio. One hundred hectares of vineyards produce 1,000 tonnes of grapes a year; most is sold to Penfolds, some skilfully made for the Chain of Ponds label. It is hard to separate the Riesling, Sauvignon Blanc/Semillon blend, Semillon or Chardonnay: all are powerfully impressive.

Galah Wine ☆☆☆¼
Tregarthen Road, Ashton, SA 5137, ☎ (08) 8390 1243,
Ⓕ (08) 8390 1243; est 1986; ❖ 750 cases; wines available for sale at Ashton Hills
A *négociant*-type mail-order business owned and run by Stephen George, here wearing his third hat. Sturdy wines, as honest as the day is long, and always offering excellent value for money.

Geoff Hardy Wines ☆☆☆☆
c/o Pertaringa Wines, Cnr Hunt and Rifle Range Roads, McLaren Vale, SA 5171, ☎ (08) 8323 8125, Ⓕ (08) 8323 7766; est 1996; ❖ NA; ?; A$; Mon-Fri 10-4
Geoff Hardy is a member of the Hardy family who has gone his own way over the past two decades as an eminently successful viticulturist. He only recently elected to have wines made under his name, including an enticing, gently spicy Shiraz.

Geoff Weaver ☆☆☆☆☆
2 Gilpin Lane, Mitcham, SA 5062, ☎ (08) 8272 2105, Ⓕ (08) 8271 0177; est 1982; ❖ 5,000 cases; No visitors
Former Hardy chief winemaker Geoff Weaver established ten hectares of close-planted vineyards between 1992 and 1998. He now fastidiously crafts classic lime-and-mineral Riesling,

fragrant gooseberry/passion fruit Sauvignon Blanc and a truly classic, long-lived grapefruit, apple and melon Chardonnay. All are packaged with the most beautiful labels in Australia.

Glenara Wines ☆☆☆½

126 Range Road North, Upper Hermitage, SA 5131, ☏ (08) 8380 5056, Ⓕ (08) 8380 5056; est 1971; ❖ 6,000 cases; ❢; A$; Mon-Fri 11-5 (closed public hols)

A property owned by the Verrall family since 1924. Not as fashionable as some of its Hills neighbours, but Trevor Jones produces full-flavoured, sturdy, ageworthy Riesling and creditable full-bodied reds that reflect their warmer vineyard site.

Grove Hill NR

120 Old Norton Summit Road, Norton Summit, SA 5136, ☏ (08) 8390 1437, Ⓕ (08) 8390 1437; est 1978; ❖ 500 cases; ❢; A$; Sun 11-5

Grove Hill is situated on the site of a heritage property established in 1846 and held by the same family since that time. The original homestead and outbuildings remain. The wines from the three hectares of vineyards are made in the full-frontal (and unpredictable) style one expects from contract-maker Roman Bratasiuk, who is best-known as the owner/winemaker of Clarendon Hills (McLaren Vale).

Hillstowe ☆☆☆

104 Main Road, Hahndorf, SA 5245, ☏ (08) 8388 1400, Ⓕ (08) 8388 1411; est 1980; ❖ 12,000 cases; ❢; A$; 7 days 10-5; café

The urbane Chris Laurie is part of the Adelaide establishment. He and his family have carefully built the business, only recently moving into their own premises at Hahndorf, where they occupy glorious 150-year-old stone buildings. The wines are good, and likely to get better.

Leland Estate ☆☆☆☆

PO Lenswood, SA 5240, ☏ (08) 8389 6928, Ⓕ; est 1986; ❖ 1,000 cases; No visitors

Former Yalumba senior winemaker Robb Cootes, with a master of science degree, deliberately opted out of mainstream life when he established Leland Estate. He lives in a split-level, one-roomed house built from timber salvaged from trees killed in the Ash Wednesday bushfires. Sauvignon Blanc is usually superb.

Lenswood Vineyards ☆☆☆☆

3 Cyril John Court, Athelstone, SA 5076, ☏ (08) 8389 8111, Ⓕ (08) 8389 8555; est 1981; ❖ 10,000 cases; No visitors

This is Tim Knappstein's third viticultural venture. Together with wife Annie, he now makes wines drawn only from the 25.5-hectare vineyard they own at Lenswood. Complex, richly flavoured, barrel-fermented Chardonnay, intense Sauvignon Blanc and Semillon, and broodingly powerful Pinot Noir are all excellent wines.

Malcolm Creek ☆☆☆⋆

Bonython Road, Kersbrook, SA 5231, ☎ (08) 8389 3235,
Ⓕ (08) 8389 3235; est 1982; ❖ 650 cases; ♈; A$; wkds, public hols
11-5; gardens

This is the low-profile retirement venture of Reg Tolley. Wines are invariably well made and age gracefully; worth seeking out.

Mawson Ridge NR

24-28 Main Road, Hahndorf, SA 5066, ☎ (08) 8362 7826,
Ⓕ (08) 8362 5240; est 1998; ❖ 200 cases; ♈; A$; by appt

The Marins have their 3.5 hectares of Chardonnay, Sauvignon Blanc and Pinot Noir contract-made at Nepenthe Vineyards.

Millers Samphire NR

Watts Gully Road, Cnr Robertson Road, Kersbrook, SA 5231,
☎ (08) 8389 3183; est 1982; ❖ 130 cases; ♈; A$; 7 days 9-6
by appt; pottery studio

Tom Miller has an interesting and diverse winemaking CV. His Riesling is a highly flavoured wine, with crushed herb-and-lime aromas and flavours.

Nepenthe Vineyards ☆☆☆☆⋆

Vickers Road, Lenswood, SA 5240, ☎ (08) 8389 8039, Ⓕ (08) 8389
8019; est 1994; ❖ 12,000 cases; ♈; A$; by appt

The Tweddell family managed to obtain rare approval to build a 500-tonne state-of-the-art winery to accompany their 25 hectares of vineyards in the ultra-sensitive Adelaide Hills water-catchment area. Winemaker Peter Leske produces some real winners: highly sophisticated oaked and unoaked wines.

Paracombe Wines ☆☆☆☆

Main Road, Paracombe, SA 5132, ☎ (08) 8380 5058, Ⓕ (03) 8380
5488; est 1983; ❖ 1,500 cases; No visitors

The 13-hectare vineyard of the Drogenmuller family has been progressively established since 1983. Much of the production is sold, but limited amounts of crisp Sauvignon Blanc, spicy/berry Shiraz/Cabernet and fragrant, sweetly minty Cabernet Franc are contract-made at Petaluma.

Perrini Estate NR

Bower Road, Meadows, SA 5201, ☎ (08) 8388 3210, Ⓕ (08) 8388
3210; est 1997; ❖ NA; ♈; A$; Wed-Sun & public hols 10-5

For Tony and Connie Perrini, their farm began as a weekend hobby; they then added a few vines, just for fun, for home winemaking. Now they have now six hectares of vineyard, replete with winery and cellar door.

Petaluma ☆☆☆☆☆

Spring Gully Road, Piccadilly, SA 5151, ☎ (08) 8339 4122,
Ⓕ (08) 8339 5253; est 1976; ❖ 30,000 cases; (see Bridgewater Mill)

Universally recognised as one of Australia's finest wineries, founded and driven by the fearsome intellect and boundless energy of Brian Croser. Adelaide Hills Chardonnay and traditional method Croser, Clare Valley Riesling and Coonawarra Cabernet/Merlot are all still hand-crafted by Croser, who does not number delegation among his many strengths.

Pibbin NR
Greenhill Road, Balhannah, SA 5242, ☏ (08) 8388 4794, ⓕ (08) 8398 0015; est 1991; ❦ 1,500 cases; ₸; A$; wkds 11-5.30
Roger and Lindy Salkeld produce White Pinot, Sparkling Pinot and Pinot Noir from their 2.5-hectare vineyard. The Pinot Noir is as dense and powerful as it is idiosyncratic.

Piccadilly Fields NR
185 Piccadilly Road, Piccadilly, SA 5151, ☏ (08) 8272 2239, ⓕ (08) 8232 5395; est 1989; ❦ 3,000 cases; No visitors
The 36-hectare vineyard owned by Sam Virgara is one of Petaluma's most important contract grape-growers. Two wines are released under the Piccadilly Fields label: a delicate, Chablis-like Chardonnay and a Merlot-dominant Bordeaux blend.

Ravenswood Lane Vineyard NR
Ravenswood Lane, Hahndorf, SA 5245, ☏ (08) 8388 1250, ⓕ (08) 8388 7233; est 1993; ❦ 1,500 cases; No visitors
Primarily a grape grower for BRL Hardy, which contract-makes a small quantity of the wine for owners John and Helen Edwards. Very stylish Chardonnay and brilliant spicy/peppery/cherryish Shiraz mark this as a special vineyard site.

Salem Bridge Wines NR
Salem Bridge Road, Lower Hermitage, SA 5131, ☏ (08) 8380 5240, ⓕ (08) 8380 5240; est 1989; ❦ NFP; No visitors
Barry Miller acquired the 45-hectare Salem Bridge property in 1989. Since then, 15 hectares have been planted with Cabernet Sauvignon, Shiraz and Merlot. A Shiraz and Cabernet Sauvignon release is in the pipeline, made off-site by contract-winemaking with input from Barry Miller.

Shaw & Smith ☆☆☆☆☆
PO Box 172, Stirling, SA 5152, ☏ (08) 8370 9911, ⓕ (08) 8370 9339; est 1989; ❦ 25,000 cases; No visitors
Martin Shaw, one of the pioneering Australian flying winemakers, and Michael Hill-Smith, Australia's first MW, make a formidable team. Immaculate Sauvignon Blanc and subtle yet powerful and textured Reserve Chardonnay are the great wines; the Unwooded Chardonnay is just that.

Talunga NR
Adelaide to Mannum Road, (PO Box 134) Gumeracha, SA 5233, ☏ (08) 8389 1222, ⓕ (08) 8389 1233; est 1994; ❦ 2,000 cases; ₸; A$; Wed-Sun & public hols 10.30-5; ❖; café
Talunga owners Vince and Tina Scaffidi are among the largest contract grape-growers in the Adelaide Hills. They operate the

Gumeracha Vineyards, planted in 165 hectares. A small part of their output is vinified under the Talunga label.

Whisson Lake NR
PO Box 91, Uraidla, SA 5142, ☏ (08) 8390 1303, ℻ (08) 8390 3822; est 1985; ❖ 300 cases; ♀; A$; by appt; wine appreciation courses

Mark Whisson is primarily a grape-grower, with 4.5 hectares of close planted vines on a steep-sloped, north-facing vineyard. A small quantity of the production is made for the Whisson Lake label by Roman Bratasiuk.

Adelaide Plains

This is one of the least appealing and most infrequently visited regions in Australia. It is laser-flat, searingly hot in summer, and not far to the east of the blue-collar industrial suburb of Elizabeth. However, with irrigation the region becomes an efficient grape producer. The very dry summer weather reduces the incidence of disease to the point where protective sprays are rarely needed; yields are high, and good sugar levels are routinely reached. Most of the production disappears into the anonymity of wine casks. The largest winery is called Barossa Valley Estate, and indeed acquires almost all of its grapes from the Barossa Valley. The most distinguished is Primo Estate.

Barossa Valley Estate ☆☆☆ⅰ
Heaslip Road, Angle Vale, SA 5117, ☏ (08) 8284 7000, ℻ (08) 8284 7219; est 1984; ❖ 60,000 cases; Mon-Fri 9-5, Sat 10-5

A substantial cooperative, and one of the few remaining, with close links to BRL Hardy. The E&E Black Pepper Shiraz and Ebenezer range (Chardonnay, Shiraz and Cabernet blend) are richly oaky flagships.

Primo Estate ☆☆☆☆☆
Old Port Wakefield Road, Virginia, SA 5120, ☏ (08) 8380 9442, ℻ (08) 8380 9696; est 1979; ❖ 20,000 cases; ♀; A$; June-Sept Mon-Fri 9-5, Sat & hols 10-4.30

Joe Grilli is little short of a magician, producing Colombard that tastes like a zesty young Sauvignon Blanc, an elegant Shiraz that utterly belies the hot growing conditions of this region, and a masterly Amarone-influenced Cabernet/Merlot made from partially dried Coonawarra and McLaren Vale grapes.

Coonawarra

The battle over the delineation of the borders of Coonawarra, brought about by the GI legislation, has continued unabated for almost five years. This is testament to the importance of the region and how valuable the name 'Coonawarra' is perceived to be. The uniform climate and flat terrain are relatively unimportant aspects. The battle rages over soil differentiation between the contested and uncontested areas. Coonawarra has three soil types. First and foremost is the prized *terra rossa*, on which the best vineyards are planted – a friable red soil (oxidised iron-stained limestone) between 100–500 cm deep, on a soft limestone base. The western side of the region has over-fertile black clays over limestone, prone to waterlogging, and on the eastern side you find duplex sandy soils over a clay base.

The problem is that the red soils do not fall exclusively within any proposed boundary. Fingers of red extrude outwards from the central cigar-shaped area (approx 15 km long) and also appear as isolated patches. The dispute is regrettable, because it distracts attention from what Coonawarra is all about: a region superbly suited to Cabernet Sauvignon (most spectacularly), Shiraz and Merlot. It is also ironic, because if ever one of Australia's wine regions deserved recognition under the GI, it's Coonawarra.

Balnaves of Coonawarra ☆☆☆☆✓
Riddoch Highway, Coonawarra, SA 5263, ☎ (08) 8737 2946, Ⓕ (08) 8737 2945; est 1975; ❖ 10,000 cases; ♀; A$; Mon-Fri 9-5, wkds 10-5
Viticultural consultant-cum-grape grower Doug Balnaves built his striking 300-tonne winery in 1996. Under the direction of former Wynns winemaker Peter Bissell, both the concentration and flavour of the wines have risen markedly: Chardonnay, Shiraz and Cabernet all shine.

Bowen Estate ☆☆☆☆✓
Riddoch Highway, Coonawarra, SA 5263, ☎ (08) 8737 2229, Ⓕ (08) 8737 2173; est 1972; ❖ 11,000 cases; ♀; A$; 7 days 10-5
The ruddy cheeks and ready smile of Doug Bowen match the temperament and visage of his golden Labrador and the generous, welcoming style of his wines. He favours late-picking, producing wonderfully rich wines in intermediate vintages where others seem to struggle.

Brand's of Coonawarra ☆☆☆☆
Main Road, Coonawarra, SA 5263, ☎ (08) 8736 3260, Ⓕ (08) 8736 3208; est 1965; ❖ NFP; ♀; A$; Mon-Fri 9-4.30, wkds 10-4
Now fully owned by McWilliam's, but with continued Brand family involvement, Brand's still seems to struggle in its efforts to attain a clear identity. The wines are never bad – sometimes very good – but never great enough to get the pulse racing.

Highbank NR
Main Penola-Naracoorte Road, Coonawarra, SA 5263, ☎ (08) 8736 3311, Ⓕ; est 1986; ❖ 4,000 cases; ♀; A$; by appt; ⛺
The shadowy label of Dennis Vice, a viticultural lecturer who owns a four-hectare vineyard. He sells most of the grapes, but with close friend Trevor Mast makes small quantities of stylish Chardonnay and a Cabernet blend to sell at the cellar door.

Hollick ☆☆☆☆✓
Riddoch Highway, Coonawarra, SA 5263, ☎ (08) 8737 2318, Ⓕ (08) 8737 2952; est 1983; ❖ 25,000 cases; ♀; A$; 7 days 9-5

Ian Hollick has been the winner of many wine trophies (including the most famous of all, the Jimmy Watson). His wines are well crafted and competitively priced, although sometimes a little on the light side these days.

Katnook Estate ☆☆☆☆☆
Riddoch Highway, Coonawarra, SA 5263, ☎ (08) 8737 2394, Ⓕ (08) 8737 2397; est 1979; ❖ 70,000 cases; Ⓨ; A$; Mon-Fri 9-4.30, wkds 10-4.30

Arguably more important as the largest contract grape-grower in Coonawarra than as a winemaker, but Katnook is going from strength to strength in the latter guise. Fragrant, Germanic-styled Riesling, long-lived, elegantly tangy Chardonnay, crisp Sauvignon Blanc, berryish, cedary Merlot, subtly oaked, cassis-driven Cabernet Sauvignon and the intense flagship Odyssey (a Reserve Cabernet) are all impressive.

Ladbroke Grove NR
Coonawarra Road, Penola, SA 5277, ☎ (08) 8737 2082, Ⓕ (08) 8762 3236; est 1982; ❖ 800 cases; Ⓨ; A$; 7 days 10-4

Has reappeared (in a small way) after a hiatus, making a Shiraz from a 2-hectare site planted by John Redman in the 1960s, and a Riesling. All sold cellar door and locally.

Leconfield ☆☆☆☆⯪
Penola Road, Coonawarra, SA 5263, ☎ (08) 8737 2326, Ⓕ (08) 8737 2285; est 1974; ❖ 17,000 cases; Ⓨ; A$; 7 days 10-5

A distinguished estate with a proud, even if relatively short, history. Long renowned for its Cabernet Sauvignon, its repertoire has steadily grown with the emphasis on single-varietal wines. The overall style is fruit- rather than oak-driven.

Lindemans (Coonawarra) ☆☆☆☆
Main Penola-Naracoorte Road, Coonawarra, SA 5263, ☎ (08) 8736 2613, Ⓕ (08) 8736 2959; est 1908; ❖ 15,000 cases; Ⓨ; A$; 7 days 10-5

Part of the Southcorp group, and one of the major brands in Coonawarra. Its trio of St George Vineyard Cabernet Sauvignon, Limestone Ridge Shiraz/Cabernet and Pyrus (a Cabernet-dominant Bordeaux blend) routinely amass gold and silver medals; they all have elegant fruit, obvious oak and soft, silky tannins in a user-friendly style.

Majella ☆☆☆☆
Lynn Road, Coonawarra, SA 5263, ☎ (08) 8736 3055, Ⓕ (08) 8736 3057; est 1969; ❖ 6,000 cases; Ⓨ; A$; 7 days 10-4.30

Brian (the Prof) Lynn was a highly successful grape-grower before deciding he would keep part of the production from his 47-hectare vineyard to make a Shiraz and Cabernet Sauvignon. He subsequently released a super-premium red called The Mallea, well worth the A$50-plus a bottle it fetches on the domestic market.

Mildara (Coonawarra) ☆☆☆✩
Penola-Naracoorte Road, Coonawarra, SA 5263, ☏ (08) 8736 3380, Ⓕ (08) 8736 3307; est 1955; ❖ 90,000 cases; ♀; A$; Mon-Fri 9-4.30, wkds 10-4

When it planted vines in 1955, Mildara was one of the first companies to proclaim its faith in Coonawarra since the turn of the century, going on to create a Cabernet Sauvignon (nicknamed Peppermint Pattie) in 1963 of legendary quality. Now, however, it seems Mildara is content with cash-cow brands such as Jamieson's Run and Robertson's Well.

Parker Coonawarra Estate ☆☆☆☆
Penola Road, Coonawarra, SA 5263, ☏ (02) 9357 3376, Ⓕ (02) 9358 1517; est 1985; ❖ 4,000 cases; No visitors

There are those, myself included, who regard the brand-name Parker Coonawarra Estate First Growth Cabernet Sauvignon as impossibly pretentious. However, I have to admit the wine can be very good, particularly when the Parkeresque 'gobfuls' of oak (no connection with Robert Parker) are toned down.

Penley Estate ☆☆☆☆☆
McLeans Road, Coonawarra, SA 5263, ☏ (08) 8231 2400, Ⓕ (08) 8231 0589; est 1988; ❖ 20,000 cases; ♀; A$; by appt

Kym Tolley was bred in the vinous 'purple', via the Penfold and Tolley families, but spent 17 years making wine for others before establishing Penley Estate (get it?). Now ranks as one of Coonawarra's finest estates, producing a succession of rich, complex, full-bodied red wines and stylish Chardonnay from the pick of 81 hectares of vines.

Punters Corner ☆☆☆☆
Cnr Riddoch Highway and Racecourse Road, Coonawarra, SA 5263, ☏ (08) 8737 2007, Ⓕ (08) 8737 2007; est 1988; ❖ 10,000 cases; ♀; A$; 7 days 10-5

Started life as James Haselgrove in 1975, and was acquired in 1992 by a group of investors with a sense of humour. Innovative packaging and the skills of contract winemaker Peter Bissell (at Balnaves) have turned this into a past-the-post favourite.

Redman ☆☆☆
Riddoch Highway, Coonawarra, SA 5253, ☏ (08) 8736 3331, Ⓕ (08) 8736 3013; est 1966; ❖ 18,000 cases; ♀; A$; Mon-Fri 9-5, wkds 10-4

I am really lost for words and don't know what to say about this chronic underperformer. Bruce and Malcolm Redman are very nice people, but they ought to be producing some of the most – not least – memorable Coonawarra reds.

Rouge Homme ☆☆☆✩
Riddoch Highway, Coonawarra, SA 5263, ☏ (08) 8736 3205, Ⓕ (08) 8736 3250; est 1954; ❖ 64,000 cases; ♀; A$; 7 days 10-5

What I have long described as the warrior brand for Lindemans, which acquired the winery in 1963 from Owen Redman. Subsequent repositioning has put it in a highly competitive ruck, but winemaker Paul Gordon cares deeply about his wines, and often makes underpriced gems.

Rymill ☆☆☆⌿
The Riddoch Run Vineyards, Coonawarra, SA 5263, ☏ (08) 8736 5001, Ⓕ (08) 8736 5040; est 1970; ⚘ 50,000 cases; ⚑; A$; 7 days 10-5; ⚐

The Rymills are descendants of John Riddoch, founding father of the region, and have long owned some of the finest Coonawarra soil, on which they have grown grapes since 1970. Present plantings cover 140 hectares. A handsome winery was built in 1991, marking a major entry into winemaking, with the best yet to come.

S Kidman Wines ☆☆☆
Riddoch Highway, Coonawarra, SA 5263, ☏ (08) 8736 5071, Ⓕ (08) 8736 5070; est 1984; ⚘ 7,000 cases; ⚑; A$; 7 days 9-5

Sid Kidman is one of the district pioneers with a fully mature 16-hectare estate vineyard. Quality has been decidedly variable; quite why I am not sure.

St Mary's NR
V & A Lane, via Coonawarra, SA 5277, ☏ (08) 8736 6070, Ⓕ (08) 8736 6045; est 1986; ⚘ 4,000 cases; 7 days 10-4

St Mary's is almost certain to fall outside the boundary of Coonawarra when this is finally determined. The vineyards, but not the brand, are partly owned by Tyrrell's.

The Blok Estate NR
Riddoch Highway, Coonawarra, SA 5263, ☏ (08) 8737 2734, Ⓕ (08) 8737 2994; est 1999; ⚘ 1,200 cases; ⚑; A$; 7 days 10-4

Di and John Blok have owned a tiny vineyard planted to Cabernet Sauvignon since 1993; the Cabernet is now released under their own label, supplemented by contract-grown grapes. The cellar door is in a renovated old stone house surrounded by newly landscaped gardens.

Wetherall NR
Naracoorte Road, Coonawarra, SA 5263, ☏ (08) 8737 2104, Ⓕ (08) 8737 2105; est 1991; ⚘ 3,000 cases; ⚑; A$; 7 days 10-4; ⎮⚉

The Wetherall family has been growing grapes for over 30 years. Son Michael's graduation from Roseworthy Agricultural College led to a limited venture into winemaking with Chardonnay, Shiraz and Cabernet Sauvignon.

Wynns Coonawarra Estate ☆☆☆☆☆ V
Memorial Drive, Coonawarra, SA 5263, ☏ (08) 8736 3266, Ⓕ (08) 8736 3202; est 1891; ⚘ NFP; ⚑; A$; 7 days 10-5

The most important winery in Coonawarra and surely its best. Part of Southcorp, its two flagships are the awesomely rich and concentrated John Riddoch Cabernet and Michael Shiraz (approach with extreme caution when less than ten years old). Supported by a spread of perfectly-crafted wines comprising a floral, crisp Riesling and subtle barrel-fermented Chardonnay (both ludicrously cheap), Shiraz, Cabernet/Shiraz/Merlot blend and Cabernet Sauvignon (great value).

Zema Estate ☆☆☆☆⊹ V
Riddoch Highway, Coonawarra, SA 5263, ☎ (08) 8736 3219, ℻ (08) 8736 3280; est 1982; ❧ 10,000 cases; ❢; A$; 7 days 9-5
One of the last outposts of hand-pruning and hand-picking in Coonawarra; winemaking practices are straightforward. If ever there were an example of great wines being made in the vineyard, this is it. Beautifully proportioned, fruit-driven Shiraz and Cabernet Sauvignon stand out.

Padthaway

Once called Keppoch, this region shares a number of things in common with Coonawarra, not least its unremarkable topography and relative isolation. It has similar patches of *terra rossa* soil, although not so restricted or regular in its distribution, and it also has underground water for irrigation and spring frost control. Its points of difference are the somewhat warmer climate, and the gentle undulations of the land, which are associated with significant changes in soil type. The suitability of the best soil was recognised by government studies back in 1944, but it was not until 1963 that Seppelt acquired land for planting. It was followed by BRL Hardy and Lindemans in 1968.

It has since become startlingly clear that, properly managed, Padthaway is capable of far, far more. The last five to ten years has seen the region gain a reputation as one of Australia's premium white wine regions. That said, it produces outstanding wines across the full spectrum, from Riesling, Sauvignon Blanc and Chardonnay to Shiraz, Merlot and Cabernet Sauvignon. Tangy Chardonnay and succulent, dark-hued Shiraz are the best.

Browns of Padthaway ☆☆⊹
Keith Road, Padthaway, SA 5271, ☎ (08) 8765 6063, ℻ (08) 8765 6083; est 1993; ❧ 35,000 cases; ❢; A$; at Padthaway Estate
The Brown family is the largest independent grape grower in a region dominated by the major Australian wine companies. The contract-made wines are light in body and flavour, but the new Myra Family Reserve Cabernet shows a quantum leap in quality.

Hardys (Padthaway) ☆☆☆☆⊹ V
Stonehaven Winery, Riddoch Highway, Padthaway, SA 5271, ☎ (08) 8765 6140, ℻ (08) 8765 6137; est 1998; ❧ NFP; No visitors
Hardy's A$18 million Stonehaven Winery opened in March 1998, the largest single winery to be built in the previous 20 years. Padthaway fruit has been an important contributor to the Eileen Hardy Chardonnay and Shiraz flagships, as well as a range of good, regionally-branded varietal wines.

Lindemans (Padthaway) ☆☆☆☆½
Naracoorte Road, Padthaway, SA 5271, ☏ (08) 8765 5155,
℻ (08) 8765 5073; est 1908; ❧ 68,000 cases; No visitors
Although the wines are made at Coonawarra, Lindemans Padthaway is an important range of regionally-branded varietal wines. The generously flavoured and oaked Chardonnay and Winemaker's Reserve Chardonnay enjoy spectacular wine show success at the highest level. Both age well over three to five years.

Orlando (Padthaway) ☆☆☆☆½
c/o Barossa Valley Way, Rowland Flat, SA 5352, ☏ (08) 8521 3111, ℻ (08) 8521 3100; est NA; ❧ NFP; No visitors
Again, the wine is made elsewhere. Lawson's Shiraz is one of two super-premium wines in the Orlando portfolio, consistently excellent, with lashings of plum/cherry/berry fruit and vanilla oak neatly whipped together. The tangy grapefruit-accented St Hilary Chardonnay is also ultra-reliable and stylish.

Padthaway Estate ☆☆☆½
Keith-Naracoorte Road, Padthaway, SA 5271, ☏ (08) 8765 5039, ℻ (08) 8765 5097; est 1980; ❧ 6,000 cases; ⚑; A$; 7 days 10-4.30
Established in a gracious old stone wool shed, this was until 1998 the only resident winery (specialising in sparkling wines). In common ownership with a Relais et Chateaux Homestead, it also offers luxurious accommodation, fine food, and a tasting centre for regional wines.

Mount Benson and Robe

Neither of these two adjoining regions can claim a viticultural history reaching back further than 1989. What they do have is their own Geographic Indication registration. This if nothing else proves that the requirement of distinctiveness is at best an elastic one. Both regions have undulating countryside (Mount Benson is a complete misnomer, incidentally) and *terra rossa* over limestone interspersed with siliceous sands on the ridges and hillside slopes.

Given the proximity of the ocean (and numerous large, shallow lakes) it is hard to imagine that frost poses a threat, but it can do so. In fact, these two regions are by far the coolest in the Limestone Coast Zone (whch also includes Coonawarra and Padthaway), and are most likely to produce better white wines than reds, unless your aim is fragrant, peppery/spicy Shiraz or leafy/minty Cabernet/Merlot. In the longer term, yield may prove the most important factor, as the potential is unquestionably there. The driving force in the establishment of Robe has been Southcorp, which now has 150 hectares planted. Over in Mount Benson, M Chapoutier & Co (of Rhône Valley fame) moved in in 1998 to produce wines for the Asian market. These are early days, but they may prove very interesting ones.

Cape Jaffa Wines NR
Limestone Coast Road, Cape Jaffa, SA 5276, ☏ (08) 8768 5053,
℻ (08) 8768 5040; est 1993; ❧ 5,000 cases; ⚑; A$; 7 days 10-5

The Hooper and Fowler families have built the first winery at Mount Benson, constructed from local paddock rock. The joint-venture includes plans to ultimately expand to 1,000 tonnes (70,000 cases), using fruit from their 20-hectare estate. The initial releases have been made from a mixture of local and McLaren Vale grapes.

Wrattonbully

Another region in the Limestone Coast Zone chosen for viticulture because of its abundance of *terra rossa* soil and the ample non-saline underground water. After a slow start in the 1970s, the region has developed dramatically. BRL Hardy, Mildara Blass and Yalumba have been in the vanguard of the vineyard growth, and are responsible for a significant part of the 1,000-plus hectares so far planted. Its climate is poised between neighbours Coonawarra and Padthaway, warmer than the former and cooler than the latter, although there is surprising variation across what is a basically flat region. The bottom line, as it were, is a temperate region ideally suited to the production of medium- to full-bodied wines based primarily on Cabernet, Merlot and Shiraz.

Heathfield Ridge Wines NR
Cnr Caves Road and Penola Highway, Naracoorte, SA 5271,
☎ *(08) 8762 4133,* ℉ *(08) 8762 0141; est 1998;* ❦ *20,000 cases;*
♀*; A$; by appt*
Built just prior to the 1998 vintage, its primary purpose is as a contract winemaking facility for others. Wines will also be released under the Heathfield Ridge label.

Koppamurra ☆☆☆ V
Joanna via Naracoorte, SA 5271, ☎ *(08) 8271 4127,* ℉ *(08) 8271 0726; est 1973;* ❦ *2,500 cases;* ♀*; A$; by appt*
John Greenshield's Koppamurra winery has been at the centre of the storm over the name of the region. Politics to one side, the wines are well priced, with Merlot and Merlot blends the winery specialities.

Mount Gambier

Mount Gambier's principal tourist attraction is its vivid blue lake in the crater of an extinct volcano. Vines were planted here back in 1982 by Sandy and Helen Haig, and there are now five grape-growers in the region. The coolest of all the Limestone Coast Zone regions, Mount Gambier lies 50 km south of Coonawarra. However, it does not seem likely it will become a significant producer in terms of volume.

Haig NR
Square Mile Road, Mount Gambier, SA 5290, ☎ *(08) 8725 5414,*
℉ *(08) 8725 0252; est 1982;* ❦ *500 cases;* ♀*; A$; 7 days 11-5*
The four hectares of estate vineyards are planted on the rich volcanic soils near the slopes of the famous Blue Lake. The wines are made at Katnook Estate.

Winters Vineyard NR
Clarke Road, O.B. Flat via Mount Gambier, SA 5290, ☎ (08) 8726 8255, Ⓕ (08) 8726 8255; est 1988; ❖ 500 cases; ⚑; A$; 7 days 10-5
Former restaurateurs Martin and Merrilee Winter have established eight hectares of vineyards; the wines are contract-made. A light, leafy but pleasant cedary Cabernet Sauvignon attests to the cool climate.

McLaren Vale

The development of viticulture in the the Southern Vales, an area stretching from Reynella to McLaren Vale to Langhorne Creek, was due almost exclusively to the efforts of three Englishmen, John Reynell, Thomas Hardy and Dr AC Kelly, with a lesser contribution from George Manning at Hope Farm. John Reynell laid the foundations for Chateau Reynella in 1838. As in the Clare Valley, the fertility of the soil was soon exhausted, and by the mid-1870s the once-thriving township of McLaren Vale was all but deserted. Thanks to the success of Thomas Hardy, by 1903 the 19 wineries in the region were producing over 3,000,000 litres of wine. Much of it was deeply coloured, high-alcohol, tannic, dry red exported to the UK. The Emu Wine Company continued this business until well into the 1950s, before being acquired by Thomas Hardy (now BRL Hardy).

At the height of the white wine boom, it became apparent that McLaren Vale could produce excellent Chardonnay, and good Sauvignon Blanc and Semillon. This discovery temporarily diverted attention from the outstanding quality of its old-vine Shiraz and Grenache, and its more than useful Cabernet. It is clear there is enough maritime influence to invest the red wines with elegance, yet sufficient warmth to guarantee a lush, velvety texture and a recurrent taste theme of fine, dark chocolate.

Over all, McLaren Vale is vying with Coonawarra and the Clare Valley to be South Australia's best red wine region (with profuse apologies to the Barossa Valley).

Aldinga Bay Winery NR
Main South Road, Aldinga, SA 5173, ☎ (08) 8556 3179, Ⓕ (08) 8556 3350; est 1979; ❖ 5,000 cases; ⚑; A$; 7 days 10-5
Nick Giralamo took over the family business after graduating from Roseworthy Agricultural College, changing the name (previously Donolga Winery) but not the enticing prices. Almost all sales direct through cellar door.

Andrew Garrett ☆☆☆☆
Kangarilla Road, McLaren Vale, SA 5171, ☎ (08) 8323 8853, Ⓕ (08) 8323 8271; est 1983; ❖ 20,000 cases; ⚑; A$; 7 days 10-4; ⌂, ⎊; conference centre
This estate bears the name of its founder, who has long since moved on. It is now a brand in the Mildara Blass empire, but thanks to the skill of winemaker Phillip Reschke produces luscious, peachy Chardonnay and scented cherryish, vanilla Shiraz with impressive regularity.

Andrew Garrett Vineyard Estates ☆☆☆⁄

*McLarens on the Lake, Kangarilla Road, McLaren Vale, SA 5171,
☎ (08) 8323 8911, ℱ (08) 8323 9010; est 1986; ❖ NA; ☯; A$; 7 days 10-5; ⚫⚫; ⇌*

Part of the personal wine business of the Andrew Garrett family, producing bright and cheerful wines designed to be quaffed without thought. Premium wines come under the Springwood Park (Adelaide Hills) and Yarra Glen (Yarra Valley) labels.

Beresford Wines ☆☆☆

*49 Fraser Avenue, Happy Valley, SA 5159, ☎ (08) 8322 3611,
ℱ (08) 8322 3610; est 1985; ❖ 158,000 cases; ☯; A$; Mon-Fri 9-5, wkds 11-5*

The flagship of a large family of labels: first the Saint (St) range, then Highwood, next Katherine Hills, and lastly Beresford. All span the major varieties, all are primarily directed at export markets, and all are cheap.

Blewitt Springs Winery ☆☆☆☆⁄

*12 Victoria Avenue, Woodcroft, SA 5162, ☎ (08) 8322 0210,
ℱ (08) 8322 0210; est 1987; ❖ 4,000 cases; No visitors*

Produces strongly flavoured and oaked wines in the bold style that gained Australian wine a reputation as exports soared in the latter part of the 1980s.

Brewery Hill Winery NR

Olivers Road, McLaren Vale, SA 5171, ☎ (08) 8323 7344, ℱ (08) 8323 7355; est 1869; ❖ 12,000 cases; ☯; A$; Mon-Fri 9-5, wkds 10-5

A change of name for the former St Francis Winery and a new address at the former Manning Park Winery. A case of Titanic deck chairs for an efficient *négociant* business.

Cascabel ☆☆☆⁄

Rogers Road, Willunga, SA 5172, ☎ (08) 8557 4434, ℱ (08) 8557 4435; est 1998; ❖ 2,000 cases; ☯; A$; by appt

Proprietors Susana Fernandez and Duncan Ferguson, although young, have made wine in seven countries. The ultimate aim here is to produce red wines with a mix of Rhône Valley and Rioja influences, using estate-grown Tempranillo, Graciano, Monastrel, Grenache, Shiraz and Viognier.

Chapel Hill ☆☆☆☆

*Chapel Hill Road, McLaren Vale, SA 5171, ☎ (08) 8323 8429,
ℱ (08) 8323 9245; est 1979; ❖ 45,000 cases; ☯; A$; 7 days 12-5*

One of the fast rising stars of the 1990s, thanks in part to the financial strength of its owner, the Gerrard family, and the winemaking skills of consultant winemaker Pam Dunsford. Consistently polished Chardonnay, Shiraz and Cabernet.

Clarendon Hills Winery ☆☆☆☆⁄

*Brookmans Road, Blewitt Springs, SA 5171, ☎ (08) 8364 1484,
ℱ (08) 8364 1484; est 1989; ❖ 10,000 cases; ☯; A$; by appt*

Roman Bratasiuk is a larger-than-life figure who makes larger-than-life wines: immense, brooding reds from small patches of old, low-yielding vines. He has a more than receptive audience with Robert Parker, the hugely influential US wine writer.

Coriole ☆☆☆☆ʲ
Chaffeys Road, McLaren Vale, SA 5171, ☏ (08) 8323 8305, ℻ (08) 8323 9136; est 1967; ❖ 30,000 cases; ♀; A$; Mon-Fri 10-5, wkds 11-5; olive oils and vineyards

Coriole neatly balances the traditional virtues of Shiraz (Lloyd Reserve from 65-year-old vines at the pinnacle) and the trendy appeal of Sangiovese. Also offers impeccable fragrant, lemony Semillon and luscious blackberry-and-plum Grenache Shiraz.

Curtis NR
Foggo Road, McLaren Vale, SA 5171, ☏ (08) 8323 8389; est 1988; ❖ 1,500 cases; ♀; A$; wkds 11-4.30

A small and relatively new producer in McLaren Vale, making wines with old-fashioned names at ludicrously low prices.

D'Arenberg ☆☆☆☆☆
Osborn Road, McLaren Vale, SA 5171, ☏ (08) 8323 8206, ℻ (08) 8323 8423; est 1912; ❖ 120,000 cases; ♀; A$; 7 days 10-5; ⓘ

The garrulous labels (front and back) should not deceive or distract you. This historic winery is doing everything right these days, with a dazzling array of richly robed reds, primarily based on Shiraz and Grenache, that exude berry, dark chocolate and balanced oak flavours.

Dennis ☆☆☆
Kangarilla Road, McLaren Vale, SA 5171, ☏ (08) 8323 8665, ℻ (08) 8323 9121; est 1970; ❖ 10,000 cases; ♀; A$; Mon-Fri 10-5, wkds & hols 11-5

Peter Dennis runs a low-profile but quite substantial winery offering a mainstream selection of wine styles, with peachy/buttery Chardonnay most frequently catching the eye.

Dowie Doole ☆☆☆☆ʲ
182 Main Road, McLaren Vale, SA 5171, ☏ (08) 8323 7314, ℻ (08) 8323 7305; est 1996; ❖ 3,500 cases; No visitors

McLaren Vale grape-growers Drew Dowie (an architect) and Norm Doole (former international banker) have 40 hectares of vines. They sell most, but have three imaginatively packaged white wines (Chenin Blanc, Semillon/Sauvignon Blanc and Chardonnay) and a Merlot made under contract.

Dyson Wines NR
Sherriff Road, Maslin Beach, SA 5170, ☏ (08) 8386 1092, ℻ (08) 8327 0066; est 1976; ❖ 2,000 cases; ♀; A$; 7 days 10-5

Allan Dyson has been making wines in the region for decades, but appears to be moving towards retirement. His small production is sold without fanfare through cellar door.

Fern Hill Estate ☆☆⋆
Ingoldby Road, McLaren Flat, SA 5171, ☎ (08) 8383 0167, ⓕ (08) 8383 0107; est 1975; ❧ 5,000 cases; ⚑; A$; Mon-Fri 10-5, wkds 10-5
Now one of three operations owned by Hill International (Marienberg and Basedow being the others), producing solid, no-frills wines at competitive prices.

Fox Creek Wines ☆☆☆☆⋆
Malpas Road, Willunga, SA 5172, ☎ (08) 8556 2403, ⓕ (08) 8556 2104; est 1995; ❧ 15,000 cases; ⚑; A$; 7 days 11-5
Has made a major impact since coming on-stream in 1995, making bold, full-bodied reds with a rich reservoir of black cherry, plum, dark chocolate and earthy fruit flavours, supported by lots of oak and tannins. The Reserve wines (Shiraz and Cabernet Sauvignon) thoroughly deserve their label status.

Geoff Merrill ☆☆☆☆
291 Pimpala Road, Woodcroft, SA 5162, ☎ (08) 8381 6877, ⓕ (08) 8322 2244; est 1980; ❧ 35,000 cases; ⚑; A$; Mon-Fri 10-5, Sun 12-5
The luxuriant moustache, the raucous laugh and the endless stream of jokes and *bonhomie* are as well known in England, Ireland and Italy as they are in Australia, for Geoff Merrill is a tireless promoter of his wines and of Australia in general. Over the years he has also accumulated an amazing number of trophies and gold medals for his wines, most of which are released with several years' bottle age.

Hamilton ☆☆☆☆
Main Road, Willunga, SA 5172, ☎ (08) 8556 2288, ⓕ (08) 8556 2868; est 1837; ❧ 45,000 cases; ⚑; A$; 7 days 10-5; vineyard; ✗
Dr Richard Hamilton now carries the winemaking mantle of [father] Burton Hamilton and [uncle] Sid Hamilton (who founded Leconfield). He produces a range of wines with considerable character, which is no more than appropriate.

BRL Hardy ☆☆☆☆☆
Reynell Road, Reynella, SA 5161, ☎ (08) 8392 2222, ⓕ (08) 8392 2202; est 1853; ❧ NFP; ⚑; A$; 7 days 10-4.30; ⎊
McLaren Vale is the headquarters of BRL Hardy, second only in size to Southcorp. Willowy Eileen Hardy Chardonnay and potent berryish, minty Shiraz are unambiguously great wines, as is the glossy Thomas Hardy Cabernet Sauvignon. Quality is maintained at all price points in the empire.

Haselgrove ☆☆☆☆
Foggo Road, McLaren Vale, SA 5171, ☎ (08) 8323 8706, ⓕ (08) 8323 8049; est 1981; ❧ 40,000 cases; ⚑; A$; Mon-Fri 9-5, wkds 10-5; ⎊
Once a tiny winery this is now the standard bearer for the Stock Exchange-listed Australian Premium Wines. Nick Haselgrove continues to make the bold, full-frontal wines, with the lusciously rich H Reserve range having conspicuous success.

Hastwell & Lightfoot ☆☆☆⁄ V
Foggo Road, McLaren Vale, SA 5171, ☎ (08) 8323 8692,
Ⓕ (08) 8323 8098; est 1990; ✦ 700 cases; No visitors
An offshoot of a 15-hectare grape-growing business, with small amounts of Chardonnay and Cabernet Sauvignon contract-made by Nick Haselgrove. Wine quality is good, the labels fun.

Hoffmann's NR
Ingoldby Road, McLaren Flat, SA 5171, ☎ (08) 8383 0232,
Ⓕ (08) 8383 0232; est 1996; ✦ 500 cases; ⚑; A$; 7 days 10-5
Peter and Anthea Hoffman have been in the wine industry for decades, which perhaps explains their cautious, toe-in-the-water approach to making wine from their vineyards. They prefer to sell most of the production to Mildara Blass.

Hugh Hamilton ☆☆☆
McMurtrie Road, McLaren Vale, SA 5171, ☎ (08) 8323 8689,
Ⓕ (08) 8323 9488; est 1992; ✦ 8,500 cases; ⚑; A$; Mon-Fri 10-5, wkds & public hols 11-5
Hugh Hamilton comes from a family with 100 years of winemaking experience behind it. There is also vigorous internal competition between members. His wines are sound but not exhilarating.

Hugo ☆☆☆
Elliott Road, McLaren Flat, SA 5171, ☎ (08) 8383 0098, Ⓕ (08) 8383 0446; est 1982; ✦ 9,000 cases; ⚑; A$; Sun-Fri 10.30-5, Sat 12-5
John Hugo burst on the scene in the 1980s with the extravagantly flavoured and oaked style that was then *de rigueur*. Less exotic and challenging wines are now the order of the day.

Ingoldby ☆☆☆☆
Kangarilla Road, McLaren Flat, SA 5171, ☎ (08) 8323 8853, Ⓕ (08) 8323 8550; est 1972; ✦ 15,000 cases; ⚑; A$; 7 days 10-5; ⚑; ⚑
Winemaker Phil Reschke performs the same magic here as he does at Andrew Garrett, making harmonious, flavoursome wines. Chardonnay and Cabernet Sauvignon lead the way.

Kangarilla Road Vineyard & Winery ☆☆☆⁄
Kangarilla Road, McLaren Vale, SA 5171, ☎ (08) 8383 0533,
Ⓕ (08) 8383 0044; est 1975; ✦ 10,000 cases; ⚑; A$; Mon-Fri 9-5, wkds 11-5
A new direction for wine-industry executive Kevin O'Brien (and wife Helen), who purchased Stevens Cambrai vineyard and winery. They renamed it, and have now released four varietal wines, including one of Australia's few Zinfandels full of spice, cigar box and blackberry.

Kay Bros Amery ☆☆☆
Kay Road, McLaren Vale, SA 5171, ☎ (08) 8323 8211, Ⓕ (08) 8323 9199; est 1890; ✦ 6,500 cases; ⚑; A$; Mon-Fri 9-5, wkds & public hols 12-5

A priceless piece of history with 100-year-old estate vineyards and a winery to match. Some of the wines are lacklustre, but not Block 6 Shiraz, redolent of the character that comes from old-vine grapes and untrammelled by overt oak.

Maglieri ☆☆☆☆✦
Douglas Gully Road, McLaren Flat, SA 5171, ☏ (08) 8383 0177, Ⓕ (08) 8383 0136; est 1972; ❖ 110,000 cases; ⚑; A$; Mon-Sat 9-4, Sun 12-4

Since its acquisition by Mildara Blass in 1999, all becomes academic: whether it's the vast production of red and white wines in the style of Italy's Lambrusco, or the much smaller output of glorious Shiraz. One can only hope the velvety, rich Shiraz – the epitome of everything great about McLaren Vale Shiraz – does not disappear into the Mildara Blass maw.

Manning Park NR
Cnr Olivers and Chalk Hill Roads, McLaren Vale, SA 5171, ☏ (08) 8323 8209, Ⓕ (08) 8323 9474; est 1979; ❖ 5,000 cases; ⚑; A$; 7 days 10-5

Former Seppelt razzle-dazzle sparkling winemaker Warren Randall acquired this low-profile business some years ago. Despite some trendy labels (Great White, Savage Grenache, Native Cabernet, or the sparkling Stormy Shiraz), he is quite content to sell almost all his wine through cellar door.

Marienberg ☆☆☆
2 Chalk Hill Road, McLaren Vale, SA 5171, ☏ (08) 8323 9666, Ⓕ (08) 8323 9600; est 1966; ❖ 30,000 cases; ⚑; A$; 7 days 10-5; ▯◉

Founded by Ursula Pridham in 1966 at a time when female winemakers were a rare species, and energetic marketers no less so. This once-prominent business now makes ordinary wines, although some effort is being made with the Reserves.

Maxwell Wines ☆☆☆☆
Olivers Road, McLaren Vale, SA 5171, ☏ (08) 8323 8200, Ⓕ (08) 8323 8900; est 1979; ❖ 8,000 cases; ⚑; A$; 7 days 10-5

This family business has come a long way since 1979, moving from cramped makeshift premises to a state-of-the-art winery in 1997. Full-flavoured Semillon, crisp, minerally Sauvignon Blanc, and sophisticated cherry and liquorice Reserve Shiraz are best.

Merrivale Wines NR
Olivers Road, McLaren Vale, SA 5171, ☏ (08) 8323 9196, Ⓕ (08) 8323 9746; est 1971; ❖ 10,000 cases; ⚑; A$; 7 days 11-5

Several recent changes of ownership have led to its acquisition by the Gerrard family (of Chapel Hill), who prefer to treat this as a completely separate exercise. Not rated as it's in transition.

Middlebrook NR
Sand Road, McLaren Vale, SA 5171, ☏ (08) 8383 0600, Ⓕ (08) 8383 0557; est 1947; ❖ 5,000 cases; ⚑; A$; Mon-Fri 9-5, wkds 10-5; ▯◉

This estate has been purchased and is being redeveloped by industry veteran Bill Clappis after his former winery, Ingoldby, was acquired by Mildara Blass.

Middleton Estate NR
Flagstaff Hill Road, Middleton, SA 5213, ☎ (08) 8555 4136, Ⓕ (08) 8555 4108; est 1979; ❦ 3,000 cases; ♀; A$; Fri-Sun 11-5; ¶
A cellar door and on-site restaurant business now owned by Nigel Catt, a highly qualified winemaker.

Mount Hurtle ☆☆☆
291 Pimpala Road, Woodcroft, SA 5162, ☎ (08) 8381 6877, Ⓕ (08) 8322 2244; est 1897; ❦ 30,000 cases; ♀; A$; Mon-Fri 10-5, Sun 12-5
A label of the Geoff Merrill/Alister Purbrick (Chateau Tahbilk) joint venture, now sold exclusively through the Australia-wide Liquorland/Vintage Cellars chain.

Needham Estate Wines NR
Ingoldby Road, McLaren Flat, SA 5171, ☎ (08) 8383 0301, Ⓕ (08) 8383 0301; est 1997; ❦ 2800 cases; No visitors
Clive Needham has two vineyards; the first (four hectares) is newly planted and will come into full production in 2001. The second has 0.5 hectares of 100-year-old Shiraz vines used to make the 120-case White Horse Shiraz.

Noon Winery ☆☆☆☆ V
Rifle Range Road, McLaren Vale, SA 5171, ☎ (08) 8323 8290, Ⓕ (08) 8323 8290; est 1976; ❦ 2,000 cases; ♀; A$; Thurs-Mon 10-5
Peripatetic Drew Noon MW returned to acquire the family business, and is making some quite spectacular Shiraz and Grenache from ultra-ripe grapes. He uses *avant garde* packaging and brand-names to heighten the impact.

Normans ☆☆☆½
Grant's Gully Road, Clarendon, SA 5157, ☎ (08) 8383 6138, Ⓕ (08) 8383 6089; est 1853; ❦ 1,100,000 cases; ♀; A$; Mon-Fri 9-5, wkds & public hols 11-5
One of the beneficiaries of the Australian Stock Exchange listing in the second half of the 1990s, Normans is growing apace. It acquired the Mount Helen Vineyard in Victoria in 1999, with positive implications for the future. Overall quality is good, that of the Chais Clarendon range especially so.

Oliverhill NR
Seaview Road, McLaren Vale, SA 5171, ☎ (08) 8323 8922; est 1973; ❦ 1,300 cases; ♀; A$; 7 days 10-5
One of the smallest and quietest wineries, selling only through cellar door and mail order.

Penny's Hill Vineyards ☆☆☆☆½
Main Road, McLaren Vale, SA 5171, ☎ (08) 8362 1077, Ⓕ (08) 8362 2766; est 1988; ❦ 3,200 cases; ♀; A$; by appt

Tony Parkinson's advertising agency background shows in the innovative red-dot labelling, mimicking the red 'sold' dot stuck on pictures at an art gallery sale. Contract winemaking at Wirra Wirra has guaranteed the quality of the Chardonnay, Shiraz and Shiraz blend.

Pertaringa ☆☆☆
Cnr Hunt and Rifle Range Roads, McLaren Vale, SA 5171, ☎ (08) 8323 8125, ℱ (08) 8323 7766; est 1980; ❦ 2,000 cases; ♀; A$; Mon-Fri 10-4

The Pertaringa label wines are made from grapes grown by leading viticulturists Geoff Hardy and Ian Leask on the Pertaringa Vineyard, acquired as a run-down 33-hectare vineyard in 1980 and since rejuvenated. The Shiraz is a classic: plum, dark cherry and chocolate abound.

Pirramimma ☆☆☆☆
Johnston Road, McLaren Vale, SA 5171, ☎ (08) 8323 8205, ℱ (08) 8323 9224; est 1892; ❦ 30,000 cases; ♀; A$; Mon-Fri 9-5, Sat 11-5, Sun & public hols 11.30-4

Pirramimma has vineyard holdings second to none in McLaren Vale. Some are old, others of more recent origin under long-term contract to Mildara Blass. Wine quality has always been good, but marketing less so. Interesting bargains are the result, such as restrained, long-lived Chardonnay and a fine Petit Verdot.

Potters Clay Vineyard NR
Main Road, Willunga, SA 5172, ☎ (08) 8556 2922, ℱ (08) 8556 2922; est 1994; ❦ 800 cases; No visitors

John and Donna Bruschi are second-generation grape-growers who assumed full ownership of the 16-hectare Potters Clay Vineyard in 1994. They are progressively establishing a winery, cellar door and ultimately a restaurant.

Reynell ☆☆☆☆☆
Reynell Road, Reynella, SA 5161, ☎ (08) 8392 2222, ℱ (08) 8392 2202; est 1838; ❦ NFP; ♀; A$; 7 days 10-4.30

The fashionably shortened name of the beautiful and historic Chateau Reynella, and headquarters for BRL Hardy. Its three basket-pressed red wines (Shiraz, Merlot and Cabernet) are richly opulent and consistently excellent.

Rosemount Estate (McLaren Vale) ☆☆☆☆☆
Ingoldby Road, McLaren Vale, SA 5171, ☎ (08) 8383 0001, ℱ (08) 8383 0456; est 1888; ❦ 100,000 cases; ♀; A$; Mon-Fri 10-5, wkds 11-5

A physically distinct and distant winery that is part of the Rosemount (Hunter Valley) empire. It produces four outstanding red wines, led by the exceptionally lush and bountiful Balmoral Syrah, packed with black cherry and blackberry fruit. Show Reserve Shiraz, GSM (a Rhône blend) and Traditional (a Bordeaux blend) are also impressive.

Scarpantoni Estate ☆☆☆☆

Scarpantoni Drive, McLaren Flat, SA 5171, ☎ (08) 8383 0186,
℻ (08) 8383 0490; est 1979; ❦ 15,000 cases; ♀; A$; Mon-Fri 10-5,
wkds 11-5

An Italian family-owned business with a range of wines, none better than the sensually rich, bitter-chocolate, red-berry and vanilla-oak Block 3 Shiraz.

Seaview ☆☆☆☆☆

Chaffeys Road, McLaren Vale, SA 5171, ☎ (08) 8323 8250,
℻ (08) 8323 9308; est 1850; ❦ 500,000 cases; ♀; A$;
Mon-Fri 9-4.30, Sat 10-5, Sun 11-4

An important part of the Southcorp empire, making some of Australia's best-known sparkling wines. From the 1999 vintage, the super-premium Edwards & Chaffey range will become an independent McLaren Vale label, making Shiraz, Cabernet Sauvignon and Chardonnay. Will continue to produce Seaview table wines that, like the sparkling range, draw on fruit from outside the region. The super-premium wines are marketed under the Edwards & Chaffey label, the lower-priced commercial wines under the Seaview label. Which offer the better value for money rests with the eye of the beholder.

Shottesbrooke ☆☆☆☆

Bagshaws Road, McLaren Flat, SA 5171, ☎ (08) 8383 0002,
℻ (08) 8383 0222; est 1984; ❦ 8,000 cases; ♀; A$; Mon-Fri 10-4.30,
wkds & public hols 11-5

Winemaker/owner Nick Holmes hand-crafts subtly oaked and invariably elegant wines, combining his own philosophy with his long experience with the grapes (and wines) of the region.

Tatachilla ☆☆☆☆☆

151 Main Road, McLaren Vale, SA 5171, ☎ (08) 8323 8656,
℻ (08) 8323 9096; est 1901; ❦ 150,000 cases; ♀; A$; Mon-Sat 10-5,
Sun & public hols 11-5; ✗

A winery with a fascinatingly convoluted history, and effectively reborn in 1995. Since then, the management and winemaking teams have made every post a winner. Best are the spicy, juicy-berry-filled Keystone (Grenache, Shiraz) and Foundation Shiraz, bursting with glossy cherry fruit and high-quality oak.

Tinlins NR

Kangarilla Road, McLaren Flat, SA 5171, ☎ (08) 8323 8649,
℻ (08) 8323 9747; est 1977; ❦ 30,000 cases; ♀; A$; 7 days 9-5

The second winery run by former Seppelt whizz-kid winemaker Warren Randall, who primarily supplies bulk wine to major wineries. A small amount is sold at the cellar door to those with BYO containers (filled to order at mouthwateringly low prices).

Wayne Thomas Wines NR

26 Kangarilla Road, McLaren Vale, SA 5171, ☎ (08) 8323 9737,
℻ (08) 8323 9737; est 1994; ❦ 4,000 cases; ♀; A$; 7 days 12-5

McLaren Vale veteran Wayne Thomas owned Fern Hill for 20 years prior to its sale in 1994. He promptly started again with contract-grown grapes sourced throughout McLaren Vale.

Wirilda Creek ☆☆☆☆ ⁄
RSD 90 McMurtrie Road, McLaren Vale, SA 5171, ☎ (08) 8323 9688, ℱ (08) 8323 9688; est 1993; ❖ 1,500 cases; ♇; A$; 7 days 10-5; ⌯, café

Kerry Flanagan has made wine in the McLaren Vale for 20 years as well as owning the famous Salopian Inn for a time. Together with partner Karen Sherlock they offer pickers lunches and accommodation. Somewhat rustic reds are the best of the bunch.

Wirra Wirra ☆☆☆☆☆
McMurtie Road, McLaren Vale, SA 5171, ☎ (08) 8323 8414, ℱ (08) 8323 8596; est 1969; ❖ 75,000 cases; ♇; A$; Mon-Sat 10-5, Sun 11-5

One of the leading wineries of the region, established by Greg Trott and family, and joined in 1999 by Dr Tony Jordan, formerly chief executive at Domaine Chandon. All the wines, white and red, are excellent, with a sophisticated polish that enhances their strong varietal character. RSW Shiraz and The Angelus Cabernet Sauvignon are usually brilliant.

Woodstock ☆☆☆☆ ⁄
Douglas Gully Road, McLaren Flat, SA 5171, ☎ (08) 8383 0156, ℱ (08) 8383 0437; est 1974; ❖ 15,000 cases; ♇; A$; Mon-Fri 9-5, wkds & hols 12-5

Winemaker/owner Scott Collett was a wild boy in his youth, and the impish devil inside still isn't far from the surface. Sturdy white wines and even sturdier (and better) red wines are ever reliable; The Stocks Shiraz (with new oak) is a good flagbearer.

Langhorne Creek

Cooled by the lake and nearby sea and easily able to ripen 15 tonnes of grapes to the hectare, producing 500,000 cases of wine a year, this is the modern face of Langhorne Creek, a paradigm of the advantages Australia has over so many of its New (and Old) World competitors. Vines were first planted here around 1860 by Frank Potts of Bleasdale, and five generations later the Potts family is better than ever. It was only in the late 1960s that the big boys took notice of Langhorne Creek. While Lindemans had begun to buy grapes from the region, it was Wolf Blass who most influenced attitudes; Orlando Wyndham arrived in 1995. It is significant that the prime function of this booming area is to grow grapes of good to very good quality with a low cost base, which go on to contribute to mega-blends like Jacob's Creek.

Bleasdale Vineyards ☆☆☆☆ ⁄
Wellington Road, Langhorne Creek, SA 5255, ☎ (08) 8537 3001, ℱ (08) 8537 3224; est 1850; ❖ 150,000 cases; ♇; A$; Mon-Sat 9-5, Sun 11-5

One of Australia's most historic wineries, drawing upon vineyards that are flooded every winter by diversion of the Bremer River, to provide moisture throughout the dry, cool, growing season (a scheme devised by founder Frank Potts in the 1860s). The wines offer excellent value for money, all showing the particular softness that is the hallmark of the Langhorne Creek region.

Bremerton Wines ☆☆☆☆
Strathalbyn Road, Langhorne Creek, SA 5255, ☏ (08) 8537 3093, ℻ (08) 8537 3109; est 1988; ❖ 15,000 cases; ⚑; A$; 7 days 10-5
Initially grape-growers, the Willsons now run a complex business both buying and selling grapes and making some delicious wines, particularly Shiraz and Cabernet Sauvignon under contract.

Lake Breeze Wines ☆☆☆☆½
Step Road, Langhorne Creek, SA 5255, ☏ (08) 8537 3017, ℻ (08) 8537 3267; est 1987; ❖ 10,000 cases; ⚑; A$; 7 days 10-5
The Follett family have been farmers at Langhorne Creek since 1880, grape-growers since the 1930s, wine producers since 1987, and opened a cellar-door facility in 1991. The quality of their wines has been exemplary, especially the rich, dense Winemaker's Selection range of red wines.

Temple Bruer ☆☆☆☆
Milang Road, Strathalbyn, SA 5255, ☏ (08) 8537 0203, ℻ (08) 8537 0131; est 1980; ❖ 12,000 cases; ⚑; A$; Mon-Fri 9.30-4.30
Known for its eclectic range of wines, Temple Bruer (which also runs a substantial business as a vine-propagation nursery) has seen a sharp lift in quality. Clean, modern, redesigned labels add to the appeal of its stimulatingly different range of red wines.

Riverland
The engine room of the Australian wine industry, producing almost 60 per cent of South Australia's grapes and hence around 30 per cent of the national grape crush. Originally developed by the Californian-born and trained Chaffey brothers (George and William), who provided the expertise for the construction of the irrigation channels that turned near desert into ideal horticultural and viticultural land, the Riverland's 100-year existence has seen the emphasis on production of the maximum possible tonnages at the minimum possible cost, an approach which served it (and Australia) well. But increasing attention is now being paid to raising quality. This is reflected in better viticultural practices, better water usage and better grape varieties and clones. The challenge for Australia is to make characterful wines with quality. Commercially, success or failure will be determined right here.

Angove's ☆☆☆☆½
Bookmark Avenue, Renmark, SA 5341, ☏ (08) 8595 1311, ℻ (08) 8595 1583; est 1886; ❖ 1,000,000 cases; ⚑; A$; Mon-Fri 9-5

Exemplifies the economies of scale achievable in the Riverland. Wines are never poor and can sometimes exceed their theoretical station in life. The white varietals are best.

Banrock Station ☆☆☆✦ V
Old Kingston Road, Kingston-on-Murray, SA 5331, ☏ (08) 8583 0235; est 1994; ✤ NFP; ⚑; A$; 7 days; conference centre, wetland conservation/interpretive centre

Owned by BRL Hardy, the property covers over 1,700 hectares. There are 230 hectares of vineyard, while the rest is a wildlife and wetland preservation area. A A$1 million visitor centre was opened in October 1998. The Unwooded Chardonnay has been of consistently good quality, and excellent value at its price.

Berri Estates ☆☆✦
Sturt Highway, Glossop, SA 5344, ☏ (08) 8582 0300, ℻ (08) 8583 2224; est 1916; ✤ NFP; ⚑; A$; Mon-Sat 9-5

Part of the BRL Hardy Group. Strictly a producer of cask and bulk wine (with much exported in bulk); no pretensions to *grandeur*.

Bonneyview ☆☆☆
Sturt Highway, Barmera, SA 5345, ☏ (08) 8588 2279; est 1975; ✤ 5,000 cases; ⚑; A$; 7 days 9-5.30; ¶

The smallest Riverland winery, selling exclusively at the cellar door, with Robert Minns, an ex-Kent cricketer and Oxford University graduate, as its owner/winemaker. The Shiraz/Petit Verdot (unique to Bonneyview) and Cabernet/Petit Verdot add a particular dimension of interest to the wine portfolio.

Kingston Estate ☆☆☆✦ V
PO Box 67, Kingston-on-Murray, SA 5331, ☏ (08) 8583 0599, ℻ (08) 8583 0304; est 1979; ✤ 100,000 cases; No visitors

Kingston Estate is a substantial and successful Riverland winery, crushing 10,000 tonnes each vintage, and exporting 80 per cent of its production. It is only in recent years that it has turned its attention to the domestic market with national distribution. Wines are well priced, and the Reserves add quality dimension.

Renmano ☆☆☆☆
Sturt Highway, Renmark, SA 5341, ☏ (08) 8586 6771, ℻ (08) 8586 5939; est 1914; ✤ 1,600,000 cases; ⚑; A$; Mon-Sat 9-5

Part of the BRL Hardy group. A radical change in winemaking technique and philosophy in 1996 has wrought miracles with the Chairman's Selection Chardonnay, the only premium wine.

South Australia: Rest of State

Looking at a map of Australia; it strikes you how close to the coastline most intensive agricultural and viticultural operations are. In the case of South Australia, only the Murray River carries viticulture inland to any significant degree. So it is that the majority of the wineries without regional homes are clustered around the coastline, adjacent (relatively speaking) to Adelaide, in the Fleurieu Zone. They thus share a strongly maritime and far cooler climate than might be expected. Predominantly on-shore winds result in high relative humidity, reducing summer vine stress and optimising growth. The risk of spring frost, too, is negligible, reflecting the generally small fluctuation in day-to-night temperatures through the growing season.

Kangaroo Island has approximately 30 hectares of vines that have been planted by ten owners, with more in the pipeline. The Florance Vineyard at Cygnet River was the first to be established in the mid-1980s. The importance of viticulture seems likely to increase in the years ahead, and cellar doors will open to take advantage of the many tourists coming to this beautiful island.

Boston Bay Wines ☆☆☆½ V
Lincoln Highway, Port Lincoln, SA 5606, ☎ (08) 8684 3600, ℱ (08) 8684 3600; The Peninsulas Zone, Port Lincoln; est 1984; ♦ 2,600 cases; ⚑; A$; wkds, school/public hols 11.30-4.30
Situated on the southern tip of the Eyre Peninsula, the vineyards offer frequent sightings of whales at play. Contract-made Riesling and Cabernet/Merlot have been consistently good.

Currency Creek Wines ☆☆☆
Winery Road, Currency Creek, SA 5214, ☎ (08) 8555 4069, ℱ (08) 8555 4100; Fleurieu Zone; est 1969; ♦ 8,000 cases; ⚑; A$; 7 days 10-5; ⫽; ⊭
Owned by the Tonkin family. Constant name changes have not helped the quest for identity, but the winery has nonetheless produced some outstanding wood-matured whites and pleasant soft reds that sell at attractive prices.

Delacolline Estate ☆☆☆
Whillas Road, Port Lincoln, SA 5606, ☎ (08) 8682 5277, ℱ (08) 8682 4455; The Peninsulas Zone, Port Lincoln; est 1984; ♦ 650 cases; ⚑; A$; wkds 9-5
Tony Bassett has three hectares of Riesling, Sauvignon Blanc and Cabernet Sauvignon. The wine style reflects the cool, maritime influence, with ocean currents sweeping up from the Antarctic.

Kangaroo Island Vines ☆☆☆☆
c/o 413 Payneham Road, Felixstow, SA 5070, ☎ (08) 8365 3411, ℱ (08) 8336 2462; Fleurieu Zone; est 1990; ♦ 600 cases; No visitors
Kangaroo Island is an utterly magical part of Australia, and the Special Reserve Cabernet/Merlot (when available) is a beautifully balanced and elegant wine. Production should increase.

Lengs & Cooter ☆☆☆☆
24 Lindsay Terrace, Belair, SA 5042, ☎ (08) 8278 3998, ℱ (08) 8278 3998; est 1993; ♦ 2,500 cases; No visitors
Carel Lengs and Colin Cooter have graduated from hobby winemaking to commercial production with great success. The Watervale Riesling, Clare Valley Semillon and Swinton Cabernet blend (from purchased grapes) are all impressive.

Macaw Creek Wines NR

Macaw Creek Road, Riverton, SA 5412, ☎ (08) 8847 2237, ⓕ (08) 8847 2237; Mount Lofty Ranges Zone; est 1992; ❖ 2,000 cases; ❡; *A$; Sun 11-4*

Rodney Hooper is a relatively young, but immensely experienced winemaker who has returned to the family's 1850 property to establish his own winery. His output includes the Yoolang Preservative-Free Cabernet Sauvignon.

Patritti Wines ☆☆❖ V

13-23 Clacton Road, Dover Gardens, SA 5048, ☎ (08) 8296 8261, ⓕ (08) 8296 5088; est 1926; ❖ 65,000 cases; ❡; *A$; Mon-Sat 9-6*

The Patrittis run a traditional, family-owned business offering wines at yesterday's prices, from substantial vineyard holdings of 40 hectares in Blewitt Springs and another 40 at Aldinga.

Peter Rumball Wines ☆☆☆❖

55 Charles Street, Norwood, SA 5067, ☎ (08) 8332 2761, ⓕ (08) 8364 0188; est 1988; ❖ 6,000 cases; ❡; *A$; Mon-Fri 9-5*

Peter Rumball has been making and selling sparkling wine for as long as I can remember. He now makes Sparkling Shiraz from Coonawarra, Barossa Valley and McLaren Vale at various wineries.

Simon Hackett ☆☆☆

PO Box 166, Walkerville, SA 5081, ☎ (08) 8232 4305, ⓕ (08) 8223 3714; est 1981; ❖ 14,000 cases; No visitors

Simon Hackett purchases grapes and makes wines at various places. The Shiraz, Old Vine Grenache and Cabernet Sauvignon are distinctly better than the Semillon and Chardonnay.

Twin Bays NR

Lot 1 Martin Road, Yankalilla, SA 5203, ☎ (08) 8267 2844, ⓕ (08) 8239 0877; Fleurieu Zone; est 1989; ❖ 1,000 cases; ❡; *A$; wkds and hols*

Adelaide doctor Bruno Giorgio has established two hectares of vines and a small winery in the Yankalilla district, one hour's drive south of Adelaide on the Fleurieu Peninsula.

Trafford Hill Vineyard NR

Lot 1 Bower Road, Normanville, SA 5204, ☎ (08) 8558 3595; Fleurieu Zone; est 1996; ❖ 300 cases

Irene and John Sanderson have established 1.25 hectares of vineyard at Normanville, near the southern extremity of the Fleurieu Peninsula. Irene tends the vineyards, and John makes the wine with help from district veteran Allan Dyson.

Will Taylor Wines ☆☆☆❖ V

1 Simpson Parade, Goodwood, SA 5034, ☎ (08) 8271 6122, ⓕ (08) 8271 6122; est 1997; ❖ 1,300 cases; No visitors

Will Taylor is a lawyer, specialising in wine law. Together with Suzanne Taylor, he has established a classic *négociant* wine business. His wines are contract-made to his specification.

Western Australia

1994 2,713 hectares 4.05 per cent of total plantings
1998 4,490 hectares 4.56 per cent of total plantings

Obviously enough, this state is a relatively small contributor to the national grape crush. The most vocal of all wine regions (the Margaret River) accounted for 0.08 per cent of the 1998 crush, but would (justifiably) assert that size doesn't matter.

Margaret River

Whether it is in part due to the subliminal sound of the name, I do not know, but I have always felt there is a feminine quality to the soft beauty of the Margaret River region. Yet at the same time it is uncompromisingly Australian. The doctors-cum-winemakers who, for some strange reason, dominated the early development of viticulture here (and still have a strong presence), were unusually sensitive to the environment. Their wineries tend to merge into the countryside rather than stand superimposed on it.

Margaret River is now one of Australia's best-regarded regions, with intensely rich but long-lived Chardonnay, and textured Cabernet Sauvignon and Merlot second to none. Yet a cloud now hangs over the Margaret River. Between 1996 and 1999, vineyard plantings have doubled, and of the new areas now under vine, some are apparently not suited to quality wine production. One of the more controversial areas is Jindong, at the northern end of the region. On the face of it, Jindong will produce pleasant, light-bodied, fast-maturing wines at a relatively low cost. This is not what the Margaret River is, or should be, about. The wineries established between 1970 and 1995, with the best vineyard sites, however, will justly retain their reputation.

Abbey Vale ☆☆☆☆
Wildwood Road, Yallingup, WA 6282, ☎ (08) 9755 2121,
℉ (08) 9755 2286; est 1986; ❖ 21,000 cases; ⚑; A$; 7 days 10-5; ⦿
Has moved from predominantly grape-growing for others to winemaking. Now produces the full spectrum of Margaret River styles, usually of good quality.

Alexander Bridge Estate NR
Brockman Highway, Karridale, WA 6288, ☎ (08) 9758 2230,
℉ (08) 9384 4811; est 1994; ❖ 3,000 cases; No visitors
Another of the fast-developing Margaret River ventures. Since 1994, 30 hectares of vines have been established, and production is planned to rise from 3,000 cases in 1999 to 24,000 cases in 2001, with an estate winery due to open in late 1999.

Amberley Estate ☆☆☆☆
Thornton Road, Yallingup, WA 6282, ☎ (08) 9755 2288,
℉ (08) 9755 2171; est 1986; ❖ 60,000 cases; ⚑; A$; 7 days 10-4.30; ⦿
Eddie Price is the winemaker at this highly successful and substantial enterprise. Slightly sweet Chenin Blanc provides the

Western Australia

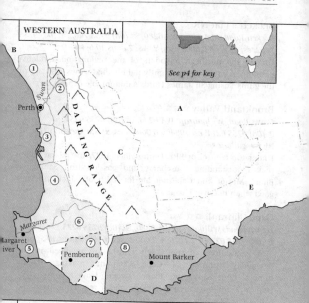

A Eastern Plains, Inland and North of Western Australia	D South West Australia	3 South West Coast
	E West Australian South East Coastal	4 Geographe
B Greater Perth		5 Margaret River
C Central Western Australia	1 Swan District	6 Blackwood Valley
	2 Perth Hills	7 Pemberton
		8 Great Southern

cash flow, excellent tangy, herbal Semillon/Sauvignon Blanc and powerful inky Shiraz the sex appeal.

Arlewood Estate NR
Harmans Road South, Willyabrup, WA 6284, ☏ (08) 9755 6267, ℻ (08) 9755 6267; est 1988; ❖ 1,800 cases; ♀; A$; Fri-Mon 11-4, 7 days during school hols; ⛳

A premier address, between Ashbrook and Vasse Felix, owned by Liz and John Wojturski. The high quality of their small production reflects the premium site. Zesty, citrous Semillon.

Ashbrook Estate ☆☆☆☆☆ V
Harmans Road South, Willyabrup, WA 6284, ☏ (08) 9755 6262, ℻ (08) 9755 6290; est 1975; ❖ 7,500 cases; ♀; A$; 7 days 11-5

This estate is one of the quietest and highest achievers in Australia, maintaining excellent viticulture and fastidious winemaking. It is hard to choose between the complex, herby, tropical Semillon, or subtly oaked, long Chardonnay, the crisp Sauvignon Blanc or powerful briar-and-cassis Cabernet.

Beckett's Flat NR
Beckett Road, Metricup, WA 6280, ☎ *(08) 9755 7402,* Ⓕ *(08) 9755 7402; est 1992;* ❖ *2,000 cases;* ⚑; *A$; 7 days 10-6;* ⛺

One of the northern outriders of the region and a relative newcomer, but its clean, slightly light-bodied wines are 'easy on the gums' (using Sir James Hardy's memorable expression).

Brookland Valley ☆☆☆☆
Caves Road, Willyabrup, WA 6284, ☎ *(08) 9755 6250,* Ⓕ *(08) 9755 6214; est 1984;* ❖ *8,000 cases;* ⚑; *A$; Tues-Sun 11-4.30;* 🍴; ⛺, *gallery*

Under the control of BRL Hardy since 1997, Brookland Valley makes outstanding gooseberry and passion fruit Sauvignon Blanc, Merlot and Cabernet/Merlot, both of which are very good when not over-oaked.

Cape Clairault ☆☆☆☆
Henry Road, Willyabrup, WA 6280, ☎ *(08) 9755 6225,* Ⓕ *(08) 9755 6229; est 1976;* ❖ *8,000 cases;* ⚑; *A$; 7 days 10-5; café*

Two generations of the Lewis family are involved in the day-to-day running of Cape Clairault, making bracing mineral/herb Sauvignon Blanc, sweeter-fruited gooseberry/tropical Semillon/Sauvignon Blanc and a red Bordeaux blend called The Clairault that takes no prisoners.

Cape Mentelle ☆☆☆☆☆
Off Wallcliffe Road, Margaret River, WA 6285, ☎ *(08) 9757 3266,* Ⓕ *(08) 9757 3233; est 1970;* ❖ *50,000 cases;* ⚑; *A$; 7 days 10-4.30*

One of the top four regional wineries, with an international reputation that must please its owner, Champagne Veuve Clicquot. Quite marvellous, seductively fruity, subtly oaked Semillon/Sauvignon Blanc; glorious figgy, melon and cashew Chardonnay; spicy, dark-plum, liquorice and gamey Shiraz; and Australia's only serious Zinfandel, a powerful turbo-charged V8.

Carbunup Estate ☆☆☆
Bussel Highway, Carbunup, WA 6280, ☎ *(08) 9755 1111; est 1988;* ❖ *NFP;* ⚑; *A$; 7 days 10-5*

Part grape-grower, part *vigneron*, with 15 hectares of estate plantings that provide fruit for two labels, Vasse River Wines and Carbunup Estate. The Chardonnay and Semillon have impressed most.

Cullen Wines ☆☆☆☆☆
Caves Road, Cowaramup, WA 6284, ☎ *(08) 9755 5277,* Ⓕ *(08) 9755 5550; est 1971;* ❖ *12,000 cases;* ⚑; *A$; 7 days 10-4;* 🍴

Mother Di and daughter Vanya preside over one of Australia's best small wineries. Concentrated, complex, flavour-packed, fig, and peach-flavoured Chardonnay and powerful, minerally Sauvignon Blanc yield only to the imperious Cabernet/Merlot, surely Australia's best, replete with luscious cassis and fine, balanced tannins.

Western Australia

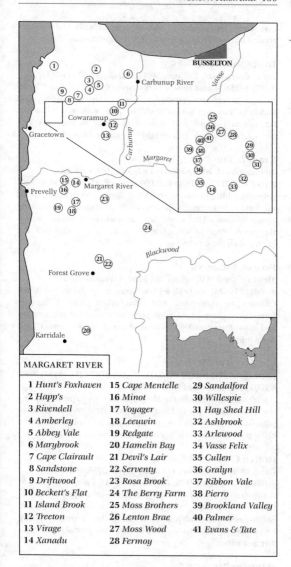

1 Hunt's Foxhaven	**15** Cape Mentelle	**29** Sandalford
2 Happ's	**16** Minot	**30** Willespie
3 Rivendell	**17** Voyager	**31** Hay Shed Hill
4 Amberley	**18** Leeuwin	**32** Ashbrook
5 Abbey Vale	**19** Redgate	**33** Arlewood
6 Marybrook	**20** Hamelin Bay	**34** Vasse Felix
7 Cape Clairault	**21** Devil's Lair	**35** Cullen
8 Sandstone	**22** Serventy	**36** Gralyn
9 Driftwood	**23** Rosa Brook	**37** Ribbon Vale
10 Beckett's Flat	**24** The Berry Farm	**38** Pierro
11 Island Brook	**25** Moss Brothers	**39** Brookland Valley
12 Treeton	**26** Lenton Brae	**40** Palmer
13 Virage	**27** Moss Wood	**41** Evans & Tate
14 Xanadu	**28** Fermoy	

Devil's Lair NR
Rocky Road, Forest Grove via Margaret River, WA 6286,
☎ *(08) 9757 7573,* ℱ *(08) 9757 7533; est 1985;* ♦ *14,000 cases;*
♀*; A$; by appt*

Not rated because of the author's winemaking involvement, but generally highly regarded for stylish, structured Chardonnay, a classic red Bordeaux blend with lingering tannins, and the jazzy second label, Fifth Leg White and Red. Striking label designs.

Driftwood Estate ☆☆☆☆
Lot 13 Caves Road, Yallingup, WA 6282, ☏ (08) 9755 6323, ℻ (08) 9755 6343; est 1989; ✦ 14,000 cases; ⚑; A$; 7 days 11-4.30; ⦿
Baroque-look Greek architecture is perhaps an appropriate backdrop for the fleshy Semillon and Battlestar Galactica Chardonnay, armed with masses of toasty/nutmeg oak and peachy/buttery fruit. It is certainly a memorable visit.

Evans & Tate ☆☆☆☆☆✓
Metricup Road, Willyabrup, WA 6280, ☏ (08) 9296 4666, ℻ (08) 9296 1148; est 1970; ✦ 100,000 cases; ⚑; A$; 7 days 10.30-4.30
Growing a little like an overcharged Topsy, this is significantly the largest producer in the region. Sophisticated winemaking shines through all the wines, but you sometimes 'wonder where the yellow went' in white wines that are elegant but lack the expected regional richness.

Fermoy Estate NR
Metricup Road, Willyabrup, WA 6280, ☏ (08) 9755 6285, ℻ (08) 9755 6251; est 1985; ✦ 15,000 cases; ⚑; A$; 7 days 11-4.30; ⌂
Changes in ownership and winemaking may bring the formidable, sharp-edged wine style back into the mainstream and allow the naturally soft fruit of the region to express itself more fully.

Flinders Bay NR
Davis Road, Witchcliffe, WA 6286, ☏ (08) 9757 6281, ℻ (08) 9757 6353; est 1995; ✦ NA; at Vasse Felix.
A joint venture between the Margaret River Gillespie family and the Ireland family (*qv* Old Station). There have been 50 hectares planted and the wines are contract-made and sold through the cellar door at Vasse Felix under the Flinders Bay label.

Gralyn Cellars ☆☆☆☆
Caves Road, Willyabrup, WA 6280, ☏ (08) 9755 6245, ℻ (08) 9755 6245; est 1975; ✦ 1700 cases; ⚑; A$; 7 days 10.30-4.30; ⦿
A substantial 25-year-old vineyard is the rock upon which the Hutton family bases its full-bodied, full-blooded Cabernet and Shiraz-based reds (with a touch of vanilla-tinged American oak). Unusually for the region, the Huttons also produce port-style fortified wines.

Hamelin Bay ☆☆☆☆
Five Ashes Vineyard, RMB 116 McDonald Road, Karridale, WA 6288, ☏ (08) 9389 6020, ℻ (08) 9389 6020; est 1992; ✦ 15,000 cases; ⚑; A$; by appt
This newly established but rapidly growing business immediately made its mark with elegant, fragrant, lemony/grassy/gooseberryish Semillon, Sauvignon Blanc and blends thereof.

Happ's ☆☆☆⯨
Commonage Road, Dunsborough, WA 6281, ☏ *(08) 9755 3300,*
℻ *(08) 9755 3846; est 1978;* ❧ *14,000 cases;* ♀; *A$; 7 days 10-5*
Erl Happ suffers fools (and critics) badly, yet is an iconoclastic and compulsive experimenter, sticking only with the Merlot which has been the winery speciality for more than a decade. The Cabernet/Merlot can also impress.

Hay Shed Hill ☆☆☆⯨
RSM 398 Harmans Mill Road, Willyabrup, WA 6280,
☏ *(08) 9755 6234,* ℻ *(08) 9755 6305; est 1987;* ❧ *12,000 cases;*
♀; *A$; 7 days 10.30-5*
This is an enterprising and innovative house, with wines such as strawberry-accented Pitchfork Pink (rosé) and Group 20 Cabernet Sauvignon (light, unoaked) providing interesting alternatives to the mainstream.

Hunt's Foxhaven Estate NR
Canal Rocks Road, Yallingup, WA 6282, ☏ *(08) 9755 2232,*
℻ *(08) 9255 2249; est 1978;* ❧ *1,000 cases;* ♀; *A$; wkds & hols 11-5*
This is a small, part-time business for David Hunt, with all sales through cellar door.

Island Brook Estate NR
Lot 817 Bussell Highway, Metricup, WA 6280, ☏ *(08) 9755 7501,*
℻ *(08) 9755 7501; est 1985;* ❧ *700 cases;* ♀; *A$; 7 days 10-5;* ⑃; *maze*
Ken and Judy Brook run a mixed business as grape-growers (selling most), café proprietors, and owners of a unique, rammed-earth maze. Their small wine production is (very competently) contract-made.

Leeuwin Estate ☆☆☆☆☆
Stevens Road, Margaret River, WA 6285, ☏ *(08) 9757 6253,*
℻ *(08) 9430 5687; est 1974;* ❧ *40,000 cases;* ♀; *A$; 7 days*
10.30-4.30; ⑃; ✗; *annual concert*
Produces Australia's best Chardonnay, immensely complex and long-lived, developing Burgundian characters with age. The second-label Prelude Chardonnay is also better than most. Cabernet Sauvignon is less consistent and less amiable.

Lenton Brae Estate NR
Willyabrup Valley, Margaret River, WA 6285, ☏ *(08) 9755 6255,*
℻ *(08) 9755 6268; est 1983;* ❧ *NFP;* ♀; *A$; 7 days 10-6*
Founded by Bruce Tomlinson, perverse political activist on all matters vinous. Son Edward has now taken responsibility for winemaking, with fine results for Chardonnay, Semillon/Sauvignon Blanc and Sauvignon Blanc.

Marybrook Vineyards NR
Vasse-Yallingup Road, Marybrook, WA 6280, ☏ *(08) 9755 1143,*
℻ *(08) 9755 1112; est 1986;* ❧ *2,000 cases;* ♀; *A$; Fri-Mon 10-5,*
7 days 10-5 school hols; ⑃

Tony Ward offers a mix of conventional Margaret River varietal wines and such oddities as Nectosia (sweet white) and Temptation (sweet red).

Minot Vineyard NR
PO Box 683, Margaret River, WA 6285, ☎ (08) 9757 3579,
℻ (08) 9757 2361; est 1600; ❖ 1,000 cases; ⚑; A$; by appt
The Miles family produces tiny quantities of two contract-made wines (Semillon/Sauvignon Blanc and Cabernet Sauvignon).

Moss Brothers ☆☆☆
Caves Road, Willyabrup, WA 6280, ☎ (08) 9755 6270,
℻ (08) 9755 6298; est 1984; ❖ 14,000 cases; ⚑; A$; 7 days 10-5
A 100-tonne rammed-earth winery produces strangely erratic wines, ranging from gloriously intense and pure Semillon to offerings such as the astringent Moses Rock Red, a blend of Merlot, Pinot Noir, Grenache and Cabernet Franc.

Moss Wood ☆☆☆☆☆
Metricup Road, Willyabrup, WA 6280, ☎ (08) 9755 6266,
℻ (08) 9755 6303; est 1969; ❖ 5,000 cases; ⚑; A$; by appt
One of the Margaret River icons. Keith Mugford produces immaculate estate-grown wines of distinctive style: rich, tropical Semillon; deep peach-honey-and-fig Chardonnay; and uniquely soft, multi-layered Cabernet Sauvignon.

Palmer Wines ☆☆☆☆
Caves Road, Willyabrup, WA 6280, ☎ (08) 9797 1881,
℻ (08) 9797 0534; est 1977; ❖ 6,000 cases; ⚑; A$; by appt
Stephen and Helen Palmer had to deal with natural hindrances such as cyclones and grasshopper plagues before ultimately bringing their 15-hectare vineyard into production. The glossy, oaky Chardonnay and powerful Merlot and Cabernet Sauvignon make it all worthwhile.

Pierro ☆☆☆☆☆
Caves Road, Willyabrup via Cowaramup, WA 6284, ☎ (08) 9755 6220, ℻ (08) 9755 6308; est 1979; ❖ 7,500 cases; ⚑; A$;
7 days 10-5
Dr Michael Peterkin makes wines in his own image: complex and concentrated (he is a doctor of medicine as well as a qualified winemaker) with towering, multi-flavoured creamy/nutty/toasty/figgy Chardonnay and a commensurately complex LTC Semillon/Sauvignon Blanc (LTC for *Les Trois Cuvées* or a little touch of Chardonnay... take your pick).

Redgate ☆☆☆☆
Boodjidup Road, Margaret River, WA 6285, ☎ (08) 9757 6488,
℻ (08) 9757 6308; est 1977; ❖ 8,000 cases; ⚑; A$; 7 days 10-5
Draws upon 20 hectares of mature vineyards to make the mainstream portfolio of austerely restrained wines. Minerally, lemony Reserve Sauvignon Blanc leads the way.

Ribbon Vale Estate ☆☆☆⌡
Lot 5 Caves Road, Willyabrup via Cowaramup, WA 6284,
☎ (08) 9755 6272, Ⓕ (08) 9755 6337; est 1977; ❖ 4,000 cases;
⚑; A$; wkds & hols 10-5

Takes its name from the unusual shape of the vineyard block, which is exceedingly long and thin. Semillon, Sauvignon Blanc and Semillon/Sauvignon Blanc are regional archetypes at their best, intense and tightly structured; blackberryish, chocolatey and earthy Cabernet Sauvignon is also impressive.

Rivendell ☆☆☆
Lot 328 Wildwood Road, Yallingup, WA 6282, ☎ (08) 9755 2235,
Ⓕ (08) 9755 2295; est 1987; ❖ 2,750 cases; ⚑; A$; 7 days 10-5

Doubtless named in honour of JRR Tolkien, Rivendell is a producer of wines such as Honeysuckle Late Harvest Semillon that would delight any hobbit. The fruit salad-accented Verdelho is good, too.

Rosa Brook Estate NR
Rosa Brook Road, Margaret River, WA 6285, ☎ (08) 9757 2286,
Ⓕ (08) 9757 3634; est 1980; ❖ 5,000 cases; ⚑; A$; Nov-Apr: 7 days 10-4, May-Oct: Thurs-Sun 11-4

Nine grape varieties on seven hectares of vineyards, with cellar-door sales now occupying what was once Margaret River's first abattoir (1930s vintage), all add up to something different.

Sandstone ☆☆☆
CMB Carbunup River, WA 6280, ☎ (08) 9755 6271, Ⓕ (08) 9755 6292; est 1988; ❖ 750 cases; No visitors

Mike and Jan Davies are the will-o'-the-wisp proprietors of the Sandstone label, usually occupied either as contract winemakers for others or off with their mobile bottling line. They make sturdy, long-lived Semillon and Cabernet Sauvignon under the Sandstone label.

Serventy ☆☆⌡
Valley Home Vineyard, Rocky Road, Forest Grove via Margaret River, WA 6286, ☎ (08) 9757 7534, Ⓕ (08) 9757 7534; est 1984;
❖ 1,500 cases; ⚑; A$; Fri-Sun & hols 10-4

The Serventy family has nurtured several generations of distinguished naturalists and pioneering conservationists. And not surprisingly, they employ strictly organic viticultural techniques, and use only minimal SO_2 in their winemaking and rudimentary winery.

Suckfizzle Augusta NR
Lot 14 Kalkarrie Drive, Augusta, WA 6290 (PO Box 570, Margaret River, WA 6285), ☎ (08) 9758 0304, Ⓕ (08) 9330 9610; est 1997; ❖ small; No visitors

The wildly improbable name comes from Rabelais. This is the joint venture of two well-known Margaret River winemakers who, in deference to their employers, do not identify themselves on any of the background material or the striking front and back labels of the wines. High-quality Sauvignon Blanc/Semillon is a certainty.

Thornhill/The Berry Farm NR
Bessel Road, Rosa Glen, WA 6285, ☎ (08) 9757 5054, ℻ (08) 9757 5116; est 1990; ❧ NFP; ⚑; A$; 7 days 10-4.30; ¶

The Berry Farm fruit wines that I have tasted are extraordinarily good, but I have yet to make my acquaintance with the grape-based wines. Names such as Tickled Pink (sparkling Cabernet Sauvignon) and Still Tickled Pink (light Cabernet Sauvignon) perhaps give a flavour of the style.

Treeton Estate ☆☆☆
North Treeton Road, Cowaramup, WA 6284, ☎ (08) 9755 5481, ℻ (08) 9755 5051; est 1984; ❧ 3,000 cases; ⚑; A$; 7 days 10-6; café

David McGowan and wife Corinne have taken the slow road in developing Treeton Estate, but have got there in the the end. The wines are fresh and light-bodied, perhaps a little too much so.

Vasse Felix ☆☆☆☆☆
Cnr Caves Road and Harmans Road South, Willyabrup, WA 6284, ☎ (08) 9755 5242, ℻ (08) 9755 5425; est 1967; ❧ 60,000 cases; ⚑; A$; 7 days 10-5; ¶

The most senior winery in the region, established by Dr Tom Cullitty but now owned by Janet Homes à Court's Heytesbury Holdings. A brand-new winery and rapidly expanding vineyard will capitalise on the strength of the brand; the flagship Heytesbury Bordeaux blend is superb.

Virage ☆☆☆
13B Georgette Road, Gracetown, WA 6284, ☎ (08) 9755 5318, ℻ (08) 9755 5318; est 1990; ❧ 1,000 cases; No visitors

The winemaking venture of former Vasse Felix winemaker Bernard Abbott, who buys grapes and rents winery space to make wines sold by mail order and direct to restaurants in Perth, Melbourne and Sydney.

Voyager Estate ☆☆☆☆☆❧
Lot 1 Stevens Road, Margaret River, WA 6285, ☎ (08) 9757 6354, ℻ (08) 9757 6494; est 1978; ❧ 20,000 cases; ⚑; A$; 7 days 10-4; ¶

The flamboyant venture of mining magnate Michael Wright, with manicured rose gardens and a Cape Dutch cellar-door sales mansion. Tucked away in the back, Stewart Pym makes wonderfully rich and skilfully oaked Semillon and Chardonnay, and powerful Reserve Cabernet/Merlot.

Willespie ☆☆☆❧ V
Harmans Mill Road, Willyabrup via Cowaramup, WA 6284, ☎ (08) 9755 6248, ℻ (08) 9755 6210; est 1976; ❧ 4,000 cases; ⚑; A$; 7 days 10.30-5

Brisk, crisp, minerally Sauvignon Blanc and Semillon/Sauvignon

Blanc have been the very successful flagbearers for the Squance family for over 20 years, providing the momentum for a substantial increase in the size of the business now underway.

Great Southern

Even by the standards of Australia, Great Southern is a large region, forming a rectangle 150 km long and 100 km wide. It embraces climates that range from strongly maritime-influenced to moderately continental, and an ever-changing topography. The suitability of the region for premium-quality table wine was pinpointed in 1955 by the distinguished Californian viticulturist Professor Harold Olmo.

It was another ten years before the first experimental vineyard was planted at Forest Hill (now owned by Janet Holmes à Court as an adjunct to Vasse Felix in the Margaret River). Vineyards spread slowly between 1965 and 1985. Most were small. The only large planting was the 100-hectare Frankland River Estate, leased by Houghton in 1981 and ultimately acquired by it. Then, in the second half of the 1980s, Goundrey Wines appeared, and the originally small Alkoomi and Plantagenet wineries flourished and grew. Howard Park, too, acquired near-icon status. All was set for the boom of the 1990s.

The two greatest wines of the region are Riesling (a serious challenge to the primacy of the Clare and Eden Valleys) and Cabernet Sauvignon. Shiraz, too, can be superb, with intense spicy, cherry flavours. Indeed, with suitable site selection, every one of the classic varieties can produce top-class wine somewhere in Great Southern.

Alkoomi ☆☆☆☆☆ V
Wingeballup Road, Frankland, WA 6396, ☎ (08) 9855 2229, ℻ (08) 9855 2284; est 1971; ❖ 50,000 cases; ⚑; A$; 7 days 10.30-5; ⇌

Through sheer hard work and experience, Merv and Judy Lange – and their children – have built a significant wine business in a remote part of the Great Southern. Racy Riesling, tangy Sauvignon Blanc, fruit-driven melon/citrous Chardonnay, currant Malbec, peppery Shiraz and finely crafted, cedary Blackbutt (Bordeaux blend) are all consistently excellent.

Castle Rock Estate ☆☆☆☆
Porongurup Road, Porongurup, WA 6324, ☎ (08) 9853 1035, ℻ (08) 9853 1010; est 1983; ❖ 5,000 cases; ⚑; A$; Mon-Fri 10-4, wkds & public hols 10-5

One of the more beautifully situated vineyards in Australia, with sweeping vistas from its hillside location in the Porongurups. Initially delicate Riesling blossoms with age, as does Chardonnay; the light-bodied reds are less convincing.

Chatsfield ☆☆☆☆
O'Neil Road, Mount Barker, WA 6324, ☎ (08) 9851 1704, ℻ (08) 9851 1704; est 1976; ❖ 10,000 cases; ⚑; A$; Tues-Sun, public hols 10-5

Mature, low-yielding vineyards are the cornerstone of this producer. The crisp, minerally Riesling and spice-and-cherry Shiraz are complemented by an excellent, early-release, unoaked Cabernet Franc, as lively a red wine as you could wish for.

Frankland Estate ☆☆☆½
Frankland Road, Frankland, WA 6396, ☎ (08) 9855 1544, ℻ (08) 9855 1549; est 1988; ❦ 12,000 cases; ▼; A$; by appt

Established on the gently rolling hills of a large sheep property by Barrie Smith and Judi Cullam. A 'slow but sure' maturing Riesling, sinewy Isolation Ridge Shiraz and elegant Olmo's Reward (Bordeaux blend) all have a devoted following, although fresher oak might help.

Gilbert ☆☆☆☆½
RMB 438 Albany Highway, Kendenup via Mount Barker, WA 6323, ☎ (08) 9851 4028, ℻ (08) 9851 4021; est 1980; ❦ 2,000 cases; ▼; A$; Wed-Mon 10-5

A part-time occupation and diversification for sheep and beef farmers Jim and Beverley Gilbert. Riesling, Chardonnay and Shiraz are very competently contract-made at Plantagenet.

Goundrey ☆☆☆☆
Muir Highway, Mount Barker, WA 6324, ☎ (08) 9851 1777, ℻ (08) 9851 1997; est 1978; ❦ 187,000 cases; ▼; A$; Mon-Sat 10-4.30, Sun 11-4.30

Now owned by Perth millionaire Jack Bendat, who has spent one or two (million) on a major, ongoing expansion programme, neatly timed with winning 'Winery of the Year' at the 1999 International Wine & Spirit Competition in the UK. Look for the Reserve wines in particular.

Harewood Estate ☆☆☆½
Scotsdale Road, Denmark, WA 6333, ☎ (08) 9840 9078, ℻ (08) 9840 9053; est 1988; ❦ 400 cases; A$; by appt

Keith and Margie Graham have established a showpiece vineyard in an idyllic setting. Part of the grape production is sold to others; a small amount is contract-made, with sophisticated barrel-fermented Chardonnay the pick.

Howard Park ☆☆☆☆☆
Lot 377 Scotsdale Road, Denmark, WA 6333, ☎ (08) 9848 2345, ℻ (08) 9848 2064; est 1986; ❦ 70,000 cases; ▼; A$; 7 days 10-4

Began a major metamorphosis in 1999, with founder John Wade moving to a consultancy role and majority owner Jeff Birch establishing a vineyard in the Margaret River region. Sublime Riesling and usually sublime Cabernet/Merlot should continue.

Jingalla ☆☆☆☆
RMB 1316 Bolganup Dam Road, Porongurup, WA 6324, ☎ (08) 9853 1023, ℻ (08) 9853 1023; est 1979; ❦ 3,000 cases; 7 days 10.30-5; ⌂, café

Another winery making decisive moves in 1999, with the announcement of the construction of a new winery to service its needs and those of others in the region.

Karrivale ☆☆☆☆✓
Woodlands Road, Porongurup, WA 6324, ☎ (08) 9853 1009, ℻ (08) 9853 1129; est 1979; ❖ 1,170 cases; ♀; A$; Wed-Sun 10-5

For long a Porongurups-based Riesling specialist, producing lovely, finely structured wines that blossom gloriously with age. Now also makes a little Chardonnay.

Karriview ☆☆☆☆
RMB 913 Roberts Road, Denmark, WA 6333, ☎ (08) 9840 9381, ℻ (08) 9840 9381; est 1986; ❖ 800 cases; ♀; A$; summer school hols 7 days 11-4, Feb-Dec: Fri-Tues 11-4

One hectare each of immaculately tended Chardonnay and Pinot Noir, capable of producing exceptionally complex and intense wines. Rating is for the successful years.

Mariners Rest NR
Jamakarri Farm, Roberts Road, Denmark, WA 6333, ☎ (08) 9840 9324, ℻ (08) 9840 9324; est 1996; ❖ 450 cases; ♀; A$; 7 days 10-5

Reincarnation of the dead Golden Rise winery, based on a 2.5-hectare vineyard planted in 1997 with Chardonnay and Pinot Noir.

Marribrook ☆☆☆
Rocky Gully Road, Frankland, WA 6396, ☎ (08) 9457 7885, ℻ (08) 9457 7885; est 1990; ❖ 2,000 cases; No visitors

Another change of name (formerly Marron View) and ownership, and with an eclectic range of wines that include light, unoaked Botanica Chardonnay, Marsanne (too delicate, perhaps) and juicy, chocolatey Cabernet/Malbec.

Matilda's Meadow ☆☆☆
Eladon Brook Estate, RMB 654 Hamilton Road, Denmark, WA 6333, ☎ (08) 9848 1951, ℻ (08) 9848 1957; est 1990; ❖ 1,500 cases; ♀; A$; Wed-Mon 10-4; ⚑

Former hotelier Don Turnbull and oil-industry executive Pamela Meldrum have established a 6-hectare vineyard producing a wide range of wines and a restaurant open all day, every day.

Merrebee Estate ☆☆☆☆✓
Lot 3339 St Werburghs Road, Mount Barker, WA 6234, ☎ (08) 9851 2424, ℻ (08) 9851 2425; est 1986; ❖ 1,000 cases; ♀; A$; wkds & public hols 10-4 and by appt

The first vintage released was 1995, ten years after the planting of its 3.5-hectare vineyard commenced. Lime-juice and honey Riesling and spicy, liquorice and vanilla Shiraz both impressive.

Millinup Estate NR
RMB 1280 Porongurup Road, Porongurup, WA 6324, ☎ (08) 9853 1105, ℻ (08) 9853 1105; est 1989; ❖ 220 cases; ♀; A$; wkds 10-5; ⚑

Pattersons ☆☆☆☆
St Werburghs Road, Mount Barker, WA 6234, ☏ (08) 9851 2063,
℻ (08) 9851 2063; est 1982; ❖ 2,000 cases; ⚑; A$; Sun-Wed 10-5
School teachers Arthur and Sue Patterson have achieved what many dream of: a beautiful rammed-earth house and cellar door on their vineyard (and grazing) property, from which they offer richly concentrated Chardonnay, powerful Shiraz and the occasional stellar Pinot Noir (such as the '94).

Plantagenet ☆☆☆☆♩ V
Albany Highway, Mount Barker, WA 6324, ☏ (08) 9851 2150,
℻ (08) 9851 1839; est 1974; ❖ 40,000 cases; ⚑; A$; Mon-Fri 9-5,
wkds 10-4; ⑩
One of the oldest and most important wineries in the region, Plantagenet has played a dual role as maker of its own consistently excellent wines (Riesling, Chardonnay, Shiraz and Cabernet Sauvignon to the fore, all combining flavour with elegance) and as a contract winemaker for numerous small grape-growers scattered throughout the Great Southern region.

Somerset Hill Wines NR
891 McLeod Road, Denmark, WA 6333, ☏ (08) 9840 9388,
℻ (08) 9840 9394; est 1995; ❖ 600 cases; ⚑; A$; by appt
Graham Lipson commenced planting nine hectares of Pinot Noir, Chardonnay, Semillon and Sauvignon Blanc in 1995 (and also lavender), opening the deliberately rustic stone cellar door in late 1998 to sell wine, lavender and crafts.

Tingle-Wood ☆☆☆☆☆♩ V
Glenrowan Road, Denmark, WA 6333, ☏ (08) 9840 9218;
est 1976; ❖ 1,000 cases; ⚑; A$; 7 days 9-5; ⑩
An intermittent producer of Riesling of extraordinary quality, although birds and other disasters do intervene and prevent production in some years.

West Cape Howe Wines NR
PO Box 548, Denmark, WA 6333, ☏ (08) 9848 2959, ℻ (08) 9848 2903; est 1997; ❖ 300 cases; No visitors
Owner/winemaker Brenden Smith was winemaker at Goundrey for years before opening his own contract-winemaking business in 1998. A small part of the annual crush is released under his West Cape Howe label.

Wignalls Wines ☆☆☆☆
Chester Pass Road (Highway 1), Albany, WA 6330, ☏ (08) 9841 2848, ℻ (08) 9842 9003; est 1982; ❖ 5,000 cases; ⚑; A$; 7 days 12-4
One of the best-known labels in the Great Southern thanks to its early success with fragrant Pinot Noir. The mantle has

slipped a little (ageing problems) but some lovely citrous, melon-like Chardonnay has helped redress the balance.

Williams Rest NR
Lot 195 Albany Highway, Mount Barker, WA 6324, ☎ (08) 9367 3277, ℉ (08) 9367 3328; est 1972; ✣ NA; No visitors
A long-established vineyard, planted way back in 1972, which is now part of the Selwyn Wine Group. The vineyard is named after Benjamin Williams, an eight-year-old boy who was accidentally killed by a mail coach in 1890, hence the name Williams Rest.

Yanwirra ☆☆☆
Redman Road, Denmark, WA 6333, ☎ (08) 9386 3577, ℉ (08) 9386 3578; est 1989; ✣ 500 cases; No visitors
Perth anaesthetist Ian McGlew and wife Liz have a little of everything planted in their 4-hectare vineyard. Part of the production is sold as grapes, part is vinified and sold at modest prices through mail order.

Zarephath Wines NR
Moorialup Road, East Porongurup, WA 6324, ☎ (08) 9853 1152, ℉ (08) 9841 8124; est 1994; ✣ 300 cases; ♀; A$; 7 days 9-4
The Zarephath vineyard is owned and operated by the Brothers and Sisters of The Christ Circle, a Benedictine community. They say the most outstanding feature of the location is the feeling of peace and tranquillity that permeates the site, something I can well believe on the basis of numerous visits to the Porongurups.

Pemberton

Everything seems to thrive in this relatively new region, from eucalyptus forests and vines to controversy. The GI legislation led to a protracted and bitter debate over the name before settling on Pemberton, but that has not been the only wrangle. First planted with vines for commercial ventures in 1977, the region was initially hailed as having the greatest potential for Pinot Noir outside Burgundy. Now it is suggested it may be best suited to Merlot and Shiraz, while the Pinot Noir often joins its more successful partner Chardonnay in sparkling wines. There has been an undercurrent of extreme disappointment running through this with the quality of some of the grapes: flavours have tended to be weak, and the wines have developed and aged with disconcerting rapidity.

The answer appears to lie partly in the annual rainfall (1,255 mm) but more importantly in the soil types, scattered across the two subregions, Pemberton and Manjimup. The best are the lateritic gravelly sands and loams overlying clay, with moderate water-holding capacity, found around Manjimup. The second are fertile Karri loams leading to excess vine vigour and crop loads. Everyone in the region is going through a steep learning curve, and Pemberton may yet live up to the lofty expectations held for it. But it won't happen overnight, nor will it happen easily.

Batista NR
Franklin Road, Middlesex, WA 6258, ☎ (08) 9772 3530,
℉ (08) 9772 3530; est 1993; ❦ 600 cases; ⚑; A$; by appt

Batista is the baptismal name of owner Bob Peruch, a Pinot Noir devotee whose father planted vines on the property back in the 1950s. Those vines are no more, and in their place are 1.5 hectares of Pinot Noir and lesser amounts of Shiraz, Cabernet and Chardonnay. The Batista Pinot Noir has been given high praise by those whose judgement is impeccable.

Black George NR
Black Georges Road, Manjimup, WA 6258, ☎ (08) 9772 3569,
℉ (08) 9772 3102; est 1991; ❦ 4,000 cases; ⚑; A$; 7 days 10.30-4.45

A relatively recent arrival on the scene, with particular aspirations to make high-quality Pinot Noir. As with so much of the Pemberton region, it remains to be seen whether the combination of soil and climate will permit this.

Chestnut Grove ☆☆☆↓
Chestnut Grove Road, Manjimup, WA 6258, ☎ (08) 9771 4255,
℉ (08) 9772 4255; est 1988; ❦ 10,000 cases; ⚑; A$; by appt

A joint venture between the Lange family of Alkoomi and Vic Kordic and his family, including grandson Darren Cook. Initial vintages were slightly weak and dilute, but increasing vine age (and, one suspects, better viticulture) has resulted in a significant lift in wine quality, particularly with the Cabernet/Merlot.

Constables ☆☆☆ V
Graphite Road, West Manjimup, WA 6258, ☎ (08) 9772 1375;
est 1988; ❦ NFP; ⚑; A$; 7 days 9-5

Father John and son Michael, together with other members of the Constable family, have established an 11-hectare vineyard at Manjimup. Most of the grapes are sold to Houghton under a long-term contract, and limited quantities are contract-made for the Constable label by Houghton.

D'Entrecasteaux NR
Boorara Road, Northcliffe, WA 6262, ☎ (08) 9776 7232; est 1988;
❦ 600 cases; ⚑; A$; by appt

This estate takes its name from the 18th-century French explorer Admiral Bruni D'Entrecasteaux. Four hectares of Chardonnay, Sauvignon Blanc, Pinot Noir and Cabernet Sauvignon, planted on rich Karri loam, produce grapes for the wines contract-made at Alkoomi.

Donnelly River Wines ☆☆☆
Lot 159 Vasse Highway, Pemberton, WA 6260, ☎ (08) 9776 2052,
℉ (08) 9776 2053; est 1986; ❦ 4,000 cases; ⚑; A$; 7 days 9.30-4.30; ⌘

Blair Miekjohn planted 16 hectares of estate vineyards in 1986, and produced the first wines in 1990. The Chardonnay has consistently been the pick of the bunch, the Pinot Noir and Cabernet Sauvignon less convincing.

Eastbrook Estate NR
Lot 3 Vasse Highway, Eastbrook, WA 6260, ☎ (08) 9776 1251, ⓕ (08) 9776 1251; est 1990; ❖ 2000 cases; ♀; A$; Fri-Sun & public hols 11-4; ¶

A weatherboard winery and restaurant made using jarrah pole, limestone and cedar have been built on the site by former Perth real-estate agent Kim Skipworth. The wines come from seven hectares of estate plantings of Pinot Noir, Chardonnay, Sauvignon Blanc and Shiraz.

Gloucester Ridge Vineyard ☆☆☆
Burma Road, Pemberton, WA 6260, ☎ (08) 9776 1035, ⓕ (08) 9776 1390; est 1985; ❖ 5,000 cases; ♀; A$; 7 days 10-5, later on Sat; café, fly fishing

Owned and operated by Don and Sue Hancock, this is the only vineyard located within the Pemberton town boundary, making it an easy walk from the centre. Quality has varied, but, as the Sauvignon Blanc shows, can be good.

Jardee NR
Old School House, Jardee, WA 6258, ☎ (08) 9777 1552, ⓕ (08) 9777 1552; est 1994; ❖ 510 cases; No visitors

A part-time interest for proprietor Steve Miolin, whose wines are made in tiny quantities from purchased fruit.

Lefroy Brook NR
Glauder Road, Pemberton, WA 6260, ☎ (08) 9386 8385; est 1982; ❖ 350 cases; No visitors

Owned by Pat and Barbara Holt, the former a graduate in biochemistry and microbiology working in medical research, but with a passion for Burgundy. The 1.5 hectares of vines are now both netted and fenced with steel mesh, producing wines that, on tastings to date, are outside the mainstream.

Merum NR
Hillbrook Road, Northcliffe, WA 6262, ☎ (08) 9777 1543, ⓕ (08) 9777 1543; est 1996; ❖ 300 cases; ♀; A$; by appt

Maria Melsom (former Driftwood Estate winemaker) and Michael Melsom (former viticulturist at Voyager Estate) have struck out on their own with wines from nine hectares that will come fully on-stream by 2003.

Mountford ☆☆☆
Bamess Road, West Pemberton, WA 6260, ☎ (08) 9776 1439, ⓕ (08) 9776 1439; est 1987; ❖ 5,000 cases; ♀; A$; Fri-Sun 10-4

English-born and trained Andrew Mountford and wife Sue migrated to Australia in 1983. They first endeavoured to set up a winery at Mudgee, thereafter moving to Pemberton with far greater success. Their strikingly packaged wines (complete with beeswax and paper seals) have been well received on eastern Australian markets, being produced from six hectares of permanently netted, dry-grown vineyards.

Piano Gully ☆☆⁄

Piano Gully Road, Manjimup, WA 6258, ☏ (08) 9772 3583,
Ⓕ (08) 9771 2886; est 1987; ❖ 450 cases; ❦; A$; wkds & public hols 10-5
The 4-hectare vineyard of Chardonnay, Pinot Noir and Cabernet Sauvignon was established in 1987 on rich Karri loam, 10 km south of Manjimup. The first releases, from the 1991 vintage, made an uncertain debut.

Picardy ☆☆☆☆☆

Cnr Vasse Highway and Eastbrook Road, Manjimup, WA 6260,
☏ (08) 9779 0036, Ⓕ (08) 9776 0245; est 1993; ❖ 4,000 cases;
❦; A$; by appt
Owned by Dr Bill Pannell and his wife Sandra, the founders of Moss Wood winery in the Margaret River region (in 1969). It is one of the relatively few wineries in Pemberton to shine, with excellent Pinot Noir, Shiraz and Merlot/Cabernet, all with rich and clearly articulated varietal character.

Salitage ☆☆☆☆

Vasse Highway, Pemberton, WA 6260, ☏ (08) 9776 1771,
Ⓕ (08) 9776 1772; est 1989; ❖ 12,000 cases; ❦; A$; 7 days 10-4; ⦿
This promised to be the pace-setter for the Pemberton region, with Chardonnay and Pinot Noir, and the early vintages were enthusiastically received by all and sundry. However, the wines appear to age in bottle with disconcerting speed, and some of the more recent releases have shown unsettling variability. The rating might be seen as a little generous.

Sinclair Wines NR

Graphite Road, Glenoran, WA 6258, ☏ (08) 9421 1399,
Ⓕ (08) 9421 1191; est 1993; ❖ 1,300 cases; ❦; A$; by appt
With five hectares of vineyard, this is the child of Darelle Sinclair, a science teacher, wine educator and graduate viticulturist from Charles Sturt University and John Healy, a lawyer, traditional jazz musician and graduate in wine marketing at Adelaide University, Roseworthy Campus.

Smithbrook ☆☆☆⁄

Smithbrook Road, Middlesex via Manjimup, WA 6258,
☏ (08) 9772 3557, Ⓕ (08) 9772 3579; est 1988; ❖ 14,000 cases;
❦; A$; 7 days 10-4
A major player in the Pemberton region, with 60 hectares of vines in production. Although majority interest was acquired by Petaluma in 1997, it will continue its role as a contract grower for other companies, as well as supplying Petaluma's needs and making relatively small amounts of wine under its own label. Perhaps the most significant change has been the removal of Pinot Noir from the current list, and the introduction of Merlot.

Tantemaggie NR

Kemp Road, Pemberton, WA 6260, ☏ (08) 9776 1164, Ⓕ (08) 9776 1164; est 1987; ❖ 110 cases; ❦; A$; wkds 9-5

Part of a mixed farming operation, with most of the grapes from the 20-hectare vineyard sold to Houghton. A light-bodied Cabernet is contract-made to the Pottinger specifications.

The Warren Vineyard NR
Conte Road, Pemberton, WA 6260, ☎ (08) 9776 1115, ⓕ (08) 9776 1115; est 1985; ❖ 600 cases; ₸; A$; 7 days 11-5

The 1.4-hectare vineyard with four varieites was established in 1985, and is one of the smallest in the Pemberton region. It came to public notice in 1992 at the SGIO Western Australia Winemakers Exhibition, when its 1991 Cabernet Sauvignon won the award for the Best Red Table Wine from the Pemberton Region. Little seen of it since then.

Treen Ridge Estate NR
Parker Road, Pemberton, WA 6260, ☎ (08) 9776 1131, ⓕ (08) 9776 1176; est 1992; ❖ NFP; ₸; A$; wkds 10-5; ⌂

A 2-hectare vineyard of Riesling, Sauvignon Blanc, Shiraz and Cabernet Sauvignon is linked to a bed-and-breakfast enterprise. The wines are contract-made and sold at the cellar door.

WoodSmoke Estate NR
Lot 2 Kemp Road, Pemberton, WA 6260, ☎ (08) 9776 0225, ⓕ (08) 9776 0225; est 1992; ❖ 1,500 cases; ₸; A$; by appt

The former Jimlee Estate was acquired and renamed by the Liebeck family in July 1998. The current plantings of a little over two hectares of Semillon, Sauvignon Blanc, Cabernet Franc and Cabernet Sauvignon are being expanded with a further two hectares of Cabernet Franc and Merlot.

Geographe

The newly created Geographe region is a far more compact and logical area than the sprawling South West Coastal Plain from which it has been divided. Its centre is Bunbury, its southern (or, more properly, southeastern) corner is Busselton, while many rivers create valleys from the hills with distinctive climates.

Geographe is an area of considerable beauty and great variation in its topography and scenery. Although not yet officially demarcated, three distinct sub-regions are strongly suggested by the topographic and climatic factors: Capel, on the coast; the Donnybrook area, cut off from the maritime influence and once famous for its apple orchards; and the Bunbury Hills, which include the scenic Ferguson Valley.

The dominant varieties are familiar enough: Chardonnay, Shiraz and Cabernet Sauvignon, with clear-cut varietal flavour in the wines. As the Margaret River continues to grow, it is expected that Geographe will, too.

Capel Vale ☆☆☆☆
Lot 5 Stirling Estate, Mallokup Road, Capel, WA 6271, ☎ (08) 9727 1986, ⓕ (08) 9727 1904; est 1979; ❖ 90,000 cases; ₸; A$; 7 days 10-4

The seemingly ever-expanding Capel Vale empire extends from Geographe to the Margaret River and to the Great Southern. A long time producer of finely honed Riesling and tangy Chardonnay, it has added super-premium Shiraz and Cabernet/Merlot at the head of a dauntingly long list of products.

Ferguson Falls Estate ☆☆☆
Pile Road, Dardanup, WA 6236, ☏ (08) 9728 1083, ℻ (08) 9728 1083; est 1983; ❖ 320 cases; ▼; A$; by appt

Peter Giumelli and family are dairy farmers in the lush Ferguson Valley. In 1983, they planted three hectares of Cabernet Sauvignon, Chardonnay and Merlot; most of the grape production was sold and it was not until 1995 that the first wines were made for commercial release. The Chardonnay, in particular, is an attractive wine.

Henty Brook Estate NR
Box 49, Dardanup, WA 6236, ☏ (08) 9728 1459, ℻ (08) 9728 1459; est 1994; ❖ NA; No visitors

One hectare each of Shiraz and Sauvignon Blanc, and 0.5 hectares of Semillon were planted in the spring of 1994. The wines are contract-made by James Pennington at Hotham Valley Estate, with commercial releases still in the pipeline.

Killerby ☆☆☆☆
Lakes Road, Capel, WA 6230, ☏ 1800 655 722, ℻ 1800 679 578; est 1973; ❖ 10,000 cases; ▼; A$; 7 days 10-4.30

The Killerby family is a long-term resident of the southwest part of this region – Ben Killerby is the fourth generation. The 21 hectares of vines were established by Ben's father, the late Dr Barry Killerby, in 1973, and are now fully mature. Both Chardonnay and Cabernet Sauvignon are highly regarded by some influential critics.

Kingtree Wines NR
Kingtree Road, Wellington Mills via Dardanup, WA 6326, ☏ (08) 9728 3050, ℻ (08) 9728 3113; est 1991; ❖ 1,000 cases; ▼; A$; 7 days 12-5.30;

Kingtree Wines, with 2.5 hectares of estate plantings, is part of the Kingtree Lodge development, a 4.5-star luxury retreat in dense Jarrah forest.

Thomas NR
23-24 Crowd Road, Gelorup, WA 6230, ☏ (08) 9795 7925; est 1976; ❖ 600 cases; ▼; A$; by appt

I have not tasted the elegant Pinot Noir and Cabernet Sauvignon of Bunbury pharmacist Gill Thomas for several years; they are only sold to a local clientele.

Wansbrough Wines NR
Richards Road, Ferguson, WA 6236, ☏ (08) 9728 3091, ℻ (08) 9728 3091; est 1986; ❖ 250 cases; ▼; A$; wkds 10-5;

Situated east of Dardanup in the picturesque Ferguson Valley, the wines are made at Willespie in the Margaret River, and are principally sold through the winery restaurant at weekends.

Swan District

Two waves of immigration by Yugoslavs, the first at the turn of the century (principally from Dalmatia) and the second after the Second World War, brought with them two claims to fame for the Swan Valley. The first, and most surprising, is that for a time it had more wineries in operation than either NSW or Victoria; the second, and more obvious, is that it joined the Barossa Valley (German) and Riverland (Italian) as a significant ethnically driven wine-producing region.

It is basically a flat alluvial river plan, bisected by the Swan River, and without much visual attraction other than the historic oasis of the Houghton winery. Its summer temperatures are fierce, often around (or above) 40°C for days on end, and vintage is underway in earnest by the end of January. Chenin Blanc and Verdelho have long been specialities, now joined by Chardonnay.

Swan Valley's importance as a grape-growing region has declined dramatically over the past 20 years from 58 per cent down to 15 per cent of Western Australian production. It is a trend which will continue, simply as a reflection of the explosive growth in the Great Southern, Margaret River and Pemberton plantings. The anchors that keep the Swan District from drifting are Houghton and Sandalford, and to a lesser extent, the small wineries serving the ever-growing wine-tourism trade.

Aquila Estate ☆☆☆
85 Carabooda Road, Carabooda, WA 6033, ☎ (08) 9561 5415,
Ⓕ (08) 9561 5415; est 1993; ❖ 19,500 cases; No visitors

As Aquila Estate has matured, so have its grape sources, centred on the Margaret River (principally) and Boyup Brook. The white wines are quite attractive, particularly the Margaret River Sauvignon Blanc and Boyup Brook Chardonnay.

Baxter Stokes Wines NR
65 Memorial Avenue, Baskerville, WA 6065, ☎ (08) 9296 4831,
Ⓕ (08) 9296 4831; est 1988; ❖ 750 cases; ♇; A$; 9.30-5 wkds
& public hols

A weekend and holiday operation for Greg and Lucy Stokes, who sell the range of Chardonnay, Verdelho, Pinot Noir, Shiraz and Cabernet Sauvignon by mail order and through cellar door. The prices are enticingly low.

Carabooda Estate NR
297 Carabooda Road, Carabooda, WA 6033, ☎ (08) 9407 5283,
Ⓕ (08) 9407 5283; est 1989; ❖ 2,000 cases; ♇; A$; 7 days 10-6

Terry Ord made his first wine in 1979, and planted the first estate vines in 1981. His first commercial vintage was 1989. The slowly, slowly approach is reflected in the range of back vintages available at the cellar door.

Cobanov NR
Stock Road, Herne Hill, WA 6056, ☎ (08) 9296 4210; est 1960;
❖ 10,000 cases; ❡; A$; Wed-Sun 9-5.30

A substantial family-owned operation producing a mix of bulk and bottled wine from 21 hectares of estate grapes. Part of the annual production is sold as grapes to other producers, including Houghton. The prices are extraordinarily low.

Coorinja ☆☆✧ V
Toodyay Road, Toodyay, WA 6566, ☎ (08) 9626 2280; est 1870;
❖ 3,200 cases; ❡; A$; Mon-Sat 8-5

An evocative and historic winery, nestling in a small gully, which seems to be in a time-warp and begging to be used as a film-set. A revamp of the packaging accompanied a more-than-respectable Hermitage (Shiraz), with lots of dark chocolate and sweet-berry flavour, finishing with soft tannins.

Garbin Estate NR
209 Toodyay Road, Middle Swan, WA 6056, ☎ (08) 9274 1747,
℻ (08) 9274 1747; est 1956; ❖ 1,000 cases; ❡; A$; 7 days 10-5.30

Peter Garbin, winemaker by weekend and design draftsman by week, decided in 1990 to substantially upgrade the family business. The vineyards have been replanted, the winery re-equipped, and the first of the new-generation wines was produced in 1994.

Henley Park Wines NR
149 Swan Street, West Swan, WA 6055, ☎ (08) 9296 4328,
℻ (08) 9296 1313; est 1935; ❖ 3,500 cases; ❡; A$; Tues-Sun 10-5;
café (Fri-Sun), playground

Like so many Swan Valley wineries, this was founded by a Yugoslav family, but is now jointly owned by Danish and Malaysian interests. The wines, made by majority owner and winemaker Claus Petersen, are principally exported to Denmark and Malaysia.

Highway Wines NR
612 Great Northern Highway, Herne Hill, WA 6056, ☎ (08) 9296 4354; est 1954; ❖ 4,000 cases; ❡; A$; Mon-Sat 8.30-6

A survivor of another era, when literally dozens of such wineries plied their business in the Swan Valley. It still enjoys a strong local trade, selling much of its wine in fill-your-own-containers and two-litre flagons, with lesser quantities sold by the bottle.

Houghton ☆☆☆☆☆ V
Dale Road, Middle Swan, WA 6056, ☎ (08) 9274 5100,
℻ (08) 9274 5372; est 1836; ❖ 300,000 cases; ❡; A$; 7 days 10-5; ⍾

The 5-star rating may seem extreme, but rests partly upon Houghton White Burgundy (aka Supreme), almost entirely consumed within days of purchase, but superlative with seven or so years' bottle age, and on the super-premium Jack Mann Cabernet blend and Reserve Shiraz.

Jane Brook Estate ☆☆☆
229 Toodyay Road, Middle Swan, WA 6056, ℡ (08) 9274 1432,
℻ (08) 9274 1211; est 1972; ❖ 20,000 cases; ▼; A$; 7 days 12-5;
|●|; playground

An attractive winery, which relies on substantial cellar-door trade and on varying export markets, with much work having been invested in the Japanese market in recent years. The white wines are usually best, although the quality of the oak isn't always up to the mark.

Lamont Wines ☆☆☆✓ V
85 Bisdee Road, Millendon, WA 6056, ℡ (08) 9296 4485,
℻ (08) 9296 1663; est 1978; ❖ 6,000 cases; ▼; A$; Wed-Sun 10-5;
|●|; gallery, playground

Corin Lamont is the daughter of the late Jack Mann, and makes her wines in the image of those made by her father, resplendent in their generosity. Lamont also boasts a superb restaurant with a gallery for the sale and promotion of local arts.

Little River Wines NR
Cnr West Swan and Forest Roads, Henley Brook, WA 6055,
℡ (08) 9296 4462, ℻ (08) 9296 1022; est 1934; ❖ 4,000 cases;
▼; A$; Fri-Wed 10-5; |●|

Following several quick changes of ownership (and of consultant winemakers) the former Glenalwyn now has as its winemaker the eponymously named Count Bruno de Tastes. I, however, have had no recent tastes.

Mann NR
105 Memorial Avenue, Baskerville, WA 6056, ℡ (08) 9296 4348,
℻ (08) 9296 4348; est 1988; ❖ 500 cases; ▼; A$; wkds 10-5 and by appt

Industry veteran Dorham Mann has established a label solely for what must be Australia's most unusual wine: a dry, only faintly pink, sparkling wine made exclusively from Cabernet Sauvignon grown on the 2.4-hectare estate surrounding the cellar door.

Moondah Brook ☆☆☆☆ V
c/o Houghton, Dale Road, Middle Swan, WA 6056, ℡ (08) 9274 5372, ℻ (08) 9274 5372; est 1968; ❖ 90,000 cases; No visitors

Owned by BRL Hardy. Most of its grapes come from the large Gingin vineyard, 70 km north of the Swan Valley, some from the Margaret River and Great Southern. Honeyed, aged Chenin Blanc and finely structured Cabernet Sauvignon are the pick of a strong portfolio.

Olive Farm ☆☆☆
77 Great Eastern Highway, South Guildford, WA 6055,
℡ (08) 9277 2989, ℻ (08) 9279 4372; est 1829; ❖ 4,000 cases;
▼; A$; Mon-Tues and Thurs-Fri 10-5, wkds 11-3; café

The oldest winery in Australia in use today, and arguably the least communicative. The ultra-low profile tends to disguise the

Paul Conti ☆☆☆✓
529 Wanneroo Road, Woodvale, WA 6026, ☎ *(08) 9409 9160,*
℉ *(08) 9309 1634; est 1948;* ❖ *8,000 cases;* ☘; *A$; Mon-Sat 9.30-5.30, Sun by appt;* ⚭

The gently-mannered Paul Conti has made some quite lovely wines in his time, the hallmarks being softness, freshness and balance. Supple Carabooda Chardonnay and chewy, cherry Marijiniup Shiraz have been the best.

Pinelli NR
18 Bennett Street, Caversham, WA 6055, ☎ *(08) 9279 6818,*
℉ *(08) 9377 4259; est 1979;* ❖ *7,000 cases;* ☘; *A$; 7 days 10-6*

Dominic Pinelli and son Robert – the latter a Roseworthy College graduate – sell 75 per cent of their production in flagons, but are seeking to place more emphasis on bottled-wine sales in the wake of recent show successes with Chenin Blanc.

RiverBank Estate NR
126 Hamersley Road, Caversham, WA 6055, ☎ *(08) 9377 1805,*
℉ *(08) 9377 2168; est 1993;* ❖ *3,500 cases;* ☘; *A$; wkds & public hols 10-5*

Robert Bond, a graduate of Charles Sturt University and Swan Valley viticulturist for 20 years, established RiverBank Estate in 1993. He draws upon 11 hectares of estate plantings and, in his words, 'the wines are unashamedly full-bodied, produced from ripe grapes'.

Sandalford ☆☆☆✓
West Swan Road, Caversham, WA 6055, ☎ *(08) 9874 9374,*
℉ *(08) 9274 2154; est 1840;* ❖ *60,000 cases;* ☘; *A$; 7 days 10-5;* ⚭; *playground*

The arrival of Bill Crappsley as winemaker, coupled with the refurbishment of the winery, has heralded major changes at Sandalford. Wine quality has improved year on year, with Chenin Blanc and Chardonnay leading the way, but not alone.

Sittella Wines NR
100 Barrett Road, Herne Hill, WA 6056, ☎ *(08) 9296 2600,*
℉ *(08) 9296 2600; est 1998;* ❖ *NA;* ☘; *A$; wkds & public hols 11-4*

Perth couple Simon and Maaike Berns acquired a 7-hectare block at Herne Hill, producing the first wine in 1998 and opening the most attractive cellar-door facility later that year.

Talijancich NR
26 Hyem Road, Herne Hill, WA 6056, ☎ *(08) 9296 4289,*
℉ *(08) 9296 1762; est 1932;* ❖ *10,000 cases;* ☘; *A$; Sun-Fri 11-5; café*

A former fortified-wine specialist (a 1969 Liqueur Tokay was released in July 1999) now making a broad range of table wines, with particular emphasis on Verdelho. Café opened late 1999.

Westfield ☆☆☆↙
Cnr Memorial Avenue and Great Northern Highway, Baskerville, WA 6056, ☏ (08) 9296 4356; Ⓕ (08) 9296 4356; est 1922; ♦ 11,000 cases; ⚑; A$; 7 days 10-5.30

John Kosovich is a consistent producer of a surprisingly elegant and complex Chardonnay; the other wines are more variable, but from time to time attractive Verdelho and excellent Cabernet Sauvignon have appeared. A family-owned vineyard at Pemberton now broadens the blend choice.

South West Coast

Left stranded by the secession of the new Geographe region to its south, what was always known as the South West Coast has been left in geographic limbo. It doesn't belong to the Swan District, but is no longer large enough to allow formal registration as a region. Thus, its official status is simply part of the Greater Perth Zone.

Its three wineries are all planted on what are known as Tuart Sands; the Tuart is a large eucalyptus gum tree which thrives on limestone-based free-draining sands that make excellent vineyard soils. The climate is strongly maritime, warmer than Margaret River but cooler – and with much lower summer temperature peaks – than the Swan District. Shiraz performs exceptionally well, Chenin Blanc likewise, and the ubiquitous Chardonnay is always ready to please.

Baldivis Estate ☆☆↙
Lot 165 River Road, Baldivis, WA 6171, ☏ (08) 9525 2066, Ⓕ (08) 9525 2411; est 1982; ♦ 6,000 cases; ⚑; A$; Mon-Fri 10-4, wkds & hols 11-5

Part of a very large, mixed horticultural enterprise on the Tuart Sands of the coastal plain. There is ample viticultural and winemaking expertise; although the wines are pleasant, soft and light-bodied, they tend to lack concentration.

Cape Bouvard ☆☆↙
Mount John Road, Mandurah, WA 6210, ☏ (08) 9739 1360, Ⓕ (08) 9739 1360; est 1990; ♦ 2,000 cases; ⚑; A$; 7 days 10-5

Doggerel poet-cum-winemaker Gary Grierson draws upon one hectare of estate plantings, but also purchases grapes from other growers for the new Cape Bouvard label. The few wines tasted have been light but inoffensive.

Peel Estate ☆☆☆☆↙
Fletcher Road, Baldivis, WA 6171, ☏ (08) 9524 1221, Ⓕ (08) 9524 1625; est 1974; ♦ 8,000 cases; ⚑; A$; 7 days 10-5

The winery rating is given for its Shiraz, a wine of considerable finesse and with a remarkably consistent track record. Every year Will Nairn holds a Great Shiraz tasting for six-year-old Australian Shirazes (in a blind tasting attended by 60 or so people), and pits Peel Estate against Australia's best. It is never disgraced. The white wines are workmanlike.

Perth Hills

The Perth Hills is a pretty region, with constantly changing vistas, and a rich profusion of exotic native vegetation. Viticulture has been carried on intermittently in the picturesque Perth Hills for over a century, but on a generally tiny scale. The longest-established of the present wineries, Hainault, dates back only to 1980. Following an ownership change it has been significantly expanded and is the only winery crushing more than 100 tonnes, processing grapes both on its own account and as a contract-maker for others.

The region has a cooler climate than the nearby Swan District, thanks to its altitude of up to 400 metres. But it could not be described as cool by any stretch of the imagination; Chardonnay, Shiraz and Cabernet Sauvignon are the most successful varieties, all showing warm-climate generosity of flavour.

Avalon Wines NR
1605 Bailey Road, Glen Forrest, WA 6071, ☎ (08) 9298 8049; est 1986; ❖ 100 cases; ♀; A$; by appt

Lyndon Crockett has 0.75 hectares each of Chardonnay, Semillon and Cabernet Sauvignon; the small production is sold by word of mouth.

Brookside Vineyard NR
5 Loaring Road, Bickley Valley, WA 6076, ☎ (08) 9291 8705, Ⓕ (08) 9291 5316; est 1984; ❖ 450 cases; ♀; A$; wkds & public hols 10-5;

One of the many miniature vineyard operations that dot the Perth Hills. It has a 0.25 hectares each of Chardonnay and Cabernet Sauvignon, selling the wine through a mailing list.

Carosa NR
310 Houston Street, Mount Helena, WA 6082, ☎ (08) 9572 1603, Ⓕ (08) 9572 1604; est 1984; ❖ 400 cases; ♀; A$; wkds & hols 11-5 or by appt; ⑩; arts & crafts

Winemaker/owner Jim Elson worked at wineries over in the eastern states before coming to the Perth Hills and setting up his own small business, offering everything from Classic Dry White to Old Tawny Port and White Port through the cellar door.

Cosham NR
101 Union Road, Carmel via Kalamunda, WA 6076, ☎ (08) 9293 5424, Ⓕ (08) 9293 5062; est 1989; ❖ 460 cases; ♀; A$; wkds & public hols 10-5

A relative newcomer, with only a tiny amount of wine available. Both the Chardonnay and Pinot Noir spend two years in French oak barriques before bottling – a long time by any standards.

Darlington Estate ☆☆☆✦
Lot 39 Nelson Road, Darlington, WA 6070, ☎ (08) 9299 6268, Ⓕ (08) 9299 7107; est 1983; ❖ 2,500 cases; ♀; A$; Thurs-Sun & hols 12-5; ⑩; monthly music events

Winemaking responsibilities have passed to Caspar van der Meer (Balt's son). He joined the family business in 1996, having spent a vintage in Bordeaux on graduating from Roseworthy in 1995. He returned to the Languedoc in 1997 to make a wine for the American market. Further improvements in wine quality seem highly probable.

Deep Dene Vineyard NR

36 Glenisla Road, Bickley, WA 6076, ☏ (08) 9293 0077, ⓕ (08) 9293 0077; est 1994; ❖ 4,000 cases; ♀; A$; by appt

Continues the near obsession of the Perth Hills *vignerons* with four hectares of Pinot Noir (0.5 hectares of Shiraz) in a climate, which, to put it mildly, is difficult for the variety. French-born and trained Celine Rousseau is the contract winemaker.

Hainault ☆☆☆

255 Walnut Road, Bickley, WA 6076, ☏ (08) 9328 6728, ⓕ (08) 9328 6895; est 1980; ❖ 2,300 cases; ♀; A$; wkds 10-5

Under new ownership the changes have come thick and fast: plantings have increased to 11 hectares, Celine Rousseau hired as winemaker, and The Barking Owl range – sourced from Pemberton, the Bickley and Swan Valleys – introduced under the Hainault Terroir range.

Jadran NR

445 Reservoir Road, Orange Grove, WA 6109, ☏ (08) 9459 1110; est 1967; ❖ NFP; ♀; A$; Mon-Sat 10-8, Sun 11-5

A quite substantial operation that basically services local clientele, occasionally producing wines of quite surprising quality from a variety of fruit sources.

Piesse Brook ☆☆☆½ V

226 Aldersyde Road, Bickley, WA 6076, ☏ (08) 9293 3309, ⓕ (08) 9443 2839; est 1974; ❖ 1,000 cases; ♀; A$; Sat 1-5, Sun & public hols 10-5 and by appt

The winemaking team of Di Bray, Ray Boyanich and consultant Michael Davies have consistently produced good wines from the four hectares of Chardonnay, Shiraz, Merlot and Cabernet Sauvignon produced on this estate.

Scarp Valley ☆☆☆☆

6 Robertson Road, Gooseberry Hill, WA 6076, ☏ (08) 9454 5748, ⓕ; est 1978; ❖ 25 cases; ♀; A$; by appt

Owner Robert Duncan presides over what has to be one of the smallest producers in Australia, with 0.25 acres of Shiraz and 30 Cabernet Sauvignon vines, yielding a single cask of wine each year (if the birds do not get the grapes first).

Walsh Family Wines NR

90 Walnut Road, Bickley, WA 6076, ☏ (08) 9291 7341, ⓕ (08) 9291 7341; est 1995; ❖ 95 cases; ♀; A$; 7 days 9-5

The aptly named partnership of the Walshes and their eight

children, one of whom is establishing a vineyard near Bridgetown in the Great Southern. Grapes from there will ultimately form part of the Walsh Family winery intake.

Rest of State

A quick glance at a map clearly shows that the official wine regions and relevant Zones of Western Australia are congregated in the southeastern corner of the State. Nevertheless, there are a handful of wineries that have found themselves outside this section of the map, although the only one located at any significant distance is Dalyup River, at Esperance. Time will tell whether some of these wineries are the harbingers of new Regions, or merely quixotic choices by their founders. What is certain is that the viticultural map of Western Australia will continue to expand over the early years of the next millennium.

Blackwood Crest Wines ☆☆☆ V
RMB 404A Boyup Brook, WA 6244, ☎ (08) 9767 3029, ℱ (08) 9767 3029; est 1976; ❖ 2,000 cases; ⚑; A$; 7 days 10-6
Max Fairbrass runs a remote and small winery that has produced one or two striking red wines full of flavour and character. The 1998 Classic White, '97 Sauvignon Blanc and '97 Shiraz are pleasant, well-crafted wines. Worth watching

Chittering Estate NR
Chittering Valley Road, Lower Chittering, WA 6084, ☎ (08) 9273 6255, ℱ (08) 9273 6101; est 1982; ❖ 12,000 cases; ⚑; A$; wkds & public hols Apr-Dec: 11-4.30
Chittering Estate was sold in late 1997, and no information has been forthcoming about its new owner's intentions.

Dalyup River Estate NR
Murrays Road, Esperance, WA 6450, ☎ (08) 9076 5027, ℱ (08) 9076 5027; est 1987; ❖ 700 cases; ⚑; A$; wkds 10-4
Tom Murray runs what is arguably the most remote winery in Australia other than Chateau Hornsby in Alice Springs. The quantities are as small as the cellar-door prices are modest. This apart, the light but fragrant wines reflect the cool climate of this ocean-side vineyard.

Hotham Valley Estate ☆☆☆☆
South Wandering Road, Wandering, WA 6308, ☎ (08) 9884 1525, ℱ (08) 9884 1079; est 1987; ❖ 12,000 cases; ⚑; A$; by appt
Impressive newcomer to the scene, situated in a region of its own 120 km southeast of Perth. It has a continental climate and sits at an altitude of 350 metres. Some exceptionally good wines have been made by former science teacher and now Charles Sturt University graduate James Pennington.

Lauren Brook ☆☆☆½
Eedle Terrace, Bridgetown, WA 6255, ☎ (08) 9761 2676, ℱ (08) 9761 1879; est 1993; ❖ 1,300 cases; ⚑; A$; 7 days 11-4; ⌂, gallery

Stephen Bullied has planted one hectare of Chardonnay on the banks of the beautiful Blackwood River. His is the only commercial winery in the Bridgetown area. An 80-year-old barn on the property has been renovated to contain a microwinery and a small gallery. The other wines are made from purchased grapes.

Scotts Brook NR
Scotts Brook Road, Boyup Brook, WA 6244, ☎ (08) 9765 3014, ⓕ (08) 9765 3015; est 1987; ❖ 1,000 cases; ⚱; A$; wkds & school hols 10-5 or by appt; ⛿

The 17.5-hectare vineyard (equidistant between the Margaret River and Great Southern regions) has been developed by local schoolteacher Brian Walker and wife Kerry. Most of the grapes are sold to other wineries; a small amount is contract-made.

Stratherne Vale Estate NR
Campbell Street, Caballing, WA 6312, ☎ (08) 9881 2148, ⓕ (08) 9881 3129; est 1980; ❖ 600 cases; No visitors

Stratherne Vale Estate stretches the viticultural map of Australia yet further. It is situated near Narrogin, which is north of the Great Southern region and south of the most generous extension of the Darling Ranges. A single red wine is made from a strange blend of Cabernet Sauvignon, Zinfandel, Merlot and Shiraz.

Wandering Brook Estate NR
PO Box 32, Wandering, WA 6308, ☎ (08) 9884 1064, ⓕ (08) 9884 1064; est 1989; ❖ 2,000 cases; ⚱; A$; wkds 9.30-6; ⊙; ⛿

In a move to diversify, Laurie and Margaret White have planted ten hectares of vines on their 130-year-old family property. The contract-made wines include such exotic offerings as Sparkling Verdelho and a port-style wine.

Tasmania

1994 362 hectares 0.054 per cent of total plantings
1998 535 hectares 0.054 per cent of total plantings
Small is beautiful, it seems; Tasmania's 1998 production of 3,136 tonnes was 0.03 per cent of the national total.

Northern Tasmania

While Jean Mignet was the first to plant grapes in northern Tasmania (at La Provence – now Providence – in 1956), modern-day viticulture and winemaking has been profoundly influenced and commercially driven by Andrew Pirie and the company he founded, Pipers Brook Vineyards. Pirie has a doctor of philosophy in viticulture and it was this that led him first to the Pipers River area, and the rich, red soils of the hillside slopes directly opposite Heemskerk. (Tasmania is still officially a Zone, with neither regions nor subregions registered as geographic indications.)

But the interaction of climate and soil is another thing again. The Bordeaux grapes – Cabernet Sauvignon *et al* – simply don't ripen reliably in Pipers River, so high-quality sparkling wine has become the focus, with three super-premium brands – Jansz, Clover Hill and (most recently) Pirie – as well as excellent Riesling, Gewurztraminer, Pinot Gris and Chardonnay. Once the clonal selection issue is sorted out, Pinot Noir will undoubtedly make its quality presence felt.

Deeds speak louder than words, and so do dollars. The Pipers Brook empire now has as much interest in the Tamar River area as it does in Pipers River. The Tamar River is more suited to the Bordeaux varieties, and to richer Chardonnay and Pinot Noir. Mind you, the map is still being drawn.

Bellingham Vineyard ☆☆☆
Pipers Brook, Tas 7254, ☏ *(03) 6382 7149; est 1984;* ❖ *700 cases;* ♀*; A$; by appt*
Dallas Targett sells most of the grapes from his 13-hectare vineyard to Greg O'Keefe, with a small selection made for the Bellingham label. Powerful, stemmy, cherryish Pinot Noir is the result and has impressed.

Brook Eden Vineyard NR
Adams Road, Lebrina, Tas 7254, ☏ *(03) 6395 6244; est 1988;* ❖ *800 cases;* ♀*; A$; 7 days 10-5*
Jan and Sheila Bezemer have planted 2.5 hectares of Chardonnay and Pinot Noir within their 60-hectare Angus beef property.

Cliff House ☆☆☆✦ V
57 Camms Road, Kayena, Tas 7270, ☏ *(03) 6394 7454,*
℻ *(03) 6394 7454; est 1983;* ❖ *2,500 cases;* ♀*; A$; by appt*
It has taken Geoff and Cheryl Hewitt some time to hit the quality button, but they have now done so with Riesling, Chardonnay and Pinot Noir. Pristine mineral-and-lime Riesling.

Tasmania 185

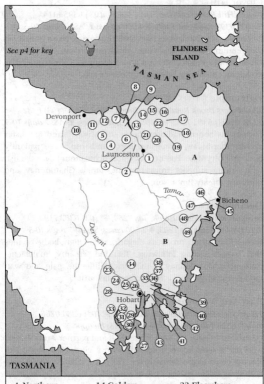

TASMANIA

A Northern Territory
B Southern Territory

1 Sharmans Glenbothy
2 Elmslie
3 Rotherhythe
4 Notley Gorge
5 Sterling Heights
6 Marion's
7 Cliff House
8 Holm Oak
9 Iron Pot Bay
10 Lake Barrington
11 Patrick Creek
12 Hawley
13 Delamere
14 Golders
15 Bellingham
16 Pipers Brook
17 Heemskerk
18 Brook Eden
19 Clover Hill
20 Providence
21 Lalla Gully
22 Dalrymple
23 Meadowbank
24 Kinvarra
25 Stefano Lubiana
26 Laurel Bank
27 Moorilla
28 Wharncliffe
29 Herons Rise
30 Geebin
31 Hartzview
32 Panorama
33 Elsewhere
34 Winstead
35 Crosswinds
36 Morningside
37 Stoney
38 Cooinda Vale
39 Palmara
40 Glen Ayr
41 Craigow
42 Wellington
43 Milford
44 Bream Creek
45 Apsley Gorge
46 Coombend
47 Freycinet
48 Criage Knowe
49 Spring Vale

Clover Hill ☆☆☆☆ɬ
Clover Hill Road, Lebrina, Tas 7254, ☎ *(03) 6395 6114,*
℻ *(03) 6395 6257; est 1986;* ❦ *4,000 cases;* ♇; *A$; 7 days 10-5*
Established by Taltarni in 1986 with the sole purpose of making a premium sparkling wine, drawing on 20 hectares of Chardonnay, Pinot Noir and Pinot Meunier. Wine quality is excellent, combining finesse with power and length.

Dalrymple ☆☆☆☆ V
1337 Pipers Brook Road, Pipers Brook, Tas 7254, ☎ *(03) 6382 7222,* ℻ *(03) 6382 7222; est 1987;* ❦ *3,300 cases;* ♇; *A$; 7 days 10-5*
Former Melbourne radio executive Jill Mitchell and her sister and brother-in-law, Anne and Bert Sundstrup, have patiently built up Dalrymple. Potent Sauvignon Blanc often heads the list, with strong support from fragrant, tangy Chardonnay and plummy, foresty Pinot Noir.

Delamere ☆☆☆
Bridport Road, Pipers Brook, Tas 7254, ☎ *(03) 6382 7190,*
℻ *(03) 6382 7250; est 1983;* ❦ *2,500 cases;* ♇; *A$; 7 days 10-5*
Richie Richardson produces elegant, rather light-bodied wines that have a strong following. Textured, creamy, malolactic-influenced Chardonnay is the pick, while the pale and wan food-loving Pinot Noir is Richardson's favourite.

East Arm Vineyard NR
111 Archers Road, Hillwood, Tas 7250, ☎ *(03) 6334 0266,*
℻ *(03) 6334 1405; est 1993;* ❦ *NA;* ♇; *A$; by appt*
Gastroenterologist Dr John Wettenhall and partner Anita James, who has a wine science degree, have a glorious, historic site sloping down to the Tamar River. They immediately struck gold with their 1998 Riesling. One to watch.

Elmslie ☆☆ɬ
Upper McEwans Road, Legana, Tas 7277, ☎ *(03) 6330 1225,*
℻ *(03) 6330 2161; est 1972;* ❦ *600 cases;* ♇; *A$; by appt*
Ralph Power has 0.5 hectares of Pinot Noir and 1.5 hectares of Cabernet; which he blends on occasion. Rustic, overall.

Golders Vineyard ☆☆☆☆ɬ V
Bridport Road, Pipers Brook, Tas 7254, ☎ *(03) 6395 4142;*
est 1991; ❦ *400 cases;* ♇; *A$; by appt*
Richard Crabtree's Pinot Noirs have gone from strength to strength since 1995. The 1.5 hectares of Pinot Noir have been followed by a hectare of Chardonnay. Worth following.

Grey Sands ☆☆☆
Frankford Highway, Glengarry, Tas 7275, ☎ *(03) 6396 1167,*
℻ *(03) 6396 1153; est 1989;* ❦ *150 cases;* ♇; *A$; by appt*
Bob and Rita Richter have very slowly established 2.5 hectares of ultra-high-density vineyards. The Pinot Gris and Merlot are sound wines.

Hawley Vineyard ☆☆☆✦
Hawley Beach, Hawley, Tas 7307, ☏ (03) 6428 6221, Ⓕ (03) 6428 6844; est 1988; ❀ 1,000 cases; ♀; A$; 7 days; ⋔; ⇌, gardens
Hawley Vineyard has a seaside location overlooking Hawley Beach and the Bass Strait to northeast. Great unoaked Chardonnay.

Heemskerk NR
40 Baxters Road, Pipers River, Tas 7252, ☏ (03) 6382 7122, Ⓕ (03) 6382 7231; est 1974; ❀ 16,000 cases; ♀; A$; Nov-Apr 10-5
In 1998 multiple ownership changes ended in the Heemskerk winery and brand being subsumed into the Pipers Brook group, which sold the sparkling wine brand Jansz to Yalumba. The dust needs to settle.

Holm Oak ☆☆☆✦
RSD 256 Rowella, West Tamar, Tas 7270, ☏ (03) 6394 7577, Ⓕ (03) 6394 7350; est 1983; ❀ 1,800 cases; ♀; A$; 7 days 12-5
Nick Butler is Tasmania's own flying winemaker, making prodigiously rich and strongly flavoured wines on the banks of the Tamar River. He hit the jackpot with a 1997 Pinot Noir. The other reds are always full-flavoured.

Iron Pot Bay Wines ☆☆☆✦
West Bay Road, Rowella, Tas 7270, ☏ (03) 6394 7320, Ⓕ (03) 6394 7346; est 1988; ❀ 2,500 cases; ♀; A$; by appt
Now part of the Rosevears Estate (*qv*) syndicate; the name comes from a bay on the Tamar River. Delicate but intensely flavoured unoaked Chardonnay, Sauvignon Blanc and Pinot Grigio are produced.

Kelly's Creek NR
RSD 226a Lower Whitehills Road, Relbia, Tas 7258, ☏ (03) 6234 9696, Ⓕ (03) 6231 6222; est 1992; ❀ 650 cases; No visitors
One hectare of Riesling, and a dash of Chardonnay, Pinot Noir and Cabernet Sauvignon are tended by majority owner Darryl Johnson. The Riesling has striking tropical fruit-salad flavours.

Lake Barrington Estate ☆☆☆☆✦ V
1133-1136 West Kentish Road, West Kentish, Tas 7306, ☏ (03) 6491 1249, Ⓕ (03) 6334 2892; est 1988; ❀ 600 cases; ♀; A$; Nov-Apr: Wed-Sun 10-5
A sparkling wine specialist owned by the vivacious Maree Taylor. The eponymous lake on the Tasmanian north coast makes a beautiful site for a picnic.

Lalla Gully Wines ☆☆☆☆✦
PO Box 377, Launceston, Tas 7250, ☏ (03) 6331 2325, Ⓕ (03) 6331 2325; est 1988; ❀ 3,000 cases; ♀; A$; at Ripples
The River Café in Launceston
Former owners Rod and Kim Ascui sold the vineyard recently, but continue to sell the delicately fragrant 1997 and 1998 Lalla Gully wines at their aesthetic Water's Edge restaurant in Hobart.

Marion's Vineyard ☆☆☆✦
Foreshore Drive, Deviot, Tas 7275, ☎ (03) 6394 7434, ⓕ (03) 6394 7434; est 1980; ❖ 2,000 cases; ♀; A$; 7 days 10-5; ⦿; ⛴, playground
The irrepressible Mark Semmens and indefatigable wife Marion have one of the most beautifully situated wineries in Australia, on the banks of the Tamar River. Wine quality bounces around, but is always full of character.

Notley Gorge ☆☆☆☆✦
West Tamar Highway, Rosevears, Tas 7277, ☎ (03) 6344 1114, ⓕ (03) 6344 1114; est 1983; ❖ 15,000 cases; ♀; A$; by appt
Part of the new Rosevears Estate group, owned by Dr Mike Beamish, that includes Iron Pot Bay and Rosevears Estate. Having had outstanding success with Chardonnay and Cabernet/Merlot made by Andrew Hood. Brand-new A$2.2 million winery.

Patrick Creek Vineyard NR
Springfield Park, North Down, Tas 7307, ☎ (03) 6424 6979, ⓕ (03) 6424 6380; est 1990; ❖ 350 cases; ♀; A$; by appt
Pat and Kay Walker have opted for high-density plantings of Chardonnay, Pinot Noir, Semillon and Sauvignon Blanc within their 1-hectare vineyard. A sturdy Pinot Noir has fared well.

Pipers Brook Vineyard ☆☆☆☆☆
Bridport Road, Pipers Brook, Tas 7254, ☎ (03) 6382 7527, ⓕ (03) 6382 7226; est 1974; ❖ 60,000 cases; ♀; A$; Mon-Fri 10-5, wkds 11-5; café
Now in public ownership, the empire has continued to grow apace, with an astonishing 220 hectares of vineyard to support the Pipers Brook, Heemskerk and Rochecombe labels. All the wines bear the stamp of founder Andrew Pirie: finesse and elegance. The Riesling seldom, if ever, misses the bull's-eye.

Providence Vineyards NR
236 Lalla Road, Lalla, Tas 7267, ☎ (03) 6395 1290, ⓕ (03) 6395 1290; est 1956; ❖ 600 cases; ♀; A$; 7 days 10-5
Provençal Jean Miguet pioneered viticulture in Northern Tasmania while working for the Hydroelectric Commission. Forty years later the EU forced a change of name from Provence to Providence Vineyards. Mature vines produce sturdy wines.

Reilly's Creek ☆☆☆
226A Lower White Hills Road, Relbia, Tas 7258, ☎ (03) 6391 8974; est 1995; ❖ 100 cases; No visitors
Reilly's Creek is the label for Relbia Vineyards, which sells most of its grapes to contract winemaker Andrew Hood. Hood makes small quantities of Reilly's Creek wines that are good quality.

Rochecombe Vineyard NR
Baxter's Road, Pipers River, Tas 7252, ☎ (03) 6382 7122, ⓕ (03) 6382 7231; est 1985; ❖ 14,000 cases; ♀; A$; 7 days 10-5; ⦿; ⚹, playground

Rochecombe, complete with newly-expanded winery, is part of the Pipers Brook group. With its excellent location and restaurant, it will continue to be a significant attraction, but the future of the brand is unclear.

Rotherhythe ☆☆☆☆⌀

Hendersons Lane, Gravelly Beach, Exeter, Tas 7251, ☏ (03) 6394 4869; est 1976; ❦ 1,600 cases; ⚑; A$; by appt

Vies with Coombend and Stoney Vineyard as the foremost producer of Cabernet Sauvignon. Rotherhythe Cabernet has the rich, blackberry and chocolate fruit of fully ripened grapes – rare for this variety in Tasmania.

Sharmans Glenbothy ☆☆☆⌀ V

Glenbothy, RSD 175 Glenwood Road, Relbia, Tas 7258, ☏ (03) 6343 0773, ℻ (03) 6343 0773; est 1987; ❦ 700 cases; ⚑; A$; by appt

Mike Sharman has pioneered a very promising region, that is situated not far south of Launceston but with a warmer climate than Pipers Brook. Three hectares of Riesling, Sauvignon Blanc, Chardonnay and Pinot Noir will tell the tale as the vines mature.

St Matthias ☆☆☆☆

113 Rosevears Drive, Rosevears, Tas 7277, ☏ (03) 6330 1700, ℻ (03) 6330 1975; est 1983; ❦ 4,000 cases; ⚑; A$; 7 days 10-5

Acquired by Moorilla Estate in 1995. The wines are made by the gifted Alain Rousseau at Moorilla and sold here through this superbly situated cellar door. Produces one of the better Cabernet/Merlots in the state.

Sterling Heights ☆☆☆☆ V

Faulkners Road, Winkleigh, Tas 7275, ☏ (03) 6396 3214, ℻ (03) 6396 3214; est 1988; ❦ 350 cases; ⚑; A$; by appt

With just over 1.5 hectares of Riesling, Chardonnay and Pinot Noir, Sterling Heights will always be a small fish in a small pond. However, the early releases had considerable success in wine shows, and the quality is all one could expect.

Tamar Ridge NR

PO Box 1513, Launceston, Tas 7250, ☏ (03) 6334 6044, ℻ (03) 6334 6050; est 1994; ❦ No visitors

Tamar Ridge is the most recent venture of beef magnate Joe Chromy. A brand-new lakeside winery will be joined by a restaurant, and the vineyards increased from 28 to 70 hectares. Expensive stuff.

White Rock Vineyard NR

1171 Railton Road, Kimberley, Tas 7304, ☏ (03) 6497 2156, ℻ (03) 6497 2156; est 1991; ❦ 500 cases; ⚑; A$; by appt

Makes light and delicate Chardonnay and Pinot Noir from one hectare, with Richie Richardson as contract maker.

Wilmot Hills Vineyard NR
407 Back Road, Wilmot, Tas 7310, ☎ (03) 6492 1193, ℉ (03) 6492 1193; est 1991; ❖ NA; ⚑; A$; 7 days 9-7

The multi-talented John and Ruth Cole have chosen a hill on the western side of Lake Barrington, not far from the Cradle Mountain Road, with marvellous views to Mt Roland and the adjacent peaks.

Southern Tasmania

The birthplace of Tasmania's wine industry is the Derwent Valley. Here, in 1827, Tasmania's first (Australia's second) commercial winemaker, Bartholemew Broughton, offered his first wine for sale. When Claudio Alcorso (of Moorilla Estate) arrived 110 years later and planted vines on the unique Derwent River isthmus, the official view of the Department of Agriculture was that viticulture was not feasible in Tasmania. Broughton and Alcorso were right; the department embarrassingly wrong. Southern Tasmania alone boasts four quite distinct (albeit unofficial) regions where grapes now flourish. The four areas are the Derwent Valley, where the Derwent River has a significant influence on vineyard siting, the hills and valleys of the beautiful Huon Valley, the Coal River/Richmond region, and the East Coast.

A pattern quickly emerges that is repeated across the regions – the best-suited varieties are Riesling, Gewurztraminer, Chardonnay and Pinot Noir (the latter two for both still and sparkling wines). On the East Coast Pinot Noir is hotly pursued by Chardonnay; Cabernet Sauvignon and Merlot are also successfully grown. The Coal River/Richmond now grows Cabernet Sauvignon and even Zinfandel thanks to irrigation. And Andrew Hood, an extaordinary winemaker, makes wines for literally dozens of producers in quantities that would elsewhere be regarded as ludicrously small and uneconomic. This has allowed many grape-growers to experiment, but also to enjoy (and sell) wines – of a quality they alone could probably not achieve – that would otherwise never see the light of day.

Apsley Gorge Vineyard ☆☆☆☆✦
Rosedale Road, Bicheno, Tas 7215, ☎ (03) 6375 1221, ℉ (03) 6375 1589; est 1988; ❖ 1,500 cases; ⚑; A$; by appt

Situated inland from Bicheno, but sharing with the other wineries of the East Coast region the capacity to produce Chardonnay and Pinot Noir of excellent richness and quality. Contract winemaking by Andrew Hood does the rest.

Bream Creek Vineyard ☆☆☆☆ V
Marion Bay Road, Bream Creek, Tas 7175, ☎ (03) 6231 4646, ℉ (03) 6231 4646; est 1975; ❖ 3,000 cases; ⚑; A$; at Potters Croft, Dunally ☎ (03) 6253 5469; ⌂, café, arts & crafts

Legendary viticulturist Fred Peacock has managed to coax this temperamental coastal vineyard into reliable production, and has been richly rewarded with Riesling, Chardonnay and a spicy, dark-plum Pinot Noir skilfully contract-made by Steve Lubiana.

Broadview NR
Rowbottoms Road, Granton, Tas 7030, ☎ (03) 6263 6882; est 1996; ❖ NA; ⚑; A$; by appt
David and Kaye O'Neil planted their vineyard in the spring of 1996. They picked the first precious 200 kg of Chardonnay in 1998, producing a fine, minerally wine.

Casa Fontana NR
4 Cook Street, Lutana, Tas 7009, ☎ (03) 6272 3180; est 1994; ❖ 300 cases; No visitors
Metallurgist Mark Fontana and Japanese wife Shige planted their first Pinot Noir in 1994, and over the following two years expanded the vineyard to its present level of 2.6 hectares. A 1998 Pinot Noir, tasted ex-barrel, was very rich and concentrated, with lovely plum and cherry fruit.

Charles Reuben Estate NR
777 Middle Tea Tree Road, Tea Tree, Tas 7017, ☎ (03) 6268 1702, Ⓕ (03) 6231 3571; est 1990; ❖ 350 cases; ⚑; A$; Thurs-Sun 10-5
Tim Krushka has planted a little bit of everything in an attempt to ascertain which varietal wine styles are best suited to the site. It's a fair bet he will come back to white wines and Pinot Noir.

Clemens Hill NR
686 Richmond Road, Cambridge, TAS 7170, ☎ (03) 6248 5985, Ⓕ (03) 6231 6222; est 1994; ❖ 500 cases; ⚑; A$; by appt
Yet another of the micro-producers served so well by Andrew Hood. It has 0.5 hectares each of Sauvignon Blanc and Pinot Noir and 0.2 hectares of Chardonnay.

Cooinda Vale ☆☆☆
Bartonvale Road, Campania, Tas 7026, ☎ (03) 6260 4227; est 1985; ❖ 300 cases; ⚑; A$; by appt
The tiny production of Riesling and Pinot Noir means that the wines are not widely known, even in southern Tasmania, and quality has been somewhat variable.

Coombend Estate ☆☆☆☆ V
Coombend via Swansea, Tas 7190, ☎ (03) 6257 8256, Ⓕ (03) 6257 8484; est 1985; ❖ 1,000 cases; ⚑; A$; 7 days 9-6; ⚐
Being graziers by background, the Fenn Smiths calculate their vineyard holdings not by area but by vine numbers. This whimsy to one side, Andrew Hood contract-makes crisp, herbal/mineral Riesling, fresh, gooseberry, Sauvignon Blanc and one of Tasmania's most reliable and best Cabernet Sauvignons, oozing cedar, cigar-box and sweet, dark-berry fruit.

Craigie Knowe ☆☆☆
Glen Gala Road, Cranbrook, Tas 7190, ☎ (03) 6223 5620, Ⓕ (03) 6223 5009; est 1979; ❖ 500 cases; ⚑; A$; wkds or by appt
John Austwick makes small quantities of wine in a tiny, rustic but charming winery as a weekend relief from a busy

metropolitan dental practice. His Cabernet Sauvignon is full-flavoured and robust, while the Pinot Noir is made in a style that will appeal to confirmed Cabernet Sauvignon drinkers.

Craigow NR
Richmond Road, Cambridge, Tas 7170, ☎ (03) 6248 5379,
℻ (03) 6248 5482; est 1989; ❖ 200 cases; No visitors

This 10-hectare vineyard sells almost all its grapes, with a nominal amount of Pinot Noir contract-made each year by Andrew Hood.

Crosswinds Vineyard NR
10 Vineyard Drive, Tea Tree, Tas 7017, ☎ (03) 6268 1091,
℻ (03) 6268 1091; est 1998; ❖ NA; ♀; A$; Oct-May: 7 days 10-5,
Sept-June: wkds

Andrew Vasiljuk makes Riesling, Chardonnay and Pinot Noir from two 1-hectare vineyards. An unoaked Pinot Noir can be surprisingly good. To prevent boredom, he also works as a consultant in Queensland each vintage.

Derwent Estate ☆☆☆☆
329 Lyell Highway, Granton, Tas 7070, ☎ (03) 6248 5073,
℻ (03) 6248 5073; est 1993; ❖ 300 cases; No visitors

The Hanigan family has a 400-hectare mixed farming property, diversifying with five hectares of vineyard planted with Pinot Noir and Riesling. The latter, contract-made by Stefano Lubiana, has been of the highest quality.

Elsewhere Vineyard ☆☆☆☆✓
40 Dillons Hill Road, Glaziers Bay, Tas 7109, ☎ (03) 6295 1509,
℻ (03) 6295 1509; est 1984; ❖ 3,000 cases; No visitors

Eric and Jette Phillips' evocatively named Elsewhere Vineyard jostles for space with their commercial flower farm. The estate-produced range comes from four hectares of Pinot Noir, three hectares of Chardonnay and two hectares of Riesling on their immaculately-tended vineyard. Concentrated, long-lived Pinot Noir leads the way.

Fishburn & O'Keefe ☆☆☆✓
16 Pioneer Avenue, New Norfolk, Tas 7140, ☎ (03) 6286 1238,
℻ (03) 6261 4029; est 1991; ❖ 3,000 cases; ♀; A$; 7 days at
Meadowbank Vineyard

A joint venture with wine consultant and contract winemaker Greg O'Keefe driving the business. In a state of transition, its future direction is yet to be revealed.

Freycinet ☆☆☆☆☆
Tasman Highway via Bicheno, Tas 7215, ☎ (03) 6257 8384,
℻ (03) 6257 8454; est 1980; ❖ 5,000 cases; ♀; A$; Mon-Fri 9-5,
wkds 10-4

The 4-hectare Freycinet vineyards are beautifully situated on the sloping hillsides of a small valley. The combination of aspect, slope, soil and heat summation produce red grapes of unusual depth of colour and ripe flavours. One of Australia's foremost producers of Pinot Noir, with a wholly enviable track record of consistency – rare with such a temperamental variety.

Geebin Wines ☆☆☆☆
3729 Channel Highway, Birchs Bay, Tas 7162, ☎ (03) 6267 4750, ℱ (03) 6267 5090; est 1983; ❖ 60 cases; ⚑; A$; 7 days 10-5; ⌂

Production is minuscule, quality consistently high. The Riesling is well made, but the interesting wine from this far southern vineyard is Cabernet Sauvignon: clearly, the vineyard enjoys favourable ripening conditions.

GlenAyr ☆☆☆½ V
Back Tea Tree Road, Richmond, Tas 7025, ☎ (03) 6260 2388, ℱ (03) 6260 2691; est 1975; ❖ 350 cases; ⚑; A$; Mon-Fri 8-5

Chris Harrington juggles management of the substantial Tolpuddle Vineyard and producing fruit contracted to Domaine Chandon with making half a dozen wines under the GlenAyr label from an adjacent 1-hectare vineyard and purchased grapes. The GlenAyr Pinot Noir is a distinguished wine that ages well.

Hartzview Wine Centre ☆☆☆
RSD 1034 Off Cross Road, Gardners Bay, Tas 7112, ☎ (03) 6295 1623; est 1988; ❖ NFP; ⚑; A$; 7 days 9-5; ⌂

A combination of wine centre, offering its own and other Huon Valley wines, and comfortable accommodation for six people in a separate, self-contained house set in mountain bushland.

Herons Rise Vineyard ☆☆☆
Saddle Road, Kettering, Tas 7155, ☎ (03) 6267 4339, ℱ (03) 6267 4245; est 1984; ❖ 300 cases; ⚑; A$; by appt; ⌂

Sue and Gerry White run a small stone country guesthouse in the D'Entrecasteaux Channel area, and basically sell the wines produced from the surrounding one hectare of vineyard to those staying at the guesthouse. Andrew Hood is contract winemaker.

Home Hill NR
73 Nairn Street, Ranelagh, Tas 7109, ☎ (03) 6228 0128, ℱ (03) 6264 1028; est 1994; ❖ 1,600 cases; No visitors

Terry and Rosemary Bennett began the development of their 4.5-hectare vineyard on gentle slopes in the beautiful Huon Valley in 1994. The first commercial releases of Chardonnay and Pinot Noir are full of promise.

Jollymont NR
145 Pullens Road, Woodbridge, Tas 7162, ☎ (03) 6267 4594, ℱ (03) 6267 4594; est 1990; ❖ 10 cases; No visitors

However briefly, Jollymont has displaced Scarp Valley (Perth Hills, WA) as the smallest wine producer in Australia, making ten cases in its first vintage, 1998. The vines are not irrigated, nor will they be, and Peter and Heather Kreet do not intend to sell any wine younger than three to four years old. Andrew Hood is contract winemaker.

Kinvarra Estate NR
RMB 5141, New Norfolk, Tas 7140, ☎ (03) 6286 1333, ℉ (03) 6286 2026; est 1990; ❦ 90 cases; No visitors

The part-time occupation of David and Sue Bevan, whose wonderful 1827 homestead is depicted on the label. The 1-hectare vineyard is split between Riesling (made by Andrew Hood) and Pinot Noir (made by Greg O'Keefe).

Kraanwood ☆☆∮
8 Woodies Place, Richmond, Tas 7025, ☎ (03) 6260 2540; est 1994; ❦ 150 cases; No visitors

Frank van der Kraan and wife Barbara run yet another doll's house-scale operation, producing Schonburger, Montage (blend) and Pinot Noir from two tiny vineyards.

Latitude Wines (or ☆☆ Bud Spur) ☆☆☆
Postal address 252 Strickland Avenue, South Hobart, Tas 7004, ☎ (03) 6224 1639, ℉ (03) 6233 3477; est 1996; ❦ NA; No visitors

Phil Barker (former chef for ten years and now a State botanist) and Anne Lasala tend a 2.5-hectare vineyard. The Sauvignon Blanc, Chardonnay and Pinot Noir are contract-made by Andrew Hood and Michael Vishacki respectively. As yet, they can't decide on the name for their venture.

Laurel Bank ☆☆☆☆∮
130 Black Snake Lane, Granton, Tas 7030, ☎ (03) 6263 5977, ℉ (03) 6263 3117; est 1987; ❦ 500 cases; ♇; A$; by appt

Laurel (hence Laurel Bank) and Kerry Carland planted their 2-hectare vineyard in 1986. The wines are released with some years' bottle age, and have far more weight than many of their counterparts, particularly the powerful plum-and-spice Pinot Noir. Andrew Hood is contract winemaker.

Meadowbank Wines ☆☆☆☆∮ V
'Meadowbank', Glenora, Derwent Valley, Tas 7410, ☎ (03) 6286 1269, ℉ (03) 6286 1133; est 1974; ❦ 3,000 cases; ♇; A$; 7 days 11-5

Now an important part of the Ellis family business on what was once (but no more) a large grazing property on the banks of the Derwent. Increased plantings are being established under contract to BRL Hardy. Andrew Hood is contract winemaker.

Milford Vineyard ☆☆☆☆ V
Richmond Road, Cambridge, Tas 7170, ☎ (03) 6248 5029, ℉ (03) 6224 2331; est 1984; ❦ 250 cases; No visitors

A single hectare of Pinot Noir grows on the largest Southdown sheep stud in Australia, which has been in Charlie Lewis's family since 1830. It is only 15 minutes from Hobart and, running to the very banks of the Coal River, it is a magic spot. The wine – made by Andrew Hood – is truly excellent.

Moorilla Estate ☆☆☆☆☆
655 Main Road, Berriedale, Tas 7011, ☎ (03) 6249 2949, Ⓕ (03) 6249 4093; est 1958; ❖ 9,000 cases; ♀; A$; 7 days 10-5; ⦿; shop; ⚔, museum

This estate is once more a glittering star. Winemaker Alain Rousseau has transformed the quality of the Pinot Noir and Merlot, and continued that of the Riesling, Gewurztraminer and Chardonnay. Owner David Walsh has established a world-class museum of eastern and African art in the former homestead designed by Sir Roy Grounds.

Morningside Wines ☆☆☆☆
RMB 3002 Middle Tea Tree Road, Tea Tree, Tas 7017, ☎ (03) 6268 1748, Ⓕ (03) 6268 1748; est 1980; ❖ 400 cases; No visitors

The name 'Morningside' was given to the old property on which the vineyard stands, as it gets the morning sun first. The Riesling, Pinot Noir and Cabernet Sauvignon have good colour, varietal flavour and length.

Orani Vineyard ☆☆☆
Arthur Highway, Sorrel, Tas 7172, ☎ (03) 6225 0330, Ⓕ (03) 6225 0330; est 1986; ❖ NA; ♀; A$; wkds & public hols 9.30-6.30

The first commercial release from Orani was of a 1992 Pinot Noir, with Chardonnay and Riesling following in the years thereafter. Solidly constructed wines have come since, produced by various contract winemakers.

Palmara ☆☆☆✓ V
1314 Richmond Road, Richmond, Tas 7025, ☎ (03) 6260 2462; est 1985; ❖ 250 cases; ♀; A$; summer 12-6; playground

Allan Bird makes tiny quantities of Chardonnay, Semillon, Ehrenfeltzer, Montage (blend), Exotica (Siegerrebe), Pinot Noir and Cabernet Sauvignon. The Exotica is one of Australia's most exotic and unusual wines, with pungent jujube, lanolin aromas and flavours.

Panorama ☆☆☆
RSD 297 Lower Wattle Grove, Cradoc, Tas 7109, ☎ (03) 6266 3409, Ⓕ (03) 6266 3409; est 1974; ❖ 250 cases; ♀; A$; 6 days 10-5

Michael and Sharon Vishacki purchased Panorama in 1997, and have since spent considerable sums in building a brand-new winery and an attractive cellar-door sales outlet, and trebling the vineyard size. They produce worthwhile Chardonnay, Sauvignon Blanc, Pinot Noir and Cabernet Sauvignon.

Pembroke NR
Richmond Road, Cambridge, Tas 7170, ☎ (03) 6248 5139, Ⓕ (03) 6234 5481; est 1980; ❖ 200 cases; No visitors

The 1-hectare Pembroke vineyard was established in 1980 by the

Spring Vale Vineyards ☆☆☆☆
Spring Vale, Swansea, Tas 7190, ☏ (03) 6257 8208, ℻ (03) 6257 8598; est 1986; ❧ 3,000 cases; ♇; A$; wkds & hols 10-5

Rodney Lyne's east-coast vineyard produces rich, Burgundian-accented Chardonnay, stylish Pinot Noir and amiable Gewurztraminer. Frost can be a problem, but not the contract winemaking of Andrew Hood.

Stefano Lubiana ☆☆☆☆✧ V
60 Rowbottoms Road, Granton, Tas 7030, ☏ (03) 6263 7457, ℻ (03) 6263 7430; est 1990; ❧ 2,000 cases; ♇; A$; Fri-Mon 10-3, or by appt

Former Riverland grower and winemaker Stefano Lubiana moved from one extreme to the other in setting up a substantial sparkling and table wine business on the banks of the Derwent River. Stefano uses a combination of both contract winemaking and his own skills to achieve unqualified success. His Primavera Riesling and Vintage Brut are both outstanding.

Stoney Vineyard ☆☆☆☆✧
Campania, Tas 7026, ☏ (03) 6260 4174, ℻ (03) 6260 4390; est 1973; ❧ 6,000 cases; ♇; A$; Mon-Fri 9-4, wkds by appt

Swiss businessman Peter Althaus has quite literally transformed Stoney Vineyard, investing millions with a long-term view. Domaine A Cabernet Sauvignon (typically with ten per cent Merlot, Cabernet Franc and Petit Verdot blended in) is Tasmania's best, heading a two-tier range of the classic white and red varietals.

Treehouse Vineyard ☆☆
257 Richmond Road, Cambridge, Tas 7170, ☏ (03) 6248 5367, ℻ (03) 6248 5367; est 1991; ❧ NA; ♇; A$; Wed-Sun 10-5; ⑩

Gradon and Margaret Johnstone planted Riesling and Pinot Noir in 1991. Andrew Hood is contract winemaker, with all the wines sold through the cellar door and by mail order. There are restaurant meals and casual food available at the Treehouse Wine Centre.

Wellington ☆☆☆☆✧ V
Cnr Richmond and Denholms Roads, Cambridge, Tas 7170, ☏ (03) 6248 5844, ℻ (03) 6243 0226; est 1990; ❧ 2,500 cases; ♇; A$; by appt

Consultant-winemaker Andrew Hood (ex-Charles Sturt University) and wife Jenny have constructed a state-of-the-art winery on land leased from the University of Tasmania. Here, Andrew Hood performs endless miracles, producing 4,500 cases for literally dozens of contract clients, often made, matured and bottled in miniscule quantities.

Wharncliffe NR
Summerleas Road, Kingston, Tas 7050, ☏ (03) 6229 7147, ℻ (03) 6229 2298; est 1990; ❖ 32 cases; No visitors

With a 0.75-hectare Chardonnay vineyard, enterprises of this size could not exist without Andrew Hood, which would be a pity, because the vineyard is beautifully situated on the doorstep of Mount Wellington and the Huon Valley.

Winstead ☆☆☆☆✤ V
Lot 7 Winstead Road, Bagdad, Tas 7030, ☏ (03) 6268 6417, ℻ (03) 6268 6417; est 1989; ❖ 400 cases; ♟; A$; Wed-Sun 11-5

The good news about Winstead is the outstanding quality of its intensely flinty Riesling and extremely generous and rich Pinot Noirs. The bad news is that production is so limited, with only 0.5 hectares of each variety being tended by fly-fishing devotee Neil Snare and wife Julieanne. Andrew Hood is winemaker.

Yaxley Estate ☆☆☆✤ V
31 Draws Field Road, Copping, Tas 7174, ☏ (03) 6253 5222, ℻ (03) 6253 5222; est 1991; ❖ 300 cases; ♟; A$; 7 days 10-6.30

While Yaxley Estate was established back in 1991, it was not until 1998 that it offered for sale each of the four wines from its vineyard plantings, which total 1.7 hectares. Once again, the small-batch handling skills (and patience) of contract winemaker Andrew Hood have made the venture possible.

Queensland

1994 1154 hectares 1.75 per cent of total plantings
1998 1405 hectares 1.42 per cent of total plantings

These figures in fact flatter Queensland, for a significant part of the plantings are of table grapes. Its wine grape crush in 1998 was less than one tenth of one per cent of the total.

Granite Belt

Although a few kilometres inside the border of Queensland, the Granite Belt looks south to NSW. It relies on the New England Highway to bring the all-important tourist traffic north across the state boundary. It is striking country, particularly in the south, where streams have deserted the granite bedrock, leaving boulder-strewn landscapes where patches of vineyard peep around the boulders and gum trees.

Lying on the western side of the Great Dividing Range, the climate is contintental yet counterbalanced by the altitude of around 800 metres. This creates moderate temperatures during the growing season and a late vintage. However, the Granite Belt is, like the Hunter Valley to its south, not a 'natural' wine-growing region. The sting in the tail is the ever-present risk of spring frosts, followed by periods of drought that are often broken by rain falling at the most inconvenient time.

But that hasn't stopped the wine boom that is sweeping Australia from taking hold here, too. A significant part of the population in the Granite Belt has always been of Italian descent: growers of orchard fruits and table grapes. In 1965, the Ricci family planted the first wine grapes – amounting to one acre of Shiraz. It then fell to Angelo Puglisi to establish Ballandean Estate, the first Granite Belt winery to secure national distribution through a fine-wine wholesaler. Others followed, and the Granite Belt has shown itself capable of great things, notably with Shiraz, Cabernet Sauvignon and Semillon. Its challenge is how to build on this for the future.

Bald Mountain ☆☆☆✓
Hickling Lane, Wallangarra, Qld 4383, ☏ (07) 4684 3186, ℱ (07) 4684 3433; est 1985; ❖ 5,000 cases; ♀; A$; 7 days 10-5

Denis Parsons is a self-taught but exceptionally competent *vigneron* who has turned Bald Mountain into the viticultural showpiece of the Granite Belt. Flinty Sauvignon Blanc and spicy Shiraz have won many show awards since 1988.

Ballandean Estate ☆☆☆
Sundown Road, Ballandean, Qld 4382, ☏ (07) 4684 1226, ℱ (07) 4684 1288; est 1970; ❖ 9,000 cases; ♀; A$; 7 days 9-5; café, concerts

The eldest and largest winery of the Granite Belt. The white wines are of diverse but interesting styles, the red wines smooth and usually well made. The estate speciality is Sylvaner Late Harvest, a particularly interesting wine of good flavour.

Queensland

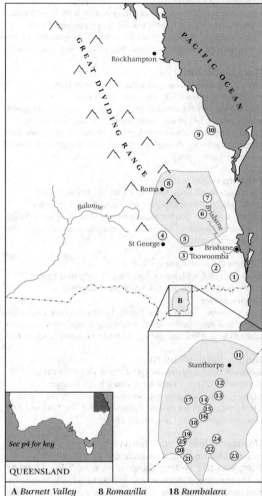

QUEENSLAND

- **A** *Burnett Valley*
- **B** *Granite Belt*

1. *Mt Tamborine*
2. *Ironbank Ridge*
3. *Preston Peak*
4. *Rimfire*
5. *Rimfire*
6. *Crane*
7. *Barambah Ridge*
8. *Romavilla*
9. *Wonbah*
10. *Tropical*
11. *Old Caves*
12. *Severn Brae*
13. *Kominos*
14. *Violet Cane*
15. *Felsberg*
16. *Stone Ridge*
17. *Mountview*
18. *Rumbalara*
19. *Ballandean*
20. *Golden Grove*
21. *Winewood*
22. *Robinsons Family*
23. *Bald Mountain*
24. *Hidden Creek*
25. *Bungawarra*

Bridgeman Downs NR
Barambah Road, Moffatdale via Murgon, Qld 4605, ☏ (07) 4168 4784, ⓕ (07) 4168 4767; est NA; ❖ NA; ♀; A$; by appt

The omnipresent Bruce Humphery-Smith contract-makes the wines from four hectares of Verdelho, Chardonnay and Shiraz.

Bungawarra NR
Bents Road, Ballandean, Qld 4382, ☏ (07) 4684 1128; est 1975; ❖ 1,300 cases; ♀; A$; 7 days 10.30-4.30

New owner Jeff Harden has five hectares of mature vineyards, which, over the years, have shown themselves capable of producing red wines of considerable character. He has joined forces with Bruce Humphery-Smith, and Bungawarra should regain its former glory.

Felsberg Winery ☆☆☆
Townsends Road, Glen Aplin, Qld 4381, ☏ (07) 4683 4332, ⓕ (07) 4683 4377; est 1983; ❖ 1,600 cases; ♀; A$; 7 days 9-5

After a slow start, former master-brewer Otto Haag is producing some very pleasant red wines, including a lifted, cherryish Shiraz and cedary, leafy Merlot.

Golden Grove Estate ☆☆☆✓ V
Sundown Road, Ballandean, Qld 4382, ☏ (07) 4684 1291, ⓕ (07) 4684 1247; est 1993; ❖ NA; ♀; A$; 7 days 9-5; ⑽; garden

Sam Costanzo has taken a family business focused on table grapes and propelled it to overnight star status, with a sweetly tangy Classic White and potent, barrel-fermented Chardonnay.

Granite Ridge Wines NR
Sundown Road, Ballandean, Qld 4382, ☏ (07) 4684 1263, ⓕ (07) 4684 1250; est 1995; ❖ 850 cases; ♀; A$; by appt

Granite Ridge has had particular success with its Cabernet Sauvignons, made by Dennis Fergusson. Both the 1995 and 1996 vintages were judged Queensland's best.

Heritage Wines of Stanthorpe ☆☆☆✓
New England Highway, Cottonvale, Qld 4375, ☏ (07) 4685 2197, ⓕ (07) 4685 2112; est 1992; ❖ 6,000 cases; ♀; A$; 7 days 9-5; ⑽; ⇌

A tourist-oriented venture (as are many of the Stanthorpe wineries), established in a painstakingly restored cool-storage shed. The estate plantings amount to two hectares each of Chardonnay and Merlot, and one hectare each of Shiraz and Cabernet Sauvignon.

Hidden Creek NR
Eukey Road, Ballandean, Qld 4382, ☏ (07) 4684 1383, ⓕ (07) 4684 1383; est 1998; ❖ 750 cases; ♀; A$; Sat 10-4, Sun 8.30-3 or by appt; ⑽

A beautifully located vineyard and winery on a ridge overlooking the Ballandean township and the Severn River valley. The boulder-strewn hills of this 70-hectare property provide only a little over six hectares of vineyard. Contract winemaker Andrew Vasiljuk travels from Tasmania for vintage.

Kominos ☆☆☆
New England Highway, Severnlea, Qld 4352, ☏ (07) 4683 4311, ℉ (07) 4683 4291; est 1976; ❖ 4,000 cases; ⌇; A$; 7 days 9-5
Tony Comino is a dedicated viticulturist and winemaker, selling all his wine by cellar door and mail order.

Mountview Wines ☆☆☆½
Mount Stirling Road, Glen Aplin, Qld 4381, ☏ (07) 4683 4316, ℉ (07) 4683 4111; est 1990; ❖ 1,200 cases; ⌇; A$; Wed-Sat 9-5, Sun 10-4; playground
David and Linda Price are refugees from the Sydney rat-race, now operating a small, neat, red-cedar farm-style winery. Various vintages of Mountview Shiraz have deservedly won trophies and gold medals at Queensland wine shows.

Old Caves NR
New England Highway, Stanthorpe, Qld 4380, ☏ (07) 4681 1494, ℉ (07) 4681 2722; est 1980; ❖ 2,200 cases; ⌇; A$; Mon-Sat 9-5, Sun 10-5
David Zanatta enjoys a strictly local, relatively uncritical and evidently loyal clientele that buys both varietal and generic wines (in bottle and flagon) at suitably low prices.

Preston Peak NR
Old Wallangarra Road, Wyberba via Ballandean, Qld 4382, ☏ (07) 4630 9499, ℉ (07) 4630 9477; est 1994; ❖ 6,000 cases; ⌇; A$; at Wyberba Vineyard
While production has doubled over the past year, the spectacular development plans of dentist owners Ashley Smith and Kym Thumpkin have slowed to a more realistic level. Winemaking continues at Wyberba; proposed Toowoomba winery is on hold.

Robinsons Family Vineyards ☆☆☆
Curtin Road, Ballandean, Qld 4382, ☏ (07) 4684 1216, ℉ (07) 4684 1216; est 1969; ❖ 2,000 cases; ⌇; A$; 7 days 9-5
The conjunction of a picture of a hibiscus and the prominently placed words 'cool climate' on the labels is a strange one, but then this has always been the nature of Robinsons Family Vineyards. The red wines can be very good, particularly when not overly extracted and tannic.

Rumbalara ☆☆☆½
Fletcher Road, Fletcher, Qld 4381, ☏ (07) 4684 1206, ℉ (07) 4684 1299; est 1974; ❖ 2,000 cases; ⌇; A$; 7 days 9-5; ⊙
Bob Gray has produced some of the Granite Belt's finest, honeyed Semillon and silky, red-berry Cabernet Sauvignon, but quality does vary. The winery incorporates a spacious restaurant, and there are also barbecue and picnic facilities.

Severn Brae Estate NR
Lot 2 Back Creek Road (Mount Tully Road), Severnlea, Qld 4352,
☏ *(07) 4683 5292,* ℻ *(07) 3391 3821; est 1990;* ❖ *300 cases;* ❢*; A$; wkds 9-5 or by appt*

This is the home estate of energetic contract winemaker Bruce Humphery-Smith. He has established 5.5 hectares of Chardonnay, relatively closely spaced and trained on a high two-tier trellis.

Stone Ridge ☆☆☆
Limberlost Road, Glen Aplin, Qld 4381, ☏ *(07) 4683 4211; est 1981;* ❖ *1,450 cases;* ❢*; A$; 7 days 10-5*

Spicy Shiraz is the speciality of the doll's-house-sized winery operated by Jim Lawrie and Anne Kennedy, but the portfolio has progressively expanded over recent years to include two whites and the only Stanthorpe region Cabernet/Malbec.

Violet Cane Vineyard ☆☆☆☆
13 Wallace Court, Glen Aplin, Qld 4381, ☏ *0418 739 257,*
℻ *(07) 4162 5328; est 1994;* ❖ *60 cases; No visitors*

The intriguingly named Violet Cane Vineyard, and no less startlingly labelled wine, is the tiny personal business of Stuart Range Estate winemaker Adam Chapman. He manages to fit in several winemaking lives, including that of Flying Winemaker in Europe each Australian spring.

Winewood NR
Sundown Road, Ballandean, Qld 4382, ☏ *(07) 4684 1187,*
℻ *(07) 4684 1187; est 1984;* ❖ *650 cases;* ❢*; A$; wkds & public hols 9-5*

A weekend and holiday activity for schoolteacher Ian Davis and town-planner wife Jeanette. The tiny winery is a model of neatness and precision planning. The 3-hectare vineyard provides some interesting wines, including Chardonnay, Marsanne and Shiraz/Marsanne.

Rest of State

The wine boom of the second half of the 1990s has led to changes in the viticultural map of Queensland on a scale unimaginable at the start of the decade. Whether all the new ventures will succeed remains to be seen. Much will depend on wine tourism, and the extent to which the owners work their way around the hazards of grape-growing in the vicinity of their wineries.

The two northern outposts near Bundaberg are Wonbah Estate and Tropical Wines. These are specialist tourism ventures, remote from the other groups. The next group, Barambah Ridge, Crane and Rimfire, are in the South Burnett and Bunya Mountain National Park areas. Then there is Ironbark Ridge and, closer to the Gold Coast, Mount Tamborine Wines, with other large-scale ventures (such as the planned Mount Cotton Winery) no less firmly aimed at the tourist market. Summer rainfall and high humidity are the principal threats to grape-growing. The obvious first line of defense is Chambourcin, the French hybrid grape that has proven so successful along the north coast of New South Wales. It is resistant to mildew, and makes deeply coloured, soft and flavoursome red wine best consumed when young. What more could anyone want?

Barambah Ridge NR
79 Goschnicks Road, Redgate via Murgon, Qld 4605,
℡ *(07) 4168 4766,* ⓕ *(07) 4168 4770; est 1997;* ❖ *10,000 cases;*
♇; *A$; 7 days 10-5;* ¶

A fast-growing business, owned by unlisted public company South Burnett Wines. A new winery for 1998 and the experience of Bruce Humphery-Smith have produced top wine-show results for the Chardonnay.

Canungra Valley Vineyards NR
Lamington National Park Road, Canungra Valley, Qld 4275,
℡ *(07) 5543 4011,* ⓕ *(07) 5543 4162; est 1997;* ❖ *NA;* ♇; *A$;*
7 days 10-5; ¶; *picnic baskets, tutored tastings*

Established in the hinterland of the Gold Coast, with a clear focus on broad-based tourism. Two hectares of vines have been established around the 19th-century homestead; in deference to the climate 70 per cent is Chambourcin, the remainder Semillon. The owners only sell a small portion of their wine.

Captain's Paddock NR
Booie-Crawford Road, Kingaroy, Queensland 4610, ℡ *(07) 4162 4534,* ⓕ *(07) 4162 4502; est 1995;* ❖ *700 cases;* ♇; *A$; wkds 9-4;* ¶

The artistic McCallum family runs this cellar-door-cum-art gallery-cum-restaurant with views over the Booie Ranges. Chardonnay and Shiraz are contract-made by Adam Chapman.

Clovely Estate NR
Steinhardts Road, Moffatdale via Murgon, Qld 4605, ℡ *(07) 3876 5200,* ⓕ *(07) 3876 5200; est 1998;* ❖ *NA; No visitors*

Although new-born, Clovely Estate has the largest vineyards in Queensland, with 174 hectares. The wines are sold in four tiers: Clovely Estate (super-premium); Left Field (to age); Fifth Row (drink now), and Outback (export).

Crane Winery NR
Haydens Road, Kingaroy, Qld 4610, ℡ *(07) 4162 7647,* ⓕ *(07) 4162 7647; est 1996;* ❖ *3,500 cases;* ♇; *A$; Fri-Tues 9-4 or by appt;* ¶

Sue Crane's grandfather planted Shiraz way back in 1898, so wine is in the blood. She and John Crane have three hectares of vineyard, but also purchase grapes from other growers in the burgeoning Kingaroy district.

Ironbark Ridge Vineyard NR
Middle Road Mail Service 825, Purga, Qld 4306, ℡ *(07) 5464 6787,* ⓕ *(07) 5464 6858; est 1984;* ❖ *250 cases;* ♇; *A$; by appt*

Vintages such as 1998 show that this estate is capable of producing Chardonnay equal to the best from Queensland.

Kenilworth Bluff Wines NR
Lot 13 Bluff Road, Kenilworth, Qld 4574, ☎ *(07) 5472 3723,*
Ⓕ *(07) 5472 3723; est 1993;* ❧ *NA;* ⚑; *A$; Fri-Sun 10-4, or by appt*

Brian and Colleen Marsh have established a 4-hectare vineyard in a hidden valley at the foot of the Kenilworth Bluff, and they have plans for a winery. The wines are currently made by Bruce Humphery-Smith.

Mount Tamborine Winery NR
32 Hartley Road, Mount Tamborine, Qld 4272, ☎ *(07) 5545 3981,*
Ⓕ *(07) 5545 3311; est 1993;* ❧ *4,000 cases;* ⚑; *A$; 7 days 10-4*

Owns vineyards in Mount Tamborine and at Stanthorpe (Granite Belt), and purchases grapes from South Australia and elsewhere. Success has been achieved with both Chardonnay and Merlot.

Rimfire Vineyards ☆☆☆✓
Bismarck Street, MacLagan, Qld 4352, ☎ *(07) 4692 1129,*
Ⓕ *(07) 4692 1260; est 1991;* ❧ *5,000 cases;* ⚑; *A$; 7 days 10-5; café*

The Connellan family has planted six hectares on its 1,500-hectare cattle stud, and enjoys one success after the other in Queensland wine shows with Chardonnay, thanks to the skill of Bruce Humphery-Smith.

Romavilla NR
Northern Road, Roma, Qld 4455, ☎ *(07) 4622 1822,* Ⓕ *(07) 4622 1822; est 1863;* ❧ *3,000 cases;* ⚑; *A$; Mon-Fri 8-5, Sat 9-12, 2-4*

An amazing historic relic, seemingly untouched since its 19th-century heyday. The table wines are ordinary but there are some extraordinary fortifieds, including a truly stylish Madeira-style wine, made from Riesling and Syrian.

Stuart Range Estates ☆☆☆✓ V
67 William Street, Kingaroy, Qld 4610, ☎ *(07) 4162 3711,*
Ⓕ *(07) 4162 4811; est 1997;* ❧ *11,000 cases;* ⚑; *A$; 7 days 9-5;* ✗

Yet another flyer, with seven growers in the South Burnett Valley, 52 hectares and a state-of-the-art winery in an old butter factory building, plus Adam Chapman as winemaker. Chardonnays stand out.

Index

Abbey Vale 156
Abercorn 35
Ada River 103
Adelaide 12
Adelaide Hills 12, 128-34
Adelaide Hills Estate 134
Affleck 47-8
Aldinga Bay Winery 142
Alexander Bridge Estate 156
Alkoomi 165
All Saints 95
Allandale 15
Allanmere 15
Allinda 56
Amberley Estate 156-7
Anderson 95
Andrew Garrett 142
Andrew Garrett Vineyard Estates 143
Andrew Harris Vineyards 35
Angove's 152-3
Antcliff's Chase 94
Apsley Gorge Vineyard 190
Aquila Estate 175
Arlewood Estate 157
Armstrong Vineyards 80
Arranmore Vineyard 129
Arrowfield 32
Arthur's Creek Estate 56
Ashbrook Estate 157
Asher 72
Ashton Hills 129
Ashwood Grove 108
Ashworths Hill 75
Auldstone 96
Austin's Barrabool 73
Avalon Vineyard 99
Avalon Wines 180

Bacchus Estate 15
Badger's Brook 56
Bago Vineyard 53
Baileys of Glenrowan 98
Bald Mountain 198
Baldivis Estate 179
Balgownie Estate 86
Ballandean Estate 198
Ballarat 85-6
Balnaves of Coonawarra 135
Bannockburn Vineyards 73
Banrock Station 153
Barak Estate 66
Barambah Ridge 203
Baratto's 44
Barbera grape 99
Barletta Bros 123
Barnadown Run 87
Barossa Ridge Wine Estate 110
Barossa Settlers 111
Barossa Valley 12, 110-20
Barossa Valley Estate 134
Barratt 129
Barretts Wines 85
Barrington Estate 32-3
Barwang Vineyard 51
Basedow 111
Basket Range Wines 129-30
Bass Phillip 104
Baxter Stokes Wines 175
Beckett's Flat 158
Belbourie 15
Belgenny Vineyard 27-8
Bellingham Vineyard 184
Belubula Valley Vineyards 42
Bendigo 11, 86-91
Beresford Wines 143
Berri Estates 153
Best's Wines 81
Bethany Wines 111-12
Beyond Broke Vineyard 15-16
Bianchet 57
Bimbadgen Estate 16
Bindi 57
Birdwood Estate 130
Birnham Wood Wines 33
Black George 170
BlackJack Vineyards 87
Blackwood Crest Wines 182

Blanche Barkly Wines 87
Blaxland Wines 16
Bleasdale Vineyards 151-2
Blewitt Springs Winery 143
Blok Estate 138
Bloodwood Estate 42
Blue Pyrenees Estate 82
Bluebush Estate 16
Boneo Plains 66
Bonneyview 153
Booth's Taminick Cellars 98-9
Boston Bay Wines 154
Botobolar 35-6
Bowen Estate 135
Boynton's of Bright 102
Brahams Creek 57
Brand's of Coonawarra 135
Brangayne of Orange 42
Branson Wines 112-13
Bream Creek Vineyard 190
Bremerton Wines 152
Brewery Hill Winery 143
Briagolong Estate 104
Brian Barry Wines 123
Briar Ridge 16
Bridgeman Downs 200
Bridgewater Mill 130
Brindabella Hills 48
Britannia Creek Wines 58
Brittens Wines 36
BRL Hardy 145
Broadview 191
Broke Estate 16
Brokenwood 16-17
Brook Eden Vineyard 184
Brookland Valley 158
Brookside Vineyard 186
Brown Brothers 99
Browns of Padthaway 139
Brushbox Vineyard 17
Bullers Beverford 108
Bullers Calliope 95-6
Bungawarra 200
Burge Family Winemakers 113
Burnbrae 36
Burramurra 92
Burrundulla 36

Cabernet Sauvignon grape 9
Calais Estates 17
Cambewarra Estate 54
Campbells 96
Canberra District 11, 47-51
Candlebark Hill 76
Canobolas-Smith 42
Canungra Valley Vineyards 203
Cape Bouvard 179
Cape Clairault 158
Cape Jaffa Wines 140-1
Cape Mentelle 158
Capel Vale 173-4
Capercaillie 17
Capogreco Estate 108
Captain's Paddock 203
Carabooda Estate 175
Carbunup Estate 158
Cargo Road Wines 42
Carindale Wines 17
Carosa 180
Casa Fontana 191
Cascabel 143
Casella 45
Cassegrain 53
Castle Rock Estate 165
Cathcart Ridge Estate 81
Catherine Vale Vineyard 17
Central Victorian High Country 94-5
Chain of Ponds 130
Chambers Rosewood 96
Chambourcin grape 54, 202-3
Chapel Hill 143
Chardonnay grape 9
Charles Cimicky 113
Charles Melton 113
Charles Reuben Estate 191
Charley Brothers 53-4
Charlotte Plains 87
Chateau Dor 87
Chateau Dorrien 113
Chateau Francois 17
Chateau Leamon 87

Chateau Pato 17
Chateau Tahbilk 92
Chatsfield 165-6
Chestnut Grove 170
Chittering Estate 182
Ciavarella 100
Clare Valley 12, 122-8
Clarendon Hills Winery 143-4
Clemens Hill 191
Cleveland 76
Cliff House 184
climate 8
Clonakilla 48
Clos Clare 123
Clovely Estate 203
Clover Hill 186
Clyde Park 73
Cobanov 176
Cobaw Ridge 76
Cockfighter's Ghost Vineyard 18
Cofield 96
Coldstream Hills 59
Connor Park Winery 87-8
Constable & Hershon 18
Constables 170
Coolnga Vale 191
Coolangatta Estate 54
Coombend Estate 191
Coonawarra 12, 134-9
Cooperage Estate 88
Coorinja 54
Cope-Williams 76
Coriole 144
Cosham 180
Cowra 40-1
Cowra Estate 40
Crabtree of Watervale 123
Craig Avon Vineyard 66
Craigie Knowe 191-2
Craiglee 79
Craigmoor 36
Craigow 192
Crane Winery 203
Craneford 120-1
Cranswick Estate 45
Crawford River Wines 85
Crisford Winery 18
Crosswinds Vineyard 192
Cruickshank-Callatoota Estate 33
Cullen Wines 158
Currency Creek Wines 154
Curtis 144

Dal Zotto Wines 100
Dalfarras 92
Dalrymple 186
Dalwhinnie 82-3
Dalyup River Estate 18
Danbury Estate 40
D'Arenberg 144
Dargo Valley Winery 104
Darling Estate 100
Darling Park 66
Darlington Estate 180-1
David Traeger 92
De Bortoli (New South Wales) 45
De Bortoli (Victoria) 59
De Iuliis 18
Deakin Estate 108
Deep Dene Vineyard 181
Delacolline Estate 154
Delamere 186
Delatite 94
Demondrille Vineyards 51
Dennis 144
D'Entrecasteaux 170
Derwent Estate 192
Devil's Lair 159-60
Diamond Valley Vineyards 59
Diggers Rest 79
Djinta Djinta Winery 104
Domaine Chandon 59
Donnelly River Wines 170
Donovan 81
Doonkuna Estate 48
Dorrien Estate 113
Dowie Doole 144
Drayton's Family Wines 18
Drews Creek Wines 18

Driftwood Estate 160
Dromana Estate 66-7
Dulcinea 85
Duncan Estate 123
Dyson Wines 144

East Arm Vineyard 186
Eastbrook Estate 171
Eastern Peake 85-6
Eden Valley 12, 120-2
Eden Valley Wines 121
Elan Vineyard 67
Elderton 113-14
Eldredge 123
Eldridge Estate 67
Elgee Park 67
Elmslie 186
Elsewhere Vineyard 192
Eltham Vineyards 59
Elyssium 18
Emerald Estate 123-4
Ensay Winery 104
Eppalock Ridge 88
Ermes Estate 67
Eurunderee Flats Winery 36
Evans & Tate 160
Evans Family 19
Evelyn County Estate 59
Excelsior Peak 52
Eyton-on-Yarra 60

Fairfield Vineyard 96
Faisan Estate 43
Far South West (Victoria) 84-5
Farrell's Limestone Creek 19
Felsberg Winery 200
Ferguson Falls Estate 174
Fergusson 60
Fermoy Estate 160
Fern Hill Estate 145
Fishburn & O'Keefe 192
Five Oaks Vineyard 60
Flinders Bay 160
Fordwich Estate 19
Fox Creek Wines 145
Frankland Estate 166
Freycinet 192-3
Fyffe Field 92

Galah Wine 130
The Gap 82
Garbin Estate 176
Garden Gully Vineyards 81
Gartleman Hunter Estate 19
Geebin Wines 193
Geelong 11, 72-5
Gehrig Estate 96
Gembrook Hill 60
Geoff Hardy Wines 130
Geoff Merrill 145
Geoff Weaver 130-1
Geographe 173-5
Giaconda 102
Gidgee Estate Wines 48
Gilbert 166
Gippsland 11, 103-7
Glaetzer Wines 114
Glen Erin Vineyard Retreat 76
Glenara Wines 131
GlenAyr 193
Glenguin 19
Glenrowan 11, 98-9
Gloucester Ridge Vineyard 171
Gnadenfrei Estate 114
Golden Grape Estate 19
Golden Grove Estate 200
Golden Gully Wines 43
Golders Vineyard 186
Goona Warra Vineyard 79
Goulburn Valley 11, 91-3
Goundrey 166
Gralyn Cellars 160
Grampians 12, 80-2
Granite Belt 198-202
Granite Ridge Wines 200
Grant Burge 114
Grape varieties 9
Great Lakes Wines 54
Great Southern 12, 165-9
Green Vineyards 63
Greenock Creek Cellars 114
Grenache grape 9

Grey Sands 186
Grosset 124
Grove Estate 51
Grove Hill 131
The Gurdies 106

Haan Wines 114
Habitat 43
Haig 145
Hainault 181
Halcyon Daze 60
Half Mile Creek 36-7
Hamelin Bay 160
Hamilton 145
Hamiltons Bluff 47
Hanging Rock Winery 76-7
Hankin Estate 92-3
Hanns Creek Estate 67
Hansen Hilltops 52
Hanson 60
Happ's 161
Harcourt Valley Vineyards 88
Hardys (Padthaway) 139
Harewood Estate 166
Hartzview Wine Centre 193
Haselgrove 145
Hastings River 11, 53-4
Hastwell & Lightfoot 146
Hawley Vineyard 187
Hay Shed Hill 161
Hayward's Whitehead Creek 93
Heathcote Winery 88
Heathfield Ridge Wines 141
Heemskerk 187
Heggies Vineyard 121
Helm's 48
Henke 94
Henkell Wines 61
Henley Park Wines 176
Henschke 121
Henty Brook Estate 174
Heritage Farm Wines 93
Heritage Wines 114
Heritage Wines of Stanthorpe 200
Hermes Morrison Wines 40-1
Herons Rise Vineyard 193
Hickinbotham 67
Hidden Creek 200-1
Highbank 135
Highland Heritage Estate 43
Highway Wines 176
Hill of Hope 19-20
Hill-Smith Estate 121
Hillstowe 131
Hilltop 51-2
HJT Vineyard 99
Hoffmann's 146
Hollick 135-6
Hollyclare 20
Holm Oak 187
Home Hill 193
Honeytree Estate 20
Horseshoe Vineyard 33
Hotham Valley Estate 182
Houghton 176
Howard Park 166
Howards Way Vineyard 20
Howarths Pycnantha Hill 124
Hugh Hamilton 146
Hugo 146
Hungerford Hill 20
Hunter Ridge 20
Hunter Valley 11, 14-31
Hunter Valley, Lower 11, 14-31
Hunter Valley, Upper 11, 32-4
Huntington Estate 37
Huntleigh Vineyards 88
Hunt's Foxhaven Estate 161
Hurley Vineyard 67-8

Ibis Wines 43
Idyll Vineyard 73
Indigo Ridge 43
Inglewood Vineyards 33
Ingoldby 146
Innisfail Vineyards 73
Iron Pot Bay Wines 187
Ironbark Ridge Vineyard 203
Irvine 121
Island Brook Estate 161
Ivanhoe Wines 20

Jackson's Hill 21
Jadran 181
James Estate 33
Jane Brook Estate 177
Jardee 171
Jasper Hill 88
Jasper Valley 54
Jeanneret Wines 124
Jeir Creek 48-9
Jenke Vineyards 114-15
Jim Barry Wines 124
Jindalee Wines 73
Jingalla 166-7
Jinks Creek Winery 104-5
John Gehrig Wines 100
Jollymont 193-4
Jones Winery 96-7

Kaesler 115
Kaiser Stuhl 115
Kalari Vineyard 41
Kangarilla Road Vineyard & Winery 146
Kangaroo Island Vines 154
Kangderaar Vineyard 89
Kara Kara Vineyard 83
Karina Vineyard 68
Karl Seppelt 122
Karrivale 115
Karriview 167
Katnook Estate 136
Kay Bros Amery 146-7
Kellermeister 115
Kellybrook 61
Kelly's Creek 187
Kenilworth Bluff Wines 204
Kennedys Keilor Valley 61
Kevin Sobels Wines 21
Kilgour Estate 73-4
Kilikanoon 124
Killawarra 124
Killerby 174
Kimbarra Wines 81
King Valley 11, 99-101
Kings Creek Winery 68
Kingsley 85
Kingston Estate 153
Kingtree Wines 174
Kinvarra Estate 194
Knappstein Wines 124
Knight Granite Hills 77
Knowland Estate 37
Kominos 201
Kongwak Hills Winery 105
Koppamurra 141
Kraanwood 194
Krondorf 115
Kulkunbulla 21
Kyeema Estate 49

La Cantina King Valley 100
Laanecoorie 83
labels 9-10
Ladbroke Grove 136
Lake Barrington Estate 187
Lake Breeze Wines 152
Lake George Winery 49
Lake's Folly 21
Lalla Gully Wines 187
Lamont Wines 177
Langanook Wines 89
Langhorne Creek 151-2
Langmeil Winery 115
Lark Hill 49
Latara 21
Latitude Wines 194
Laurel Bank 194
Lauren Brook 182-3
Lavender Bay 68
laws 9-10
Lawson's Hill 37
Leasingham 125
Leconfield 136
Leeuwin Estate 161
Lefroy Brook 171
Leland Estate 131
Lengs & Cooter 154
Lenswood Vineyards 131
Lenton Brae Estate 161
Leo Buring 116
Liebich Wein 116
Lillydale Vineyards 61

Index

Lillypilly Estate 45
Lindemans (Coonawarra) 136
Lindemans (Hunter Valley) 21-2
Lindemans (Karadoc) 108-9
Lindemans (Padthaway) 140
Lirralirra Estate 61
Little River Wines 177
Little's Winery 22
London Lodge Estate 33-4
Long Gully Estate 61
Longleat 93
Longview Creek Vineyard 80
Lost Valley Winery 80
Louis-Laval Wines 22
Lovey's Estate 61
Lowe Family Wines 37
Lyre Bird Hill 105

McAlister Vineyards 105
Macaw Creek Wines 155
Macedon Ranges 11, 75-9
McGuigan 22-3
McIvor Creek 89
McLaren Vale 12, 142-51
McManus 45
Macquariedale Estate 22
McWilliam's 45
McWilliam's Mount Pleasant 23
Madew Wines 49
Maglieri 147
Main Ridge Estate 68
Mair's Coalville 105
Majella 136
Malcolm Creek 132
Mann 177
Manning Park 147
Mansfield Wines 37
Mantons Creek Vineyard 68
Margan Family Winegrowers 22
Margaret River 12, 156-65
Marienberg 147
Mariners Rest 167
Marion's Vineyard 188
Maritime Estate 68
Markwood Estate 100
Marribrook 167
Marsh Estate 22
Martins Hill Wines 37
Marybrook Vineyards 161-2
Massoni Main Creek 69
Mataro grape 9
Matilda's Meadow 167
Mawarra 77
Mawson Ridge 132
Maxwell Wines 147
Meadowbank Estate 194
Meerea Park 34
Merlot grape 9
Merrebee Estate 167
Merricks Estate 69
Merrivale Wines 147
Merum 171
Miceli 69
Michelini Wines 100-1
Middlebrook 147-8
Middleton Estate 148
Milbrovale 23
Mildara (Coonawarra) 137
Milford Vineyard 194-5
Milimani Estate 49
Millers Samphire 132
Millinup Estate 167-8
Minimbah 34
Minot Vineyard 162
Mintaro Cellars 125
Minya Winery 75
Miramar 38
Miranda (King Valley) 101
Miranda (Riverina) 46
Miranda Rovalley Estate 116
Mistletoe Wines 23
Mitchelton 93
Molly Morgan Vineyard 23
Monbulk Winery 61-2
Monichinno Wines 93
Montague View Estate 23
Montara 81
Montrose 38
Moondah Brook 177

Moorebank Vineyard 23
Moorilla Estate 195
Moorooduc Estate 69
Morning Cloud Wines 69
Morningside Wines 195
Mornington Peninsula 12, 65-72
Mornington Vineyards Estate 69
Morris 97
Moss Brothers 162
Moss Wood 162
Mount Alexander Vineyard 89
Mount Anakie Wines 74
Mount Avoca Vineyard 83
Mount Beckworth 86
Mount Benson 140-1
Mount Charlie Winery 77
Mount Duneed 74
Mount Eyre Vineyard 24
Mount Gambier 141-2
Mount Gisborne Wines 77
Mount Horrocks 125
Mount Hurtle 148
Mount Ida 89
Mount Langi Ghiran Vineyards 81-2
Mount Macedon 77
Mount Majura Wines 50
Mount Mary 62
Mount Prior Vineyard 97
Mount Tamborine Winery 204
Mount View Estate 24
Mount Vincent Mead 38
Mount William Winery 77-8
Mountadam 122
Mountain Creek Wines 83
Mountford 171
Mountilford 38
Mountview Wines 201
Mourvedre grape 9
Mudgee 11, 35-9
Mudgee Wines 38
Munari Wines 89
Murray Darling 107-9
Murray Robson Wines 24
Murrindindi 94-5
Murrumbateman Winery 50
Muscat grape 95, 98

Narkoojee 105
Nashdale Wines 44
Nebbiolo grape 9
Needham Estate Wines 148
Nepenthe Vineyards 132
New South Wales 14-55
  vintages 11
Newstead Winery 89
Nicholson River 105-6
Noon Winery 148
Normans 148
Notley Gorge 188
Nuggetty Ranges Winery 90

Oakridge Estate 62
Oakvale 24
Old Barn 116
Old Caves 201
Old Station Vineyard 125
Olive Farm 177-8
Oliverhill 148
Ollsens of Watervale 125-6
Orange 11, 41-4
Orani Vineyard 195
Orlando (Barossa Valley) 116
Orlando (Padthaway) 140
Osborns 69-70
Ovens Valley 101-3

Padthaway 12, 139-40
Padthaway Estate 140
Palmara 195
Palmer Wines 162
Pankhurst 51
Panorama 195
Paracombe Wines 132
Paradise Enough 106
Paringa Estate 70
Park Wines 102
Parker Coonawarra Estate 137
Passing Clouds 90
Patrick Creek Vineyard 188
Patritti Wines 155

Pattersons 168
Paul Conti 178
Paul Osicka 90
Paulett 126
Peacock Hill Vineyard 24
Pearson Vineyards 126
Peel Estate 179
Peerick Vineyard 83
Pemberton 169-73
Pembroke 195-6
Pendarves Estate 24
Penfolds 116
Penley Estate 137
Penny's Hill Vineyards 148-9
Pennyweight Winery 102
Penwortham Estate 126
Pepper Tree 24-5
Peppers Creek 25
Perrini Estate 132
Pertaringa 149
Perth Hills 180-2
Petaluma 132-3
Peter Lehmann 117
Peter Rumball Wines 155
Peterson Champagne House 25
Petersons 25
Pewsey Vale 122
Pfeiffer 97
Phillip Island Vineyard 106
Piano Gully 172
Pibbin 133
Picardy 172
Piccadilly Fields 133
Pierro 162
Piesse Brook 181
Pieter van Gent 38
Piggs Peake 25
Pikes 126
Pinelli 178
Pinot Noir grape 9
Pipers Brook Vineyard 188
Pirramimma 149
Pizzini 101
Plantagenet 168
Platt's 39
Plunkett 85
Pokolbin Estate 25
Poole's Rock 25
Poplar Bend 70
Port Phillip Estate 70
Portree 26
Pothana 26
Potters Clay Vineyard 149
Preston Peak 201
Primo Estate 134
Prince Albert 74
Providence Vineyards 188
Punters Corner 137
Pyrenees 12, 82-4

Queen Adelaide 117
Queensland 198-204
  vintages 13
Quelltaler 126

Ravenswood Lane Vineyard 133
Ray-Monde 80
Reads 101
Red Clay Estate 39
Red Edge 90
Red Hill Estate 70
Red Rock Winery 74
Redgate 162
Redman 137
Reg Drayton Wines 26
Reilly's Creek 188
Reillys Wines 127
Renmano 153
Reynell 172
Reynolds Yarraman 34
Ribbon Vale Estate 163
Richmond Grove 117
Riesling grape 9
Rimfire Vineyards 204
Rivendell 163
RiverBank Estate 178
Riverina 11, 44-7
Riverina Wines 46
Riverland 152-3
Robe 140-1

Roberts Estate Wines 109
Robinsons Family Vineyards 201
Robinvale 109
Rochecombe Vineyard 188-9
Rochford 78
Rockford 117
Romavilla 204
Rosa Brook Estate 163
Rosemount Estate (Hunter Valley) 34
Rosemount Estate (McLaren Vale) 149
Rosewhite Vineyards 102-3
Rossetto 46
Rothbury Estate 26
Rothbury Ridge 26
Rotherhythe 189
Rouge Homme 137-8
Ruker Wines 50
Rumbalara 201
Rutherglen 11, 95-8
Ryland River 70
Rymill 138

S Kidman Wines 138
Saddlers Creek 26
St Gregory's 85
St Hallett 118
St Huberts 62-3
St Leonards 97
St Mary's 138
St Matthias 189
St Peter's Edenhope Winery 46
Salem Bridge Wines 133
Salisbury Estate 109
Saltram 117
Sandalford 178
Sandalyn Wilderness Estate 26
Sandhurst Ridge 90
Sandstone 163
Sandy Farm Vineyard 78
Sangiovese: grape 99
Sarsfield Estate 106
Sauvignon Blanc: grape 9
Scarborough 27
Scarp Valley 181
Scarpantoni Estate 150
Schmidts Tarchalice 117
Scotchmans Hill 74
Scotts Brook 183
Sea Winds Vineyard 70
Seaview 150
Seldom Seen Vineyard 39
Semillon: grape 9
Seppelt 117-18
Seppelt Great Western 82
Serventy 163
Sevenhill Cellars 127
Severn Brae Estate 202
Seville Estate 62
Shantell 62
Sharmans Glenbury 189
Shaw & Smith 133
Shiraz: grape 9
Shoalhaven 54-5
Shottesbrooke 150
Silos Estate 55
Silvan Winery 62
Simon Hackett 155
Sinclair Wines 172
Sittella Wines 178
Skillogalee 127
Smithbrook 172
soils 8
Somerset Hill Wines 168
Sorrenberg 103
South Australia 110-55
  vintages 12
South West Coast (Western Australia) 179
Southern Grand Estate 34
Spring Vale Vineyards 196
Stanley Brothers 118
Stanton & Killeen Wines 97
Staughton Vale Vineyard 74-5
Steels Creek Estate 63
Stefano Lubiana 196
Stein's 39
Stephen John Wines 127
Sterling Heights 189

Stone Ridge 202
Stoney Vineyard 196
Stonier's Wines 71
Stratherne Vale Estate 183
Strathkellar 93
Straws Lane 78
Stringy Brae 127
Stuart Range Estates 204
Stumpy Gully 71
Sucknizzle Augusta 163-4
Summerfield 84
Sunbury 79-80
Surveyor's Hill Winery 50
Sutherland 27
Sutherland Smith Wines 97-8
Swan District 13, 175-9
Swan Hill 107-9

Tait Wines 118
Talijancich 178
Tallara 39
Taltarni 84
Talunga 133-4
Tamar Ridge 189
Tamburlaine 27
Tanglewood Downs 71
Tannery Lane Vineyard 90
Tantemaggie 172-3
Tarrawarra Estate 63
Tarwin Ridge 106
Tasmania 184-97
  vintages 13
Tatachilla 150
Tawonga Vineyards 103
Taylors 127-8
Temple Bruer 152
Templer's Mill 44
Tempus Two Wines 27
Terrace Vale 27
T'Gallant 71
Thalgara Estate 27
Thistle Hill 39
Thomas 174
Thornhill/The Berry Farm 164
Tim Adams 128
Tim Gramp 128
Tingle-Wood 168
Tinklers Vineyard 28
Tinlins 150
Tinonee Vineyard 28
Tintilla Wines 28
Tipperary Hill Estate 90-1
Tokay: grape 95, 98
Tollana 118
Toorak Estate 46
Torbreck Vintners 118
Trafford Hill Vineyard 155
Treehouse Vineyard 196
Treen Ridge Estate 173
Treeton Estate 164
Trevor Jones 119
Trio Station 78
Tuck's Ridge 71
Tulloch 28
Tumbarumba 52-3
Tumbarumba Wine Cellars 52-3
Tumbarumba Wine Estates 53
Turkey Flat 119
Turramurra Estate 71
12 Acres 91-2
Twin Bays 155
Twin Valley Estate 119
Tyrrell's 28

Undercliff 28-9

Van de Scheur 29
Vasse Felix 164
Veritas 119
Verona Vineyard 29
Vico 46
Victoria 56-109
  vintages 11-12
Victorian Alps Wine Co 101
Villa Primavera 71-2
Vinden Estate 29
  vintages 11-13
Vintina Estate 72
Violet Cane Vineyard 202
Virage 164
Virgin Hills 78-9
Voyager Estate 164

Wa-De-Lock 107
Wallington Wines 41
Walsh Family Wines 181-2
Wandering Brook Estate 183
Wandin Valley Estate 29
Waninga 128
Wansbrough Wines 174-5
Wantirna Estate 63
Wards Gateway 119
Warrabilla 98
Warramate 63
Warraroong Estate 29
Warren Vineyard 173
Warrenmang Vineyard 84
Water Wheel 91
Waybourne 75
Wayne Thomas Wines 150-1
Wellington 196
Wendouree 128
West Cape Howe Wines 168
Westend 46-7
Western Australia 156-83
  vintages 12-13
Westfield 179
Wetherall 138
Wharncliffe 197
Whispering Hills 91
Whisson Lake 134
White Rock Vineyard 189
Whitehorse Wines 86
Wignalls Wines 168-9
Wild Dog 107
Wild Duck Creek Estate 91
Wilderness Estate 31
Wildwood Vineyards 79
Will Taylor Wines 155
Willespie 164-5
Williams Rest 169
Willow Bend 119
Willow Creek 72
The Willows 118
Wilmot Hills Vineyard 190
Wilson Vineyard 128
Wilton Estate 47
Wimbaliri Wines 50
Windara 31
Windowrie Estate 41
Windy Ridge Vineyard 107
Winewood 202
Winstead 197
Winters Vineyard 142
Wirilda Creek 151
Wirra Wirra 151
Wolf Blass 119
Wood Park 101
Woodend Winery 79
Woodonga Hill 52
WoodSmoke Estate 173
Woodstock 151
Wrattonbully 141
Wyanga Park 107
Wyldcroft Estates 72
Wyndham Estate 31-2
Wynns Coonawarra Estate 138-9

Yaldara Wines 120
Yalumba 120
Yanwirra 169
Yarra Burn 63-4
Yarra Edge 64
Yarra Ridge 64
Yarra Track Wines 64
Yarra Valley 12, 56-65
Yarra Valley Hills 64
Yarra Yarra 64
Yarra Yering 64-5
Yarrabank 65
Yass Valley Wines 50-1
Yaxley Estate 197
Yellowglen 86
Yering Farm 65
Yering Grange Vineyard 65
Yering Station 65
Yeringberg 65
Yunbar Estate 120

Zappacosta Estate 47
Zarephath Wines 169
Zema Estate 139
Zuber Estate 9